Critical Studies Series

THE NOVEL AND AUTHENTICITY

THE NOVEL AND AUTHENTICITY

by
David Holbrook
Fellow of Downing College, Cambridge

VISION
and
BARNES & NOBLE

Vision Press Limited
Fulham Wharf
Townmead Road
London SW6 2SB

and

Barnes & Noble Books
81 Adams Drive
Totowa, NJ 07512

ISBN (UK) 0 85478 156 0
ISBN (US) 0 389 20711 X

Library of Congress Cataloging-in-Publication Data

Holbrook, David.
  The novel and authenticity.

  (Critical studies)
  1. English fiction—History and criticism.
2. Truthfulness and falsehood in literature. 3. Literature
and morals. I. Title. II. Series: Critical studies
series.
PR830.M67H65   1987   823'.009'353   86-32027
ISBN 0-389-20711-X

For my students

Printed and bound in Great Britain by
L.R. Printing Services Ltd.,
Crawley, W. Sussex.
Phototypeset by Galleon Photosetting,
Ipswich, Suffolk.
MCMLXXXVII

Contents

Introduction

This book has emerged out of my work in various directions—
in literary criticism, in university teaching, as a creative writer,
and as a student of philosophy and psychology. I have been
obliged to ask myself, 'What is a novel?' The answer must be
given in attending to actual novels, and so I have found myself
engrossed in attention to particular works, often those I was
teaching. It seemed to me that there was something that needed
to be said, in answer to that question, which bore on the present
situation, in which the word 'novel' has become a vague term,
embracing all kinds of manifestations, many of which have
nothing to do with the novel as a work of art, as we study it in
the university. There is also the problem that while at best the
novel is a medium of the quest for authenticity, it has now
become, even in areas of serious attention to literature, a vehicle
for inauthenticity. I shall try to show what I mean by the word
'authenticity', and to discuss it as the focus of a certain kind of
moral concern. Again, here, it needs to be said that the novel, in
today's culture, in some areas, has become a medium of
immorality, a vehicle for the deliberate assault on values,
meaning and truth.

This is a serious problem. Before it can be tackled, however,
it is necessary to redefine 'the novel', and it is with that I try to
confine myself here. The novel is a serious mode of thought, of a
certain kind, about human experience, and if we lose it as that,
we lose a great deal. In order to deal with this problem I
propose, once more, to evoke what I call philosophical anthropology, as I did in *Lost Bearings in English Poetry*. Fortunately,
other works by the present author are now to appear in which I
elaborate on philosophical anthropology and its findings, and
their relevance to the Humanities, so that my attention to the
subject here can be brief. But a little needs to be said, for my
whole approach to literary criticism depends upon it. The

7

expedition into consideration of models of man and knowledge is not a substitute for responsive literary criticism, but it gives a base for serious concern about truth and human need.

Philosophical anthropology includes a number of disciplines—psychoanalytical thought, existentialist philosophy, existentialist psychotherapy, phenomenology, post-critical philosophy, post-Kantian philosophy devoted to the question, 'What is man?', and attempts to devise a form of psychotherapy which is influenced by the philosophy of Martin Heidegger, known as *Daseins*-analysis. We may call all these disciplines 'subjective' disciplines, because they endeavour to explore the nature of human reality by methods which include the inner life, the subjective experience of man and woman. So, they involve us in a reconsideration of the nature of knowledge, and if we are to regard the novel as a mode of knowing, then they will be found of great relevance to our study.

I am particularly interested, in this sphere of discourse on existentialism and phenomenology, in the findings of psycho-therapists, and the kind of debate they engage in. Important instances of this kind of debate may be found in *Existence: A New Dimension in Psychiatry*, edited by Rollo May, Ernest Angel and Henri F. Ellenberger (Basic Books, 1958); *True and False Experience*, Peter Lomas (Allen Lane, 1973); *Playing and Reality*, D. W. Winnicott (Tavistock, 1971); and the works of Marion Milner. These are not primarily theoretical works, though they do explore the nature of knowledge, and in this they may be seen as parallel to works such as Susanne Langer's *Mind: An Essay in Human Feeling* (Johns Hopkins, 1967) and Michael Polanyi's *Personal Knowledge* (Routledge and Kegan Paul, 1958). There are certain elements from all these works which I want to invoke here.

One is the element of *integrity*; there can be no question but that all those engaged in this kind of philosophical anthropology are concerned with the truth, and this is often within the context of care, often with people to whom this is a life-or-death matter. In this there is a particular kind of *moral concern*, and this is of great importance to us in cultural criticism, since there are many attempts to undermine or dismiss such concern with human welfare in the arts today.

Moreover, such work represents an important implicit critique

8

of our prevalent modes of knowledge, and with this our concept of *what 'truth' may be*, and how it may be found. This in turn may be linked with the concept of the *true self*, of being true to oneself, which is the theme of authenticity. These questions need to be examined in the light of the wider question of *what we think of ourselves*.

The predominant mode of thought about life and human nature in the West is positivistic and mechanistic. The word 'subjective' in our vocabulary tends to be pejorative, and there are strong movements—not least in Cambridge—which urge that anything subjective must be distrusted and probably rejected, because it cannot be verified in terms of things to be seen and measured. Psychoanalysis especially comes in for some powerful rejection, because, it is claimed, it cannot be shown 'objectively' to have any 'real' effect. As Susanne Langer says, in some psychology and philosophy, the problems of the relationship between subjective and objective factors in mental activity are removed from the sphere of investigation (yet, as Erwin Straus points out in *The Primary World of Senses*, they remain there in a concealed form, since consciousness is necessary to conduct the experiments). Phenomenology attempts to deal with the phenomena of consciousness, and to devise disciplines by which these may be understood. But in much modern psychology, there is an enigma:

> These relationships [i.e. between the subjective and objective factors in mental activity] and the terms that develop in conjunction with them—symbols, concepts, fantasy, religion, speculation, selfhood and morality—really represent the most exciting and important topics of the science of mind. . . . To exclude such relationships for the sake of sure and safe laboratory methods is to stifle human psychology in embryo. (Susanne Langer, *Mind: An Essay in Human Feeling*)

The very terms and perspectives of modern scientific psychology thus tend to prevent it from encountering the very subject of its explorations. And insofar as this is so, the model of man which emanates from such human sciences is one from which consciousness and the inner life is missing. Since science is the one remaining authority in a world in which most sources of authority have disappeared, it seems moreover that man is a mere mechanism, the product in the first place of some cosmic 'error' of mutation, developed through the processes of ruthless 'survival' through 'natural selection', a product of his genes, hormones, instincts, defence mechanisms or his environment, or the processes of the class struggle or whatever. In this there is no sphere of *being*, and we have no philosophy of being. The effects are seriously nihilistic, and it is against this that the existentialist movement has protested. Kierkegaard, for example, for such reasons, pronounced it 'blasphemy' to approach man in the perspectives of the natural sciences, because of their implicit denial of uniqueness, in human existence. And there has been a parallel protest on behalf of being, running through-out English literature itself, as in the work of Charles Dickens, William Blake, S. T. Coleridge, and D. H. Lawrence. F. R. Leavis made profound criticisms of the utilitarian mode of thought about man, as in his Introduction to the volume *Mill on Bentham and Coleridge*.

One of the gravest elements in positivistic and mechanistic approaches to the nature of man is that they tend to destroy 'intentionality': that is, creativity in life is implicitly denied. This is certainly true of Darwinian evolutionary theory (see the present author's *Evolution and the Humanities* (Gower, 1987)). This theory—elevated into a dogmatic philosophy of existence—had a devastating effect on some authors, such as Thomas Hardy and Tolstoy, for this very reason. Life and the universe seemed to them futile as a result, if not, as in Hardy's case, a terrible mistake. In general, it may be said, the effect of a philosophy of existence coming across to us from physicalist science has been a sense of bleakness, as if we were accidentally thrust into a universe which is alien to us, and in which we were not at home. The psychotherapist Karl Stern has tried to trace this view of existence to the philosophies of certain individuals who erected a psychopathological element in their own psyches into a philosophy, mostly to do with rejection by their mothers: Réné Descartes, Schopenhauer, and Jean-Paul Sartre especially. His *The Flight from Woman* tries to link the prevalent tendency to view the universe (or Mother Earth) as alien if not hostile, to a deep fear of woman in those who had been let down in an absolute way, by the woman as mother—notably Descartes, whose mother died when he was a baby.

But, be that as it may, there are elements in the predominant modes of thought about man and his predicament, based on the 'scientific view', which can be critically examined for their failures to apprehend the truth of things as they really are. For instance, it would seem, from critiques of Darwinian mechanistic evolutionary theory, that there are many reasons why the theory of 'accidental' mutation and survival by the elimination of unsuccessful forms, cannot be held to be the basis of the development of life. Even when mathematical calculations are made, of the probable occurrences of new forms, it is found that there has not been time enough for these to happen by random chance processes. Many things in the development of life require recognition of an 'innovative principle' in the universe, while science itself is interested in life in the universe because of the order displayed there, and the 'intrinsic' interest which living creatures have.

The word 'intrinsic' is important here, because one of the most significant themes in phenomenology is not only that of 'intentionality', that is the creativity in life which seeks towards fulfilment in the future, but its emphasis on the *uniqueness of the experience of being in the one living creature.* In psychotherapy, this becomes an emphasis on the one I AM, the individual in his living now, and his own life-process and the pattern he seeks to fulfil—an emphasis which, of course, Dickens's Sissy Jupe was well aware of, in the face of the statistics offered by Mr. Gradgrind. The self which we know to be valid in its living existence and thus unsusceptible to 'objective' calculation and impingement, *is* the true self, and only in terms of our own intentional pattern does life 'count' for us. Moreover the primary need of this true self is to find meaning in existence. In the realm of consciousness, which philosophical anthropology recognizes as the main focus of our existence, what matters primarily to us is to explore the possible meaning of our existence and the agency by which this is done is *culture*—by the use of symbols.

It is this emphasis which makes psychotherapy based on philosophical anthropology so different from Freudian psychoanalysis which has always tended to attempt to root therapy and the human dynamics of personality in the organic life of the organism. Freud, in his attempts to persuade the doctors of his

11

time, who wanted to follow a 'scientific' path, developed a metapsychology which relied, in the end, on instinct theory and which included the 'death instinct' to explain human hate and destructiveness. These negative dynamics were in his 'model' ineducable, and so Freud's social and political implications tended to be pessimistic (see: Ian D. Suttie, *The Origins of Love and Hate*; Harry Guntrip, *Personality Structure and Human Interaction*; David Holbrook, *Human Hope and the Death Instinct*). The work of D. W. Winnicott is most important here, because he has virtually reversed this 'model', and, even as a Freudian, came to the conclusion that what was primary in human needs was not the satisfaction of instincts at all, but the need for culture. Culture in man is a primary need, and the child, as soon as it develops the capacity to use symbolism in its play and inter-subjective life with the mother, exerts this instrument on the questions: What is it to be human? and What is the point of life? These are the questions which are explored by the adult culture of its civilization, which the child takes on, through the meeting of union and separateness as a condition of all human existence; and they are the essential questions asked in such an art form as the novel.

Thought about psychotherapy has thus become also thought about the development of normal life in us, and about the nature of man himself. Under the influence of existentialist thought and other philosophies, the emphasis has come to be on this search in the individual for his fulfilment, in terms of the *meaning* of his life. Martin Heidegger's concepts here have become important, especially that of 'being-unto-death'—the fact that we are all moving, and know ourselves to be moving, towards death and nothingness. It is urgent for us to find some sense of *having meaningfully existed*. Every choice and act which gives us some sense or definition in this way, so that we can say that 'here and in this I have existed', enables us to bear the dreadfulness of our tragic predicament. So, the word *Dasein* has been seized on, the term which means 'being there'; we need to give a sense of being here-and-now meaningfully in existence, as a counter-assertion to our inevitable nothingness. Obviously, no mere manic display can count in the face of such a need; and so we come to the need to make an *authentic* assertion of the *Dasein*, and our reparative-creative achievements must be real ones.

These concepts are of great importance for literary criticism, since they provided a new moral basis for discrimination.

We may turn now to the question of what *knowledge* is. We cannot confine our knowledge of ourselves as living beings to a reductionist paradigm which knows everything only in terms of particulate analysis and measurable facts. In the end these all come down to mathematical entities, and the spaces between things, the positions of the atoms in the universe. To define such abstractions answers none of the real questions at all, least of all about our experience. There must be 'other' ways of knowing, and the puzzle, of course, is what these might be. One answer, I believe, is that a work of art like the novel represents that *other mode of knowing*, and it is important to note that this other mode of knowing such as we have in a work of art is *ineffable*; it can never be found in ultimate terms, accounted for fully, or put into explicit form (such as objective science demands, in its Cartesian emphasis on 'clear and distinct ideas'). This kind of knowledge admits that *being itself* is intractable and ineffable. In such a concept of knowledge we may find great relief, since it allows for intentionality, for potentialities yet to be realized, for the mystery of existence, and for the essential *freedom of being*. Here I cannot do better than lift one of Peter Lomas's most important quotations, which is from the work of an important phenomenologist, Maurice Merleau-Ponty:

> I am not the outcome or the meeting-point of numerous causal agencies which determine my bodily or psychological make-up. I cannot conceive of myself as nothing but a bit of the world, a mere object of biological, psychological or sociological investigations. I cannot shut myself up within the realm of science. All my knowledge of the world, even my scientific knowledge, is gained from my own particular point of view, or from some experience of the world without which the symbols of science would be meaningless. The whole universe of science is built upon the world as directly experienced. . . . I am, not a 'living creature' nor even as a 'man', nor again even a 'consciousness' endowed with all the characteristic which zoology, social anatomy or inductive psychology recognize in these various products of the natural or historical process—I am the absolute source, my existence does not stem from my antecedents, from my physical and social environment; instead it moves out towards them and sustains them, for I alone bring into being for myself (and

13

therefore into being in the only sense that the word can have for me) the tradition which I elect to carry on, or the horizon whose distance from me would be abolished . . . if I were not there to scan it with my gaze. . . .

(The Phenomenology of Perception, pp. viii–ix)

One might even say that this is what the novel *says*: that only that which is valid to the self is what one alone 'brings into being for oneself' and that the world only exists insofar as one is there 'to scan it with one's gaze'.

To which I will add another quotation lifted from Lomas's book, from Susanne Langer, on the same page: 'The direct perception of artistic import, however, is not systematic and cannot be manipulated according to any rule. It is intuitive, immediate, and its deliverances are ineffable . . .' (op cit.). It is important to note that both these quotations in Lomas go with his particular kind of human emphasis on the nature of psychotherapy. Whatever abstract philosophical account we give of such a human process, the actual practice must be rooted in direct experience. Theoretical writings may clarify our understanding. But we are dealing with both 'personal knowledge' (the work of Polanyi is relevant) and also with the intuitive practice of a living process. The living self of the being is ineffable and living its own dynamics; the novelist in creation lives through his exploratory experience, and so does the teacher of his novel, and the critic. All are engaged in existential processes, and a common fundamental element is the uniqueness of the living 'I'.

However, certain realities emerge from these processes, and in therapy Lomas draws these to our attention. Existential therapy regards the person as 'a unique, spontaneous being who cannot be adequately described in those terms which have proved useful in our assessment of the inanimate world'. The important question is what the patient is experiencing, and the therapist is concerned with finding his way into the perceptual world of the patient. Philosophical anthropology, as a background to this approach, does not offer an exact formulation or theoretical basis. But it does seem to be possible to find in this body of thought an important distinction, between true and false self, and true and false experience. Here Lomas believes that D. W. Winnicott was the most creative recent thinker in the sphere of psychotherapy since Freud. His most important contribution was his conception of a 'true self'. This is that self which has a sense of its own reality and integrity, and seeks to fulfil its potentialities. Where this true self cannot be realized, it may be protected by a 'false self' which may make a successful adaptation to society, and may keep things going—but the individual is left with a feeling that while the 'true self' may remain intact, it has never had the chance to come fully into being, in its own right. Lomas says,

> The true self, I take it, is that which develops directly from the original being of the child. It is imperfect and ill-defined (because we live in an imperfect and ill-defined world) but it remains roughly true to our innate potential. When, beyond a certain degree, the true self is so crushed or impoverished by the environment, it develops, for its own sake and for the sake of others, an alternative or false self which appears to function adequately. (Lomas, *True and False Experience*, p. 93)

This false self acts as 'caretaker' to the true self, concealing it and protecting it, in the hope that one day circumstances may become sufficiently favourable for it to take a step into the world again. The progress by which the true self seeks to manifest itself may be hindered by all kinds of false meanings. Lomas reports that he often finds 'the search for more hopeful conditions, a search which, because of previous reverses, may take such tentative and distorted forms that its true meaning can easily be overlooked' (ibid., p. 97). The patient may subject his therapist to all manner of tests with the aim of finding out if he can be trusted and these 'experiments' may be very destructive. Then again there is the problem of dropping the false but successful patterns which have enabled the patient to survive so far. But the therapist's aim is to foster the rejection of those parts of the personality which stand in the way of healthy development: 'that which is false and sterile has to go.' These processes may be very confusing, and Lomas provides some fascinating case-histories to demonstrate the problems which may arise. But his emphasis must be noted: the 'dead and diseased wood' is 'gradually shed' in the name of a sense of 'true being' which is there in the patient. If it were not there, as a universal human dynamic, no therapy could succeed.

I often wonder whether the psychotherapists have fully pondered the implications of their work and their reflections on it. If we take the implications of the work of therapists like Lomas, Rollo May and Marion Milner, we must surely accept that there is, in every human being, a primary need to become the being one has a sense, within one, that one can become. There is a 'true self' which, however ill-defined or confused, knows that there is an 'I' which seeks to become itself. I suppose religious believers would call this the soul, but it does seem to be an energy which is the manifestation of that unique, uncompromising being such as Merleau-Ponty expresses in his passage above. The universal model of man which predominates in an age of 'science' *menaces* that true being in all of us, because it implies that we are the 'product' of other forces or processes, when we know, at the heart of being, that we are not. We are *only*—that is, the only significance for us lies in the recognition of this—our 'true self' and the potentialities it represents. *Nothing else will do.* And on this we can, surely, build a morality which is based on the truth about human beings.

Moreover, something else needs to be said about that true self being; it has a sense of its own *pattern*, and thus is a *formative dynamic*. Here we may look at the wider problem of how we see life in the universe. The predominant view of life in the universe is that it is an 'accidental' product of matter in motion. The modern scientific view is that there must be no teleological element in our thinking—no direction, aim or purpose in nature. Yet this is in clear contradiction of the facts, which are that natural phenomena represent what can only be called 'achievements'; the eye, the brain, flight, must surely be called achievements, and, as Polanyi puts it, there is a sense in which 'life strives'. Some scientists thus speak of a 'formative principle' in the universe, an innovative dynamic, and even a primary 'intelligence'. It does seem to be an undeniable aspect of the universe of matter that it tends to organize itself into higher forms, and, as Polanyi sees it, these forms are in a hierarchy of significance, the human mind representing the highest achievement of such significance of form, so remarkable that it gives meaning to the universe (see *Meaning* by Michael Polanyi and Harry Prosch).

If we accept this, then the dynamic by which each human

being seeks to realize a 'true self' may be seen as belonging to a fundamental principle of the universe. We may even perhaps take in here F. R. Leavis's word '*Ahnung*' by which he seemed to mean a fundamental sense of obligation, of a dynamic of conscience, by which we must feel a sense of duty to the universe of created life. In her remarkable study of a long psychoanalysis, *In the Hands of the Living God*, Marion Milner writes of how she finds patients 'moving towards a direct kind of inner face-to-face contact with the "other" in themselves which is yet also themselves' (p. 384). 'Increasingly in my clinical work I found myself needing to find what verbal concept in psycho-analytical thinking corresponded with what L. L. Whyte has called the formative principle.' She discusses whether one should call this the id; but, surely, in Freudian instinct theory, this dynamic can have no other function than to bring about organic relief by detensioning, as a purely physical force? Marion Milner is evidently groping about for a different kind of force, which cannot really be brought into the sphere of instinct theory, unless one were to see an organizing pattern-making aspect in instinct itself, which is surely impossible. She speaks of

> something that is shown in a person's own particular and individual rhythms and style. . . . Or is the term 'unconscious integrating aspect of the ego' more appropriate? Or a primal undifferentiated ego-id force? Certainly, some patients seemed to be aware, dimly or increasingly, of a force in them to do with growth, growth towards their own shape, also as something that seemed to be sensed as driving them to break down false inner organisations which do not really belong to them; something which can also be deeply feared, as a kind of creative fury that will not let them rest content with merely compliant adaptation; and also feared because of the temporary chaos it must cause when the integrations on a false basis are in the process of being broken down in order that a better one may emerge. (pp. 384–85)

As with Peter Lomas's case-histories, one feels a parallel between them and a good novel, so here perhaps one exclaims to oneself—Yes! That is what *Wuthering Heights* is about—and in saying this, one is recognizing that the novel can be the record of a quest for the realization of the true self, either in a character with whom the novelist identifies, or by using the novel as a kind of creative dream, in which the problems of true self being are explored. If these can be made universal, then the novel will be recognized as such, by us all as readers, at the tacit level—and the satisfactions will be great. I believe this dynamic of authenticity is found in all great novels.

What I have tried to show is that in philosophical anthropology, especially in its applications to psychotherapy, we have a vindication of the serious novel. It can be a mode of exploration of the same critical problem which emerges as the main necessity in the therapeutic consulting-room—the search for authenticity of being. In this way the novel is a special mode of thought. It belongs to a certain way of knowing, and the great achievement of the English novel, such as Q. D. Leavis delineates in her marvellous essay 'The Englishness of the English Novel', was the creation of a literary form which could deal with authenticity in its most complex and profound aspects.

No novel can be great unless it attends to this problem of authenticity, in the manner of utter integrity. That is, to put it in a traditional way, the true novel is only written out of intense moral concern, not about good and bad behaviour, so much as about what it is human beings find to be true to themselves. What engages our attention to a novel is its pursuit of 'true self being'. The novel recognizes, because of its realism, that there will be 'false self solutions'—and one aspect of these will be egoism that lives at the expense of others. So, here, there is another profound moral concern; but the roots of the morality are in the way in which 'wicked' or failed behaviour originates in the betrayal of the true self. The strategies of false solutions may be adopted to protect the true self; or they may simply be false out of confusion and tendencies to moral inversion, or out of inadequacy. But the theme is always authenticity, and this, as I have suggested, seems to be a manifestation of life displaying itself in the universe. The lessons for us are profound, and the connections I have tried to make between philosophy, psychology and literature, should, I believe, suggest a new validity for the creation of novels, for their subjection to literary criticism, and for their study in education—for they offer insights, in an experiential way, into some of the deepest problems of human existence.

There was a time when this emphasis would have been taken for granted, but there have been various developments which have undermined our confidence, in our interest in the novel. One has been the development of certain forms of literary theory which have tended to dismiss the kind of relationship between author and reader on which my kind of emphasis depends. This problem I also hope to deal with elsewhere; here it will be enough to say that since philosophical anthropology so powerfully brings to the forefront of the human picture the primary need for culture and the exploration of experience by symbolism, in relation to the quest for authenticity, we have in this field of study sufficient support for our kind of emphasis. Moreover, there have been developments in the novel itself, of various kinds, which at one level have meant the abrogation of standards in the face of commercial requirements for 'success', and at another have meant that the novel has become the vehicle of a deliberate assault on human values. These have both been made possible by a decline in criticism—indeed, by the virtual absence of any kind of serious and responsible criticism. Those of us who teach the novel in the university know differently, although even there the influences of the world of fashionable literature are often felt. There is a continual problem, as we find in conversations with both students and colleagues, of having to deal with manifestations in which discrimination has to be made. The word 'novel' now covers such a multitude of sins that it is almost impossible to use it sensibly at all. And this is compounded by the strange manifestations by which a professional in an English department (say) can write a superb critical essay on a novel in the great tradition, but also write an appalling novel which insults the human spirit, and encourage elsewhere forms of writing which seem to threaten the reputation of the novel with what can only be called corruption, while spoiling the atmosphere in which that kind of work of art can be enjoyed. The absence of good criticism allows such chaos.

In an old-fashioned spirit we need to indicate the way in which a great novelist such as George Eliot gave herself up to that formative principle which deals with authenticity and truth:

in all that she considered her best writing, there was a 'not herself' which took possession of her, and that she felt her own personality

19

to be merely the instrument through which this spirit, as it were, was acting. Particularly she dwelt on this in regard to the scene in *Middlemarch* between Dorothea and Rosamund, saying that, although she knew that they had, sooner or later, to come together, she kept the idea resolutely out of her mind until Dorothea was in Rosamund's drawing room.

From the Reverend Cross's *Life of George Eliot*

And then to insist, where the effect of the novel is concerned, that the same author was right when she wrote:

But man or woman who publishes writings inevitably assumes the office of teacher or influencer of the public mind. Let him protest as he will that he only seeks to amuse, and has no pretension to do more than while away an hour of leisure or weariness—he can no more escape influencing the moral taste, and with it the action of intelligence, than a setter of fashion, in furniture and dress, can fill the shops with his designs and leave the garniture of persons and houses unaffected by his industry.

The findings of philosophical anthropology, especially psycho-therapy, have shown us that in the exercise of their powers of exploring existence through cultural symbolism, human beings are engaged in pursuing their most fundamental freedom. There are two aspects of this freedom: it expresses a need to find one's own conscience at a very deep level—for as the therapist E. K. Ledermann has argued, existentialist therapy is the process of fostering that 'unconscious' or natural conscience in the patient, which enables him to make those choices and decisions about action which contribute to the fulfilment of being.[1] The other aspect is thus that of defining oneself, of finding out one's authentic nature, and so one's own 'meanings'. If we are dis-inherited from the tradition of the great novel, and if the novel becomes something else, or an instrument of inauthenticity, then our freedom suffers, for we lose a source of touch with truth and the possibility of meaning. The question is as serious as that, and that is why the novel 'matters'.

NOTES

1. E. K. Ledermann, *Mental Health and Human Conscience: The True and the False Self* (Avebury, 1984).

1

The Novel and Moral Concern: *Mansfield Park*

Till this moment I never knew myself—Elizabeth Bennett in *Pride and Prejudice*.

Returning again recently to teaching the novel, I was surprised to find what a passionate moral concern underlies the greatest novels. I came back to this teaching after a long expedition into existentialist philosophy; and what I find is that when I say 'moral' as in my opening sentence, what I mean is something of course very different from moralizing, discriminating between Goodies and Baddies and promoting the triumph of virtue. We have seen that existentialist psychotherapists postulate a primary dynamic in every human being, which seeks to fulfil the particular and unique potentialities that lie latent in the unfolding self. But, when we are weak, or emotionally deprived, or wounded, or frustrated, we are capable of developing a false self, to ward off the world's knocks, and to cope with experience as best we can. This 'false self' may be called false, because it often tends to inhibit the realization of the best potentialities; it is often obliged to frustrate the best possibilities of being; it knows it is a compromise or a making do; but it is the only way to hold a self together, in relationship to reality—and it may even be heroic. But it is still false,[1] to what the being could be; and so, in most people's lives, there comes a time when there must be an upheaval, a revolution, so that the true self can find its realization. This is the problem of ethical living—understanding what in oneself one really wants, and how that can be fulfilled in the world.

21

The moral turmoil may cause much pain; but so, too, can the frustration of all true self possibilities. Our delight, as we experience one of the great traditional novels, is in watching the characters discover, often in pain and distress, full of an awareness of their vulnerability, what it is to be true to the deepest promptings of their hearts. This seems to me to be what happens when we read one of Jane Austen's novels, and this explains why they are read with such fascination in the strangest foreign parts of the world, by people whose civilization is vastly remote from hers.

I therefore begin with a novel which has been the subject of a characteristic rejection in our time, *Mansfield Park*. I want to suggest that it made many novels that followed possible, by the very gravity of its theme of authenticity. I do not propose to engage in a discussion of the comments of Kingsley Amis; it would distract me too much from my aim to engage with the views of those I would not expect to understand Jane Austen. But I noted last year that her most recent biographer,[2] an American, found *Mansfield Park* 'unpleasant'.

Jane Austen is, perhaps, too honest and penetrating to be acceptable to our age. Her primary preoccupation, one is sometimes surprised to remind oneself, is with pain; the pain caused by the effects on the emotional life, of egotism, neglect, or trivial attitudes. At the opposite pole is the grave discovery of authenticity, and the joy of its fulfilment. Typically 'modern' questions which students raise today, about the narrowness of her milieu, or her failure to write about the Napoleonic Wars, are hugely beside the point; one might as well complain that Emily Dickinson does not write about hobos on the railroads, or that Lady Macbeth does not spend enough time visiting the sick. Jane Austen's attention was given to the heart and to self-realization: to the existential question of what one really needs in one's innermost being, in whatever age or circumstance.

D. W. Harding has discussed the problems she had, of living in a closed, intimate society,[3] and we misread Jane Austen if we do not take in the problem of 'hate' and its 'regulation'. Here we may find abundant clues to this underlying problem:

> Lady Bertram did not at all like to have her husband leave her:
> but she was not disturbed by any alarm for his safety, or

solicitude for his comfort, being one of those persons who think nothing can be dangerous or difficult or fatiguing, to anybody but themselves.

The whole end of that chapter (Chapter 3 of *Mansfield Park*) seems as if it were written in an outburst of anger at the very society she appreciated so much (Sir Thomas is leaving): 'The Miss Bertrams were to be pitied . . . not for their sorrow, but for their want of it. . . . they felt themselves . . . to have every indulgence within their reach. . . .' Over some rather deprecatory remark of Edmund's on the occasion, Fanny weeps (not because of Sir Thomas . . .). Seeing this, 'her cousins, on seeing her with red eyes, set her down as a hypocrite. . . .' Throughout the novel one cannot but note passages which deal with the discomforts of proximate living; those speak of 'disquiet', 'gross ignorance', 'meanness', 'distressing vulgarity of manner', this or that one is 'stupid', 'her cousins were deficient in the less common acquisitions of self-knowledge, generosity, and humility'. 'She had received no kindness from Mrs. Norris and could not love her. . . .' 'Admiral Crawford was a vicious man. . . .' Another is described as 'an undersized, little, mean-looking man'. The most terrible things are said about people: of Fanny, Mrs. Norris cries that she is obstinate, especially 'considering who and what she is . . .'—meaning she is a poor relation indebted to her adoptive family; Edmund says of Miss Crawford, 'she does not think evil, but she speaks it'; Crawford 'wanted the glory as well as the felicity, of forcing her to love him'. Fanny becomes aware that 'her mother was a partial, ill-judging parent, a dawdle, a slattern. . . .' Finally, Crawford is guilty of a 'dreadful crime', while Miss Crawford gives a 'sanction to vice' and in the end, Mrs. Norris, whom Emma has experienced as an 'hourly evil', goes off to live with Maria, so that 'their tempers became their mutual punishment'. Mr. Crawford and Mrs. Rushforth hope to marry, but in the end she is obliged to be convinced that such hope is vain, and then

> the disappointment and wretchedness arising from the conviction rendered her temper so bad, and her feelings for him so like hatred, as to make them for a while each other's punishment. . . .

Any reader trying to read Jane Austen for escape, into a charming Dresden world of eighteenth-century elegance, must either not read these distressing words and phrases, or be blind to their disturbing meanings.

On the other hand, once we become aware that there is plenty of hate and pain about, we should not suppose that the novels are a vehicle for Jane Austen's revenge on her society. She wants to discover whether it is possible to live, by the values of Augustan society which she respected so much, and in the wider sense to enquire by what values, then, can we hope for a well-regulated society—given man's (and woman's) nature? This is, of course, Shakespeare's question, too.

The words 'pain', 'misery', and 'punishment', however, often point to a specific crux. The existential problem found one of its main crises in matrimony. The whole of a woman's life depended upon the critical moment, of being made an 'offer'. It is no good deriding the 'system', or pointing out sardonically that in the *Gentleman's Magazine* the dowries were given in the marriage announcement columns; the predicament of Jane Fairfax in *Emma* makes it plain what was involved, in the failure to marry: 'to retire from all the pleasures of life, or rational intercourse, equal society, peace and hope, to penance and mortification for ever'. It was the end of one's hopes in life, and the danger is that of women's lives being ruined.

The opportunity to avoid the fate of blight came only by chance, and sporadically, at the moment of bloom; Fanny Price is only 18 at the end of *Mansfield Park*. Beyond 24 or 25, the moment was gone for ever; as is clear from *Persuasion*, a woman over 26 was in danger of losing her 'bloom' and so her hopes of a possible potentiality for the rest of her days. In *Sense and Sensibility* Marianne declares, 'A woman of seven-and-twenty can never hope to feel or inspire affection again. . . .'

The whole structure of the close society about which Jane Austen writes depends upon this matrimonial problem being satisfactorily solved. A woman had to make her judgement between her inward emotional life and the necessity of making a good enough match to sustain her in security.[4] Fanny's mother's marriage is an example of the consequences of getting it wrong. Whereas Miss Maria Ward with only £7,000 had the good luck to captivate Sir Thomas Bertram, and to be thereby raised to the rank of baronet's lady 'with all the comforts and conse- quences of an handsome house and large income' (she being 'at

least three thousand pounds short of any equitable claim to it'),
Miss Francis married 'to disoblige her family' by 'fixing on a
lieutenant of marines, without education, fortune or connections'. In eleven years' time she had 'a large, and still increasing
family, an husband disabled for active service, but not the less
equal to company and good liquor, and a very small income'.

It was out of this dismal situation that the Bertrams rescued
Fanny: 'Give a girl an education, and introduce her properly
into the world, and ten to one she had the means of settling well,
without farther expense to anyone.'

This problem then exacerbates the problem of emotional
authenticity and integrity, which Jane Austen makes the theme
of her art, and which, developed by great artists who came after
her, became the theme of *Middlemarch, Daniel Deronda, Portrait of
a Lady* and *Dombey and Son*; Dorothea Brook, Gwendolen
Harleth, Isabel Archer and Edith Dombey all make errors of
choice and authenticity which severely damage their lives and
fulfilment.

In making this reference I am, of course, implying that many
novelists who came later learnt from Jane Austen this central
theme. An example will be discussed later: Henry James's *The
Awkward Age*. In that novel there is, in the heroine, a complete
failure of authenticity, and this is due to the triumph of what in
Mansfield Park the Crawfords embody—'London'. 'London' is
the mode of explicit, charming, self-conscious but destructive
talk—and the 'free' comment of sophisticated discourse that
cannot take authenticity seriously, or cherish it. Vanderbank
speaks thus of this 'London':

> ... she has in her expression all that's charming in her nature.
> But beauty, in London . . . staring, glaring, obvious, knock-down
> beauty, as plain as a poster on a wall . . . fetches such a price in
> the market that the absence of it . . . constitutes . . . a sort of
> social bankruptcy. London doesn't love the intent, or the lurking,
> has neither time, nor taste nor sense for anything less discernable
> than the red flag in front of the steam-roller. It wants cash over
> the counter and letters ten feet high. . . .

'London' is an enemy in *Mansfield Park* in a somewhat
different way, though there is a clear line running from
Restoration London through the Crawfords and Mrs. Fraser's

entourage to that of the Buckingham Crescent to which Mr. Longdon's Beccles is juxtaposed. The opponent of 'London' in *Mansfield Park* is Sir Thomas Bertram, the country gentleman. As Lionel Trilling says in his interesting essay in the *Pelican Guide to English Literature*, 'the Crawfords are of London': 'their manner is the London manner, their style is the *chic* of the metropolis.' They represent a distinctly modern type, the kind of person who cultivates the style of sensitivity, virtue and intelligence—but whose charm and elegance are their main preoccupation, not principles or integrity. With Henry Crawford we have someone who is (as Trilling declares) 'a prey to his own charm'. But it is also more than that; he is a prey to his own egotism:

> I have a plan for the intermediate days. . . . I do not like to eat the bread of idleness. No, my plan is to make Fanny Price in love with me. . . . I cannot be satisfied . . . without making a small hole in Fanny Price's heart. . . . in that soft skin of hers, so frequently tinged with a blush as it was yesterday, there is decided beauty. . . .

He cannot understand her; 'London' cannot understand such sincerity, and must exert on it that will which seeks to reduce everything to triviality and thereby subdue the exigencies of life, in manic denial:

> Never met with a girl who looked so grave on me! I must try to get the better of this. Her looks say, 'I will not like you, I am determined not to like you'; and I say she shall.

It is to Miss Crawford's credit that she replies

> I do desire that you will not be making her really unhappy; a *little* love, perhaps may animate her and do her good, but I will not have you plunge her deep, for she is as good a little creature as ever lived, and has a great deal of feeling.

Henry, however, has only a fortnight to give to it:

> It can be but for a fortnight . . . and if a fortnight can kill her, she must have a constitution which nothing could save. No, I will not do her any harm, dear little soul.

He only wants, he declares, to produce an effect which will mean that 'when I go away that she shall never be happy again. I want nothing more.'

It is difficult if not almost impossible for us, to read such passages properly. We tend perhaps to read them 'playfully' as we read the dialogue in Restoration comedy. But Restoration comedy depends, in a special kind of fantasy, on our not admitting either the pain and woe caused by the exploitation of feeling, promiscuities and infidelities—while also failing to admit the human need to love. As L. C. Knights has argued, it reduces sexual emotion to the level of triviality and falsification;[5] and that is what Jane Austen is saying. The flippant tone of the Crawfords denies the real hate and harm; in the circumstances it was only too possible to spoil a woman's life. The London 'brightness' hides hate and hostility. While the Crawfords' attitudes to personal relationships are those of Restoration comedy, the play from light German melodrama rehearsed at Mansfield Park is Kotzebue's *Lover's Vows* which deals with illicit love and a bastard. Jane Austen does not object to such a work because she is a prude (a point Trilling makes), but because the performance of it involves the amateurs in impersonation; not only does this mean that Mr. Crawford and Maria are given the excuse to make love in public, but there is a danger that by entering into the character and attitudes of the people in the play, individuals may *find the integrity of the real self diminished. Impersonation* is the danger, and the falsification of authenticity it may lead to.

If falsification happens (and it does of course happen), then there could be serious hurt. And there are plenty of indications throughout the novel that individuals *are* hurt; the triumph of the Crawfords is followed by such consequences:

> Julia *did* suffer. . . . She had loved, she did love still, and she had all the suffering which a warm temper and a high spirit were likely to endure under the disappointment of a dear, though irrational hope, with a strong sense of ill-usage. Her heart was sore and angry, and she was capable only of angry consolations.

Her sister becomes her enemy: 'they were alienated from each other', and Julia was 'not superior' to the hope of 'some distressing end to the attentions . . . some punishment to Maria for conduct so shameful . . .'. There is a fear of 'public disturbance'—which, of course, later ensues. Fanny and Julia never communicate about it all, but they are 'two solitary sufferers'. In the end, the lives of Maria, Julia, and even

27

Crawford, *are* ruined; their social selves are destroyed, and their fulfilment precluded.

So, we are meant to take it seriously, and not playfully when, after the conversation referred to above, Jane Austen writes

> she left Fanny to her fate, a fate which, had not Fanny's heart been guarded in a way unsuspected by Miss Crawford, might have been a little harder than she deserved. . . .

A girl 'with so much tenderness of disposition' could not have 'escaped heart-whole' had not her affection been engaged elsewhere. He was (and the word is significant) '*attacking*' her peace of mind. Yet, of course, he is 'entertaining' and 'his manners were . . . so seriously and blamelessly polite . . . that it was impossible not to be civil to him in return. . . .'

The predicament of the heroine is such that we today find it hard to grasp. She is, so to speak, trapped. At Mansfield she must try to uphold her integrity, even though the Bertram children lack 'active principle' and proper education (Lady B having totally neglected this task). There, she is an adopted child of a poor relation, as Mrs. Norris viciously points out from time to time. Her own home has become a place where she could no longer live; among its vulgarity, she finds smallness of mind, insufficiency of awareness of others and their needs and rights, a mother who is a slattern, and a father who makes her the object of coarse jests; she finds a milieu (as Trilling emphasizes) where it has become customary *to devalue the human worth of other people*, and she has learnt at Mansfield Park to respect this.

But that is also the effect of the chic, flippant attitude to other people which the Crawfords embody. They come from a 'vicious' background: 'Admiral Crawford was a man of vicious conduct, who chose, instead of retaining his niece, to bring his mistress under his own roof.' Admiral and Mrs. Crawford have spoiled the pair as children: they '*though agreeing in nothing else, were united in affection for these children, or, at least, were no farther adverse in their feelings than that each had their favourite. . . .*' Mary Crawford is pretty; Henry, though not handsome, had air and countenance; the manners of both were lively and pleasant. But such exposure to favouritism and 'vice' (Jane Austen clearly implies) has made them selfish and, morally, 'light'; their attitudes appear at once (Chapter 5) to be those of 'London' chic, and are meant to seem dangerous:

> 'And besides, Miss Bertram is engaged. Remember that, my dear brother. Her choice is made.'
> 'Yes, and I like her the better for it. An engaged woman is always more agreeable than a disengaged. She is satisfied with herself. Her cares are over, and she feels that she may exert all her powers of pleasing without suspicion. All is safe with a lady engaged; no harm can be done. . . .'

The danger is there in their 'light' attitudes: '. . . if one scheme of happiness fails, human nature turns to another; if the first calculation is wrong, we make a second better; we find comfort somewhere. . . .' Marriage, Mary declares, 'is a manoeuvring business'—and speaking of dashed hopes she cries, 'What is this but a take in?' These remarks on marriage ('You have been in a bad school for matrimony, in Hill Street') are clearly meant to relate to the Crawfords' unhappy experience of divided parents, and are meant to appear so, seriously out of tune with the atmosphere of Mansfield Park, and especially with Edmund's serious calling.

Edmund is the antithesis of 'London'. When Miss Crawford wants to know if Fanny is 'out', he declares, 'My cousin is grown up. She has the age and sense of a woman, but the outs and not outs are beyond me.'[6]

Very early on in the novel, then, we have been introduced to two conflicting moral worlds. In Chapter 7, Fanny and Edmund discuss the Crawfords' attractiveness; but, Edmund asks:

> '. . . was there nothing in her conversation that struck you, Fanny, as not quite right?'
> 'Oh, yes! she should not have spoken of her uncle as she did. I was quite astonished. . . .'
> '. . . It was very wrong; very indecorous. . . . I do not censure her *opinions*; but there certainly *is* impropriety in making them public. . . .'

The Crawfords, says Edmund, have been under 'disadvantages', and Mrs. Crawford has simply not brought up her niece to understand what was due from her to the Admiral who brought her up. But now, with Miss Crawford's prettiness and her harp, Edmund is soon falling in love, and Fanny is surprised 'that he could spend so many hours with Miss Crawford, and not see more of the sort of fault which he had already observed'. And it is painful to Fanny to see the quiet mare which he had promised her supplied to Miss Crawford. Jane Austen is developing a situation which engages the attention of the reader, that of a woman being in love with a man without fully acknowledging it to herself, while the man begins to fall in love with an un-suitable other woman, who is likely to ruin *his* life.

That Miss Crawford is unsuitable begins to become plain in Chapter 8:

> She had none of Fanny's delicacy of taste, of mind, of feeling; she saw Nature, inanimate Nature, with little observation; her attention was all for men and women; her talents for the light and lively. . . .

That again is 'London' as against 'Mansfield Park'; and the difference between Fanny and Mary is discussed in relation to their response to architecture and landscape: in which perspective we may even sense Pope in the background, and all that Augustan feeling about the relationship between landscape, sensibility and values.[7]

When it comes to the regulation of the household, Mary Crawford reveals her 'London' contempt for the moral virtues. In the chapel, Fanny cries, 'A whole family assembling regularly for the purpose of prayer is fine!' Mary derides it:

> . . . It must do the heads of the family a great deal of good to force all the poor housemaids and footmen to leave business and pleasure and say their prayers here twice a-day, while they are inventing excuses themselves for staying away.

Miss Crawford is decidedly 'modern': '. . . it is safer to leave people to their own devices on such subjects. Everybody likes to go their own way. . . . The obligation of attendance . . . is what nobody likes. . . .' Of the young women of the past, she says, they were

> starched up into seeming piety, but with heads full of something very different—especially if the poor chaplain were not worth looking at—and, in those days, I fancy parsons were very inferior even to what they are now.

The 'light' and playful irony, which clearly derives from Restoration comedy, belongs to that almost cynical impulse to

30

unmask all pretensions; only, in her course of playful derision, she cannot stop herself making a comparison deeply offensive to Edmund, who is going to be ordained.

To Jane Austen, ordination and Edmund's 'calling' are no joke. Writing a letter at the time she received her first copies of *Pride and Prejudice*, she wrote 'Now I will try and write something else, and it shall be a complete change of subject— ordination.' The question of ordination, as Trilling makes clear, is of essential importance to the novel; and Edmund's taking on the office runs parallel as a theme to the way the characters take on rôles in their amateur theatricals, and the way Henry Crawford takes on a part to play, in trying to make Fanny love him.

Edmund is so angry with Mary Crawford that it takes him some time to reply: 'Your lively mind can hardly be serious even on serious subjects.' He tries to defend both the influence of chapel ('the influence of the place and of example may often rouse better feelings than are begun with') and the need for the mind to struggle against worldly distraction: 'The mind which does not struggle against itself under *one* circumstance, would find *objects* to distract it in the other, I believe.' We may relate this to the fundamental moral question in the novel, which is that of 'active principle'. There is a need for *conscience* and for conscience to be heard and applied, without taking flight into 'lightness' as Mary does, in the end, when she tries to be flippant about her brother's 'crime', in the outcome.

At the moment in the chapel, however, Miss Crawford shows herself capable of being chastened; when it is clear to her Edmund is an ordinand, she declares, 'If I had known this before, I would have spoken of the cloth with more respect.'

Miss Crawford, however, soon regains her playful composure: 'So, you are to be a clergyman, Mr. Bertram. This is rather a surprize to me.' She thought this was always the lot of the youngest brother; Edmund rejoins:

> 'Do you think the church itself never chosen, then?'
> '*Never* is a black word. But, yes, in the *never* of conversation, which means *not very often*, I do think it. For what is to be done in the church? Men love to distinguish themselves, and in either of the other lines distinction may be gained, but not in the church. A clergyman is nothing.'

Words do not mean in 'conversation' what they really mean; and in Miss Crawford's perspective, not to be socially distinguished in the worldly way is to be nothing. Edmund responds ironically that the clergyman may not set 'the tone' in dress or be 'high in state or fashion',

> But I cannot call that situation nothing which has the charge of all that is of the first importance to mankind individually or collectively considered, temporally and eternally, which has the guardianship of religion and morals, and consequently of the manners which result from their influence. . . .

'Manners' here has the meaning it has in 'manners makyth man': civilized modes of conducting oneself; or as in 'evil communications corrupt good manners'. How, asks Miss Crawford, can a couple of sermons a week 'govern the conduct and fashion the manners of a large congregation for the rest of the week? One scarcely sees a clergyman out of his pulpit . . .'. Responds Edmund, '*You* are speaking of London, *I* am speaking of the nation at large. . . . *We do not look in great cities for our best morality* . . .' (my italics).

In the local community, the clergyman has an influence:

> The *manners* I speak of might rather be called *conduct*, perhaps, the result of good principles; the effect, in short, of those doctrines which it is their duty to teach and recommend; and it will, I believe, be everywhere found, that as the clergy are, or are not what they ought to be, so are the rest of the nation.

Fanny concurs with 'gentle earnestness', but Miss Crawford still urges him to do something 'better'. 'You really are fit for something better. Come, do change your mind. . . .' There follows the highly significant episode of the women squeezing through the fence, leaving Mr. Rushworth, who has had a long trek to get the key, mortified and displeased; Maria has gone with Crawford to a distant knoll from which to get a view of the house. Julia is in a temper with everyone and snaps at Fanny ('you always contrive to keep out of these scrapes'). Mr. Rushforth declares that Henry Crawford is 'an ill-looking fellow. . . . In my opinion, these Crawfords are no addition at all. We did very well without them.' At last Edmund and Miss Crawford reappear, and all is 'disappointment and depression' to Fanny. Mrs. Norris, however, is of the opinion that the day

32

for Fanny has been 'Nothing but pleasure from beginning to end!' 'Their spirits were in general exhausted; and to determine whether the day had afforded most pleasure or pain, might occupy the meditations of almost all.' 'Pain' is a recurrent word in Jane Austen, and it is often clear that in her world even quite small forms of selfishness, neglect, wrong judgement or thoughtlessness could cause serious pain to others; and even this scene of a walk round the park thus becomes an indication of the greater pain to come, for it reveals the latent faults in many of the characters, and the potential chaos in the indulgence of selfishness.

The Crawfords triumph, in urging the company towards the injudicious and improper rehearsal of the play. Even Edmund takes part:

> To be acting! After all his objections—objections so just and so public! After all that she had heard him say, and seen him look, and known him to be feeling. Could it be possible? Edmund so inconsistent! Was he not deceiving himself? Was he not wrong? Alas! it was all Miss Crawford's doing. She had seen her influence in every speech, and was miserable.

Fanny is, of course, jealous, and there is some small irony at this. But what troubles Fanny is the way in which Edmund's integrity is being eroded, just as the play-acting itself is undermining people's sense of who and what they are: undermining *principle*, the capacity for ethical living.

Fanny, however, though she never ceases to know where *she* stands, and refuses to act, suffers greatly. She is 'full of jealousy and agitation'. Her rival is triumphant:

> Miss Crawford came with looks of gaiety which seemed an insult, with friendly expressions towards herself which she could hardly answer calmly. . . . She alone was sad and insignificant. . . . she could almost think anything would have been preferable to this. . . .

Julia is another to suffer: 'Henry Crawford had trifled with her feelings.' The play is having its effect—even as Sir Thomas returns. Crawford is going; Maria reflects:

> The hand which had so pressed hers to his heart! the hand and the heart were alike motionless and passive now! Her spirit supported her, but the *agony of her mind* was severe. . . . (my italics)

We live in a very different age, in which perhaps the key note is a somewhat schizoid suppression of feelings. As Rollo May declares in *Love and Will*, in America today people have taught themselves even to have sexual intimacy while not allowing their feelings to be engaged. Can we even understand the feelings of an engaged girl like Maria Bertram, who experiences a fictional relationship with another man in a play rehearsal, and suffers 'severe' 'agony of mind'? Whatever we feel about it, we must surely take Jane Austen's word for it, that there *was* suffering?

Sir Thomas is burning every copy of the play. Mr. Rushworth has gone away to tell those at Sotherton that he has returned. Maria hopes that Crawford will 'lose no time in declaring himself, and she was disturbed that even a day should be gone by without seeming to advance the point.' But Crawford is going, 'and so ended all the hopes his selfish vanity had raised in Maria and Julia Bertram.' In the last pages of Chapter 21, we may study the full effects of the attitude and culture of the Crawfords.

Maria's life *is* ruined. Her marriage is a false compensation for the loss of the hopes perfidiously aroused by the trifling and egotistic Crawford. In dismay she grasps at the security she has risked, by her flirtation with the richer man, and so her marriage is made in a false compromise from the beginning, in consequence.

Sir Thomas discerns some part of the truth: that 'Mr. Rushforth was an inferior young man, as ignorant in business as in books, with opinions in general unfixed, and without seeming much aware of it himself'. Sir Thomas tries to understand her feelings (though he knows nothing, of course, of the flirtation with Crawford).

> . . . Little observation there was necessary to tell him that indifference was the most favourable state they could be in. Her behaviour to Mr. Rushforth was careless and cold. She could not, did not like him.

Advantageous as would be the alliance, and public as the engagement was, her happiness should not have been sacrificed to these considerations; Jane Austen and her milieu adhere strongly to the principle that it is disastrous to marry without love. Mr. Rushforth, she believes, was accepted on too short an acquaintance, in any case.

Sir Thomas talks to Maria. For a moment she has a struggle—but only for a moment. She does not have the smallest desire to break off her engagement: 'She had the highest esteem for Mr. Rushforth's character and disposition, and could not have a doubt of her happiness with him.' But the reader knows she is desperate; there is now, after Crawford's defection, no other alternative but that of the kind of humiliation faced by Jane Fairfax in *Emma*. Sir Thomas (Jane Austen reports) is 'glad to be satisfied', and we proceed to a wedding as inauthentic as it could be.

> Her feelings, probably, were not acute. . . . A well-disposed young woman, who did not marry for love, was in general but the more attached to her own family . . . such and such-like were the reasonings of Sir Thomas, happy to escape the embarrassing evils of a rupture, the wonder, the reflexions, the reproach that must attend it; happy to secure a marriage that would bring him such an addition of respectability and influence, and very happy to think anything of his daughter's disposition that was most favourable for the purpose. . . .

So subtle is the depiction of the corruption, of Maria's feelings, and of Sir Thomas in his complacency, that we might feel for a moment we are reading George Eliot or Henry James; but then we realize where they learned their art. The inauthenticity becomes more and more complex as Maria Rushforth's life becomes falsified. At last to her it is now more important to cheat Crawford of his triumph than to examine her relationship with Rushforth. She is glad

> that she was safe from the possibility of giving Crawford the triumph of governing her actions, and destroying her prospects: and retired in proud resolve, determined only to behave more cautiously to Mr. Rushforth in future, that her father might not be again suspecting her.

Had the question come up earlier with Sir Thomas, she might have given a different answer; but Maria now enters upon her disastrous compromise, made cold by the absence of any further communication from Crawford: 'her mind became cool enough to seek all the comfort that pride and self-revenge could give.' At every step, Jane Austen's account reveals the pain and hatred bound up with feelings damaged by the light trifling of egotism, in such a milieu:

> Henry Crawford had destroyed her happiness, but he should not know that he had done it: he should not destroy her credit, her appearance, her prosperity too. He should not have to think of her as pining . . . for *him* . . . rejecting . . . independence and splendour, for *his* sake. . . .

There is a grave irony here beneath Jane Austen's terms: what 'independence' and 'splendour' is there, in being married to a man you hate? In what does woman's freedom lie?

> *Independence* was more needful than ever; the want of it at Mansfield more sensibly than ever. She was less and less able to endure the *restraint* which her father imposed. The *liberty* which his absence had given was now become absolutely necessary. She must *escape* from him and Mansfield as soon as possible, and find consolation in future and consequence, bustle and the world, for a *wounded* spirit. (my italics)

She prepares for the marriage in 'the misery of disappointed affection and *contempt* of the man she was to marry'. Could anything be more horrible, ominous and inauthentic? Maria's is a disastrous false solution: 'It was a very proper wedding. The bride was elegantly dressed; the two bridesmaids were duly inferior. . . .' The carriage was thought to be unsmart, but 'In everything else the etiquette of the day might stand the strictest investigation. . . .' Mrs. Norris 'had done everything'; she had made the match, and

> no-one would have supposed, from her confident triumph, that she had ever heard of conjugal infelicity in her life, or could have the smallest insight into the disposition of the niece who had been brought up under her eye.

Maria's only consolation is the renewed friendship of her sister, now the rivalry between them was ceased. But to anyone interested in human beings with respect for their capacity to be true to themselves, these pages must be painful, as the record of a not uncommon form of disastrous falsity. And while there is no suggestion that Maria would have been completely happy with her Rushforth had it not been for Henry Crawford, it is to the latter's inhuman selfishness that the key words point: 'misery', 'wounded', 'destroyed happiness' and 'contempt'.

With the departure of the Bertram daughters, 'the family circle became greatly contracted', and attention thus focusses on Fanny, who becomes 'the only young woman in the drawing room' and thus the centre of attention around the ever-present question of a marriageable girl's future prospects.

By accident, Fanny develops a new intimacy with Miss Crawford: a rainshower obliges her to shelter at the Parsonage at a dull moment in 'the gloom and dirt of a November day'; seeing her, Miss Crawford was 'all alive again directly' and plays her her cousin's favourite piece on the harp.

> Such was the origin of the sort of intimacy which took place between them . . . an intimacy resulting principally from Miss Crawford's desire of something new, and which had little reality in Fanny's feelings.

Fanny goes to her every two or three days—'it seemed a kind of fascination.' 'She could not be easy without going, and yet it was without loving her, without ever thinking like her.' She does derive 'occasional amusement', but 'that often at the expense of her judgement, when it was raised by pleasantry on people or subjects which she wished to be respected'.

The modern word for the Crawfords is *manic*. They cannot bear to be bored, to have an emptiness in their hours; essentially, they lack inner resources. By contrast, Fanny has had plenty of occasion to be alone, to occupy herself, to reflect. Here again is the difference between 'London' and Mansfield Park; and one of the important differences is that to Fanny certain people and subjects should be 'respected': the London flow of conversation is always corrosive. (We are on the way to the ever self-conscious but destructive talk of Mrs. Brookenham's dining room.) As we have seen, the difference extends to the perception of Nature; Fanny declares, about the shrubbery,

> How beautiful, how welcome, how wonderful the evergreen! when one thinks of it, how astonishing a variety of nature! . . . One cannot fix one's eyes on the commonest natural production without finding food for a rambling fancy.

Miss Crawford sees 'no wonder in this shrubbery equal to seeing myself in it'. She can hardly conceive that she would ever spend so long in such a quiet place ('the quietest five months I have ever passed'):

> '*Too* quiet for you, I believe.'
> 'I should have thought so, *theoretically*, myself, but,' and her eyes brightened as she spoke, 'take it all and all, I never spent so happy a summer. But then,' with a more thoughtful air and lowered voice, 'there is no saying what it may lead to.'

So, she is more reconciled to a country residence than she had ever expected to be. Miss Crawford, however, has a remedy for all the problems of housekeeping and bills.

> 'I mean to be too rich to lament or to feel anything of the sort. . . .'
> 'You intend to be very rich?', said Edmund, with a look which, to Fanny's eye, had a great deal of serious meaning.
> 'To be sure. Do you not? Do not we all?'

Edmund, however, proclaims that his intentions 'are only not to be poor'. But Miss Crawford is soon back again at urging him into Parliament or the Army. Edmund replies,

> . . . there *are* distinctions which I should be miserable if I thought myself without any chance—absolutely without chance or possibility of obtaining—but they are of a different character.

The difference between 'London' and Mansfield Park, then, is a profound difference between the choice of life-tasks, and solutions to the problem of existence. About this Jane Austen is quite 'straight' and serious—and Christian; when (as Fanny and he walk home) Edmund is 'thoughtful', he is reflecting upon the conflict between his fascination with the charming Miss Crawford, and his principles as an ordinand—and his recognition of the moral limitations of Mary's attitudes.

The manic element in the life of the Crawfords becomes plain when Henry arrives on a visit, and Fanny is the 'principal lady in company'. Edmund proclaims himself very glad to see him; but Fanny cannot forget the damage the man has done to the daughter's emotions, which Fanny was able to observe. Significantly, he sees the play rehearsal as a 'dream' when they were all 'alive':

> 'It is as a dream, a pleasant dream!' he exclaimed. . . . There was such an interest, such an animation, such a spirit diffused. Everybody felt it. We were all alive. There was employment, hope,

solicitude, bustle, for every hour of the day. Always some little objection, some little doubt, some little anxiety to be got over. I never was happier. . . .'

'Distraction from distraction by distraction' seems an appropriate comment, on Crawford's love of such a 'flight from reality'. I suppose our age's trouble with a novel like *Mansfield Park* is that our age itself is given over to distraction and the manic—while scruples and emotional realities seem to us mere 'little objections, some little doubt, some little anxiety to be got over'—which is Miss Crawford's ultimate attitude to her brother's adultery.

To some, Fanny appears 'prissy'. But, as here, Fanny (as we have seen) is aware of the suffering caused by Henry Crawford's unprincipledness. So, she repeats to herself: 'Never happier!—never happier than when doing what you must know was not justifiable!—never happier than when behaving so dishonourably and unfeelingly! Oh! what a corrupted mind!' Again, these are strong terms; but the reality of Fanny's predicament gives them point: as the principal lady in the drawing-room her future is the cynosure of all attention, and it is important that she shall be fully aware that Crawford is *dishonourable, unfeeling, corrupt* and liable to do what he could never justify— yet be flippant about it all and, indeed, to find such conduct 'vital'.

He is unaware of her feelings and startled when she angrily responds, that in her opinion everything had gone quite far enough, as her uncle disapproved it all so entirely. Crawford, she reflects, after another conversation in Edmund's office, 'can feel nothing as he should'.

Crawford has a fortnight to spare; he 'does not like to eat the bread of idleness', so he has a plan 'to make Fanny Price in love with me'. We have seen how Mary defends her—but then leaves her to her fate.

Crawford is nothing if not elegant and courteous: after dinner he offers to teach Lady Bertram and Fanny 'speculation'; he is in high spirits. A conversation ensues on Thornton Lacey, the home that goes with Edmund's future living. Behind this, again, we may sense Pope's values: '"Tis use alone that justifies expense.' Crawford is all for alterations:

the house must be turned to front the east instead of the north. . . .
And *there* must be your approach, though what is at present the
garden. . . . Then the stream—something must be done with the
stream. . . .

Edmund protests that what needs to be done must be done
without any very heavy expense and this, he hopes, 'may suffice
all who care about me'—a note which makes Miss Crawford
'suspicious and resentful of a certain tone of voice'. Fanny has
never seen the place, and tries to hide her interest; the chapter
(25) conveys all the complexities of interrelationships in a close-
knit community. Yet Crawford is by now anxious that Fanny
should think well of him; when the painful subject of their day
at Sotherton comes up, he murmurs to her:

> I should be sorry to have my powers of *planning* judged of by the
> day at Sotherton. I see things very differently now. Do not think
> of me as I appeared then.

But he comes up sharp against Mansfield Park, when Sir
Thomas makes it plain how soon and how completely Edmund
is to take on his residence: Edmund, he says

> . . . knows that human nature needs more lessons than a weekly
> sermon can convey; and that if he does not live among his
> parishioners, and prove himself, by constant attention, their
> well-wisher and friend, he does very little either for their good or
> his own.

Hearing this, Miss Crawford is disconcerted, because she cannot, to sustain her fancies, 'shut out the church, sink the
clergymen'—and yet she does not dare to relieve herself by a
single attempt to throw 'ridicule' on his cause.

A ball is planned; Edmund has serious problems: 'but the
whirl of a ballroom, perhaps, was not particularly favourable to
the excitement or expression of serious feelings.' The passage
again makes it clear (Chapter 26) that Jane Austen's theme is
authenticity: 'He knew his own mind, but he was not always
perfectly assured of knowing Miss Crawford's.' He had many
anxious feelings, many doubtful hours; as to the result of a
proposal:

> when he thought of her acknowledged disinclination for privacy
> and retirement, her decided preference for a London life, what

could he expect but a determined rejection? unless it were an
acceptance even more to be deprecated, demanding such sacri-
fices of situation and employment on his side as conscience
must forbid.

Did she love him well enough?

The ball intensifies the problems of choice. Miss Crawford
offers Fanny a choice of gold chains, for her to wear a cross her
brother William has given her. The chain she chooses, to her
confusion, turns out to be one which Henry Crawford has given
his sister. Miss Crawford believes she has 'never seen a prettier
conscience':

> 'My dear child', said she, laughing, 'what are you afraid of? . . .
> or perhaps—looking archly—you suspect a confederacy between
> us, and that what I am doing is with his knowledge and at his
> desire?'

Fanny is persuaded, but 'there was an expression in Miss
Crawford's eyes which she could not be satisfied with.' As we
know, Miss Crawford realizes that Henry intends to amuse
himself by making Fanny Price in love with him. But Fanny
suspects that 'he wanted, she supposed, to cheat her of her
tranquillity as he had cheated [her cousin].' It is hardly 'prissy',
surely, to wish to avoid the consequences of a man's cruelty
when you are so vulnerable?

The irony of the chain is deepened by the discovery that
Edmund is giving her a plain gold chain, too. Fanny is in
raptures; but what shall she do with Miss Crawford's? Edmund,
in turn, is delighted by Miss Crawford's kindness. Return the
necklace! It would be mortifying her severely. It would seem an
act of ingratitude; Fanny should wear the Crawford gift:

> I would not have the shadow of a coolness between the two
> whose intimacy I have been observing with the greatest pleasure
> . . . between the two dearest objects I have on earth. . . .

Fanny has never heard Edmund speak so openly; it was a stab:
'He would marry Miss Crawford.' But Fanny sees that he was
deceived in her: 'he gave her merits which she had not; her
faults were what they had ever been, but he saw them no
longer.'

Authenticity thus lies at the heart of the comedy continually,

41

in all its complexity. Fanny knows Crawford to be 'corrupt'; she suspects Miss Crawford, for all her charm, to be contemptuous of the good values embodied in Edmund's future office, and possibly capable of duplicity in her attitude to her brother's intrigues. But because she loves her cousin Edmund, Fanny is asked to wear a jewel, over which she has been tricked into acceptance, following Edmund's persuasion that the gift came from Mary's generosity and sympathy—which gift seems likely to involve her in an intimacy with Crawford she could only find painful, since she regards him as unprincipled and cruel.

Moreover, Fanny is in love with Edmund. The note he had begun but had left unfinished, to accompany the necklace, was locked away with it, as the best part of the gift: 'there was a felicity in the flow of the first four words . . . which she could have looked at for ever.'

But she struggles against hope. She tries to 'overcome all that was excessive, all that bordered on selfishness', in her affection for Edmund.

> To call or to fancy it a loss, a disappointment, would be a presumption for which she had not words strong enough to satisfy her own humility. To think of him as Miss Crawford might be justified in thinking, would in her be *insanity*. (my italics)

She tries to regulate her thoughts and comfort her feelings by a happy mixture of reason and weakness. On the eve of the ball, however Edmund has been pained by Miss Crawford's manner; he wished to engage Miss Crawford for the first two dances, but she told him it was the last time she would ever dance with him:

> She is not serious. I think, I hope, I am sure she is not serious; but I would rather not hear it. She has never danced with a clergyman, she says, and she never *will*. . . .

Edmund declares that he knows her disposition to be as sweet and faultless as Fanny's,

> but the influence of her former companions makes her seem— gives to her conversation, to her professed opinions, sometimes a tinge of wrong. She does not *think* evil, but she speaks it, speaks it in playfulness; and though I know it to be playfulness, it grieves me to the soul.

Jane Austen points to a dissociation between word and act. 'The effect of education', says Fanny gently: and, indeed, in one sense, as we shall see, *Mansfield Park* is an 'educational' book, because one of the problems is Lady Bertram's failure to educate her daughters properly, while the Admiral, his mistress and that milieu have miseducated Mary. But where, we may ask, was Fanny educated? What was it in Fanny's upbringing, that made her so principled and insightful? Perhaps privation, gratitude, and the kindly influence of Edmund himself? But Fanny's gift is to be in touch with her true conscience, with dogged integrity.

'London' playfulness is destructive, Jane Austen sees, because it is egotistical; it prefers (as does Henry) to live in a dream of its own vanity. But it is not only a question of not being able to be 'serious'; Mary Crawford displays a disastrous incapacity to extend enough sympathy to recognize what grief she is giving to Edmund's soul by deriding the very choice he has made in his life: his 'office'—the office which has become the focus of his integrity and the meaning of his existence. We can surely only demur if we are indifferent to people giving one another pain, or are to suppose it does not matter when individuals are assailed in the very area where they believe they are most likely to fulfil themselves? The tendency in our time to reject *Mansfield Park* is a mark of our failure to recognize the deepest human realities and existential needs. Fanny finds it hard to exert 'all the heroism of principle' in her own case, however much she is determined to do her duty; and now she has to try to be equally brave in soliciting comfort in the man she loves: 'Do not ask advice of *me*. I am not competent', she declares, when Edmund suggests that 'it appears as if the mind itself was tainted.' She warns him against saying too much: 'Take care *how* you talk to me ... the time may come—.' But, he avows, the time will never come. And even if it did, he would not be ashamed of his own scruples. He has not been blinded.

'He had said enough to shake the experience of eighteen.' In passing, we may reflect that Jane Austen clearly has faith in the capacity for wisdom in each new generation; she displays a profound belief in human nature and its capacity for integrity. Edmund's admission now had made everything 'smiling', and, to make her happiness complete, Crawford's chain will not go through the ring of William's cross, so Edmund's must be worn.

At the ball, Fanny is principal lady, and is admired by

everyone; Sir Thomas is proud of his niece. Edmund and Miss Crawford, however, part in mutual vexation, because of offensive remarks she continues to make about the clergy.

A slack period follows the ball, during which Edmund is away. Suddenly, however, Henry Crawford returns, announcing to his sister that he is 'quite determined to marry Fanny Price.' His affections, he declares, are firmly fixed, and his sister is pleased. At this moment the Crawfords are quite sincere; one might say that they have been 'educated' by Mansfield Park. There is no calculation or cynicism. Mary says

> From my soul I do not think she would marry you *without* love; that is, if there is a girl in the world capable of being uninfluenced by ambition, I can suppose it her; but ask her to love you, and she will never have the heart to refuse.

He, says Jane Austen, 'had too much sense not to feel the worth of good principles in a wife, though he was too little accustomed to serious reflexion to know them by their proper name'. He had been impressed by her steadiness and regularity of conduct, her high notion of honour, and her observance of decorum; he depended fully on her faith and integrity, and in saying as much he 'expressed what was inspired by the knowledge of her being well principled and religious'. Indeed, Crawford is captivated exactly by the Fanny who sees him as unprincipled.

He even sees that his 'light' project to make her love him was 'bad, very bad in me'. He believes he can make her very happy, 'happier than she has ever been yet herself, or ever seen anybody else'. When he announces his plans, Mary cries 'then we shall all be together'—meaning herself and Edmund included. She even declares it an advantage to Henry, that he should soon get away from the Admiral 'before your manners are hurt by the contagion of his'. He is much in love; he is going to do marvellous things for Fanny, and he is going to show Maria and Julia Bertram how wrong they were to neglect Fanny and be so unkind to her. His attitude now is no longer selfish vanity; but it still has a strong current in it of the desire to see himself, and to be seen, as Fanny's benefactor and promoter, with great approval, and so there is falsification in his motives, and the egotism is still there.

Crawford has secured William's promotion to Lieutenant;

that has been his business in London. But while Fanny's heart is beating with gratitude, he declares his love and she is astonished and confused to find that he really means it: 'It was so; he had said it.' 'It was all beyond belief! He was inexcusable, incomprehensible! But such were his habits, that he could do nothing without a mixture of evil.' He has just made her the happiest of human beings, but now he had insulted her. How could *she* have excited serious attachment in a man who had seen so many, and had been admired by so many, and flirted with so many? Fanny had never known such a day of agitation.

The modern reader, I believe, finds it hard to respond adequately for various reasons. Jane Austen has two major concerns—pain and the moral coarseness which leads to one person inflicting pain on another, and integrity and the relationships between egotism, vanity and duplicity; so, she uses a language which invokes moral standards: 'evil', 'insulted', 'agitation'. It is almost impossible for us to return to respond adequately to a word such as 'serious' as used by Jane Austen. So much of our literature is based on the appeal of enjoying the insult, and the language in which it is gloated upon, that we no longer even notice the moral issues involved, when one individual inflicts pain on another; rather, because of the moral inversions in our literature and its ethos, we laugh. Even with a serious novelist like Saul Bellow, we are led to take it as so 'normal' for a father to threaten his son with a gun, for the protagonist to fantasize shooting his ex-wife, for him to have been raped by a homosexual and so on (in *Herzog*), that the behaviour of hate and cruelty seems only 'realistic', while the only hope is to survive, bruised and traumatized, in a world in which the pain of being violated is endemic. The language becomes itself a vehicle for a kind of defensive dissociation.

Yet in truth, to be more realistic, and to be more closely attentive to what (say) the psychotherapists tell us about the everyday lives of their patients, our central concern is still not to suffer pain at the hands of others, and, if we can, to find joy, and that which is right and proper for ourselves. It is for this reason that we shall always return to Jane Austen's novels; they are essentially existential, about fundamental problems of being and meaning. Her language is at one with a firm grasp on these things.

The Novel and Authenticity

Fanny's worst trial, over the proposal of Mr. Crawford, is a masterpiece of complex and subtle plot. Fanny is an adopted member of the Bertram family and so owes them a great allegiance—and, indeed, she fully and gratefully acknowledges Sir Thomas's values. But she is in love with Edmund, though no one is aware of it, and she has not yet acknowledged it to herself. Crawford she knows to have done serious harm to Julia and Maria, and has shown himself vain and unprincipled with them, and in his conduct in Sir Thomas's absence. Yet Crawford is now seriously in love with Fanny, and offers his hand (and his considerable wealth) openly, liberally and properly. Sir Thomas is happy at this excellent offer for Fanny, who is, after all, an intimate friend of Crawford's sister, and Crawford has secured preferment for her dearest brother. Yet the proposal—first communicated to her by Sir Thomas with all his weight of approval behind it—throws her into 'perturbation and dismay'.

'What is all this?' asks Sir Thomas, 'what are your scruples *now?*'

Fanny protests that she has given Crawford no encouragement.

'Am I to understand . . . that you mean to *refuse* Mr. Crawford?' It is beyond Sir Thomas's comprehension. And Fanny feels 'almost ashamed of herself, after such a picture as her uncle had drawn, for not liking Mr. Crawford.'

Sir Thomas wonders whether her affections are engaged else- where, and sees her, her face like scarlet, form her lips into a *no*. As for early marriages, does she not agree that Edmund has seen the woman he could love—a painful moment indeed? Has she any cause to think ill of Mr. Crawford's temper?

> 'No, sir.'
> She longed to add, 'but of his principles I have'; but her heart sank under the appalling prospect of discussion, explanation, and probable non-conviction. . . .

It is only later, when Crawford shows at last what kind of unprincipled man he is, that Fanny is vindicated. At the moment, she must simply endure the opprobrium, and live with the pain of being thought badly of, without there being any possibility of revealing her true reasons for not accepting Crawford. Sir Thomas's daughters are so closely involved in the truth that she cannot tell him; she could not tell Sir Thomas the truth without betraying them. She hopes it will be enough for him to learn she does not like Crawford; but she finds 'to her infinite grief' it was not.

Whatever changes there have been in the position of women and in matrimonial relationships, Fanny's is still a kind of situation in which we all—men and women—may well find ourselves: unable to make a clear moral position known, because to declare everything openly would cause greater distress or evil, or be met with sheer incomprehension. At such a moment, we must simply endure, as Fanny endures, and hope that the truth will ultimately prevail (as in life it does not always prevail). She must be discreet, to preserve the very fabric of mutually trusting relationships which she (and her author) admires.

Sir Thomas declares, with cold sternness, that Fanny has 'disappointed every expectation' of her conduct and has proved her character the very reverse of what he had supposed. The moral irony is that this extremely painful reprimand for Fanny has been brought about by the one commendable and proper action taken by the vain and unprincipled Henry Crawford! She is now accused of 'temper, self-conceit' and that 'independence of spirit' which 'prevails so much in modern days' (1814!) 'which in young women is offensive and disgusting beyond all common offence'. She is 'wilful and perverse' and inconsiderate of the judgement of her betters. But *we* know that Fanny's judgement is better than that of her betters.

Sir Thomas dismisses her refusal as a 'wild fit of folly', in which she is throwing away an honourable opportunity—one which Sir Thomas would gladly have accepted for one of his own daughters; it was a 'gross violation of duty and respect' for her to refuse Crawford, and a mark of *ingratitude*. Fanny cries bitterly, and declares that she knows Crawford would only make her miserable; Sir Thomas, however, takes hope that perhaps, if the man persists, he might eventually persuade her. She, however, 'was miserable for ever'.

One of Fanny's main concerns is whether Edmund might think her selfish and ungrateful; he was away, otherwise he might have softened his father's wrath. But Sir Thomas is not entirely without understanding and sympathy; when Fanny returns from the shrubbery she finds a fire in her room, and he has given orders for this to be lit daily.

We must today feel satisfaction, that women are not now in such a position, to feel obliged to secure their future, under such pressures in the sphere of the emotional life. The independence of spirit which Sir Thomas deplores has become a real independence, or nearly so, after over a hundred and fifty years of struggle. Yet, of course, there are other pressures and other circumstances, in which an individual, man or woman, may still be faced with the need to maintain integrity, when even their nearest and dearest, and those to whom they have obligations, cannot be put in the true picture, and some anguish may have to be endured; and our cry may still be Fanny's:

'Heaven defend me from being ungrateful!'

> She trusted, in the first place, that she had done right; that her judgement had not misled her. For the purity of her intentions she could answer . . .

. . . and she hopes her uncle will see, as a good man, 'how wretched, how unpardonable, how hopeless, and how wicked it was, to marry without affection'. As for Crawford, she worries at first whether perhaps he really loved her and was unhappy, but later consoles herself:

> London would soon bring its cure. In London he would soon learn to wonder at his information, and be thankful for the right reason in her which had saved him from its evil consequences.

But Crawford is not going to give up so easily. His vanity will not allow him to let up. He was in love, very much in love:

> and it was a love which, operating on an active, sanguinary spirit, of more warmth than delicacy, made her affection appear of greater consequence because it was withheld; and determined to have the glory, as well as the felicity, of forcing her to love him.

Crawford displays what D. H. Lawrence called 'will'; he believes he must succeed (he has no suspicion that her heart is previously engaged). Jane Austen's psychology is superb, in her depiction of the development of Fanny's manner, in the face of the development of Crawford's love.

> Mr. Crawford was no longer the Mr. Crawford who, as the clandestine, insidious, treacherous admirer of Maria Bertram,

had been her abhorrence, whom she had hated to see or to speak to, and whose power, even of being agreeable, she had barely acknowledged.

He is a Mr. Crawford who is addressing her with ardent, *disinterested*, love, whose feelings have, apparently, become all that was honourable and upright. She herself has to become both more compassionate, and also must feel a sense of being honoured. Yet as he persists she becomes angry, because his perseverance reveals itself as selfish and ungenerous.

> Here was again a want of delicacy and regard for others which had formerly so struck and disgusted her. . . . How evidently was there a gross want of feeling and humanity where his own pleasure was concerned; and, alas! how always known, *no principle to supply as a duty what the heart was deficient in*! (My italics.)

The last phrase is a key one in Jane Austen; and (which is all my point) it is a key phrase in the whole development of the novel as a great work of art. There is the same want of principle 'to supply as a duty what the heart was deficient in' in Gwendolen Harleth, in Grandcourt, in Gilbert Osmond and Mrs. Brookenham, in Sir Claude and Miss Overmore. However further developed these are, the moral roots of the humane concern with how human beings can live without giving pain to one another, and destroying one another's lives, are in Jane Austen, not least in *Mansfield Park*.

Sir Thomas, who remains puzzled, declares that she is not to suppose that he is trying to persuade her to marry against her inclinations. Lady Bertram, however, tells Fanny: 'it is every young woman's duty to accept such a very unexceptional offer as this.' But this was 'almost the only rule of conduct, the only piece of advice, which Fanny had ever received from her aunt in the course of eight years and a half'!

To this Fanny decides it would be unprofitable to respond; but when Edmund returns and has obviously learnt about the matter, and takes her hand, she thinks that 'but for the occupation and the screen which the tea-things afforded, she must have betrayed her emotion in some unpardonable excess.' But Edmund is entirely on his father's side—which is ironical, since he himself has decided against Mary Crawford because of *her* lack of principle!

An important opportunity comes, however, for Edmund to talk to Fanny in Chapter 35. She finds, at least, that Edmund does not blame her. He cries,

> 'How could you imagine me an advocate for marriage without love? . . . You did not love him; nothing could have justified your accepting him.'
>
> Fanny had not felt so comfortable for days and days.

But when Edmund hopes for Crawford's success, she cries out, 'Oh! never, never, never! he never will succeed with me', and astonishes Edmund with her 'irrationality', for he is blind to her attachment to him.

The scene is subtly ironic, again, since as Edmund presses Fanny towards unauthenticity, he shows that 'Miss Crawford's power was all returning.' Yet she, of course, cannot tell the truth, even if she admitted it to herself, that she loves Edmund. But Fanny can make it a little more plain than she could to Sir Thomas, that she has doubts about Crawford's character. At the play,

> I then saw him behaving, as it appeared to me, so very improperly and unfeelingly . . . so improperly by poor Mr. Rushworth, not seeming to care how he exposed or hurt him, and paying attentions to my cousin Maria. . . .

But, says Edmund, 'let not any of us be judged by what we appeared at that period of general folly'; the heart of the problem (as Lionel Trilling says) is the way in which everyone had been caught up in a false ethos which the play had created. Miss Crawford, who is angry with Fanny, tries to convince her that, despite his earlier tendency to flirtation, Henry is now a changed man; but Fanny doggedly insists, 'I cannot think well of a man who sports with any woman's feelings; and there may often be a great deal more suffered than a stander-by can judge of. . . .' Mary insists that 'he is attached to you in a way that he never was to any woman before . . .'—but all Fanny can manage is a faint smile. References to William touch her deeply; but, as we are aware throughout Chapter 36, there is still a radical difference between the manic ebullience of Miss Crawford's ('London') attitude to life, love and marriage, and Fanny's gravity.

The youthfulness of Fanny and her uprooted predicament is underlined when, after spending half her life at the Bertram household, she goes back to her old home—where everything is noise and disorder. The point seems to be to throw the (Augustan) values which Mansfield Park embodies at best into sharp contrast; at home she reflects sadly on Mansfield:

> The elegance, propriety, regularity, harmony, and perhaps, above all, the peace and tranquillity of Mansfield, were brought to her remembrance every hour of the day, by the prevalence of everything opposite to them *here*.

It is not only living in incessant noise that is the disadvantage of Fanny's Portsmouth home; at Mansfield, it is true, there were 'no sounds of contention, no raised voice, no abrupt bursts, no tread of violence.' But it is the respect for persons that she misses: 'and proceeded in a regular course of cheerful orderliness; everybody had their due importance; everybody's feelings were consulted.' The irritations represented by a Mrs. Norris were nothing 'compared with the ceaseless tumult of her present abode'. Her authentic self cannot now exist without all that is meant by 'Mansfield Park'.

Without that reference, the kind of moral discrimination Fanny persists in over Henry Crawford would have been impossible to sustain; yet he is so much in love with her that he braves the humbleness of her home, to visit her, and press his suit again.

> She was sorry, really sorry; and yet in spite of this and the two or three other things which she wished he had not said, she thought him altogether improved since she had seen him; he was much more gentle, obliging and attentive to other people's feelings than he had ever been at Mansfield. . . .

The interval while Fanny is at Portsmouth is crucial. She parts from Crawford on sympathetic terms, though his hopes of her must clearly be at an end. Has Edmund come any closer to proposing to Miss Crawford? In Chapter 44 comes a crucial letter from him. It is a very confiding letter, and has the air of intimacy, as between brother and sister, or cousins—and more: 'you know the weak side of her character. She was in high spirits, and surrounded by those who were giving all the support of their bad sense to her too lively mind.' That is, Mary Crawford is in her 'London' setting. 'I do not like Mrs. Fraser. She is a cold-hearted, rash woman. . . .' This Mrs. Fraser married from

51

convenience, and she and her sister Lady Stornaway are determined supporters of everything 'mercenary and ambitious'. Edmund is appalled at the influence these 'London' characters have on Miss Crawford: 'they have been leading her astray for years.'

Yet Edmund declares 'she is the only woman in the world whom I could ever think of as a wife', and he cannot give her up. Yet 'It is the influence of the fashionable world altogether that I am jealous of. It is the habits of wealth that I fear.' Edmund wonders how he should propose: by letter? But he also says to Fanny. 'I miss you more than I can express.'

The letter irritates Fanny: 'he will marry her, and be poor and miserable.' She even flies into resentment: 'Fix, commit, condemn yourself.' However, Tom Bertram becomes seriously ill, and everything is temporarily disturbed. But while Edmund goes to be with his brother, Tom's sisters prefer to remain in town.

Fanny now becomes 'disposed to think the influence of London very much at war with all respectable attachments', and she gets a very 'London' letter from Mary Crawford, which fills her with disgust. Miss Crawford, writing in a totally inappropriate light vein ('Fanny, Fanny, I see you smile and look cunning, but upon my honour I never bribed a physician in my life'), reflects on the chances of Edmund inheriting Tom's estate. It is all written in the witty style of Restoration comedy; but to Fanny it is wholly in bad taste, and displays an unpardonable deficiency of genuine emotion and human sympathy at such a moment. Yet Mary offers to convey Fanny to Mansfield in their carriage—an offer she realizes she must instantly decline. But on pondering Miss Crawford's letter she sees that the most sinister aspect of it is that Miss Crawford would be willing to consider Edmund as a clergyman, 'under certain conditions of wealth'; schooled by her mercenary and ambitious London friends 'she had learnt to think nothing of consequence but money.'

The next communication is a bombshell—a letter from Miss Crawford rejects 'a most scandalous, ill-natured rumour' about Henry: 'I am sure it will be all hushed up, and nothing proved but Rushworth's folly. If they are gone, I would lay my life they are only gone to Mansfield Park. . . .' Had there been some indiscretion, in Henry's marked display of attentions to her cousin?

Ironically, the devastating revelation comes from Fanny's father, from the newspaper he would sit reading, usually paying her no attention except for some coarse jest:

> 'What's the name of your great cousins in town, Fan?'
> A moment's reflection enabled her to say, 'Rushworth, sir.' . . .
> 'Then there's the devil to pay among them, that's all! . . . I don't know what Sir Thomas may think of such matters . . . But, by G—! if she belonged to *me*, I'd give her the rope's end as long as I could stand over her. . . .'

This must be the most brutal note in all Jane Austen, and parallel to her father's punitive cruelty is Fanny's shock:

> The horror of a mind like Fanny's, as it received the conviction of such guilt, and began to take in some part of the misery that must ensue, can hardly be described. At first it was a kind of stupefaction; but every moment was quickening her perception of the horrible evil.

Jane Austen's position is quite clear from her language: to run away in an adulterous relationship with a married woman is a 'sin of the first magnitude', and to attempt to 'gloss it over and desire to have it unpunished' (as Mary Crawford does) is corrupt. But Jane Austen is not being simply prudish or adhering dogmatically to the Christian commandments; it is the misery caused to others that concerns her: 'It was too horrible a confusion of guilt, too gross a complication of evil, for human nature, *not in a state of utter barbarism*, to be capable of!' It is not the decorum of Mansfield Park that is threatened, but all those values by which people can live in harmony, peace and trust—a forfeiture of *principle*, by which alone one can live truly:

> *His* unsettled affections, wavering with his vanity, *Maria*'s decided attachment, and no sufficient principle on either side, gave it possibility. . . . what would be the consequence? Whom would it not injure? . . . Whose peace would it not cut up for ever. . . .

Sir Thomas and Edmund, she supposed, might find it 'scarcely possible to support life and reason under such a disgrace' while 'as far as this world alone was concerned' (it appeared to her) 'the greatest blessing to every one of kindred with Mrs.

Rushworth would be instant annihilation'. There is nothing ironic in Jane Austen's presentation of Fanny's shock here; she means it, and endorses it. Edmund says 'There is no end of the evil let loose upon us'—Julia, to cap everything, has run off with Mr. Yates, whom Sir Thomas thought so badly of.

It is a long time before Edmund can speak of Miss Crawford. At last he tells Fanny that when he met her (at Lady Stornaway's) she began by exclaiming, 'What can equal the folly of our two relations?' Edmund comments:

> No harsher name than folly given! So voluntarily, so freely, so coolly to canvass it! No reluctance, no horror, no feminine, shall I say, no modest loathings? This is what the world does. For where, Fanny, shall we find a woman whom nature had so richly endowed? Spoilt, spoilt!

The moral ground in Jane Austen's novel is as firmly based, fair and square Christian, as John Bunyan's: 'Thou shalt not commit adultery.' Miss Crawford is of London, the world, Vanity Fair; and she compounds evil: 'She saw it only as folly, and that folly stamped only by exposure. . . . it was the detection, not the offence, which she reprobated. . . .'

Miss Crawford made it worse at every moment; turning to Fanny, she declares she would never forgive her for being such a 'simple girl' as to turn Henry Crawford down. If he had married her, he would have forgotten Maria: 'It would have all ended in a regular standing flirtation, in yearly meetings at Sotherton and Everingham.' 'Cruel!' said Fanny, 'quite cruel. At such a moment to give way to gaiety, to speak with lightness, and to you! Absolute cruelty.' No, says Edmund, hers was not a cruel nature; she did not mean to wound his feelings:

> The evil lies deeper, in her total ignorance, unsuspiciousness of there being such feelings; in a perversion of mind which made it natural of her to treat the subject as she did.

She was speaking as she had heard others speak (Mrs. Fraser, Lady Stornaway)—*and*, we may perhaps suggest, as people speak in Restoration comedy. The language goes with a corruption of sensibility: 'Hers are faults of principle, Fanny; of blunted delicacy and a corrupted, vitiated mind. . . .' 'Perversion of mind,' 'a corrupted, vitiated mind': these are strong words, and bring to mind St. Paul's phrase, 'evil communications corrupt good manner'; *that* is what *Mansfield Park* is about, and the corruption means *pain, hurt* and *wounding*, in its consequences.

As Miss Crawford goes on, proposing marriage for Henry and Maria, Edmund is more and more deeply hurt: 'she had been inflicting deeper wounds in every sentence.' He had not supposed it possible that anything could occur to make him suffer more, but he did suffer more. He went on to suggest the overcoming of the *'dreadful crime'* by 'a defiance of decency and impudence in wrong', recommending to everyone 'a compliance, a compromise, an acquiescence in the continuance of the sin . . .'. When Edmund responds to put his point of view she laughs at him, affecting carelessness, but obviously confused and dismayed, and yet accusing him of 'sermonizing'.

Her final appeal to him is a 'saucy playful smile', 'seeming to invite in order to subdue me'; but Edmund walks out on her. 'How have I been deceived!' he finally exclaims. Now, 'Fanny's friendship was all that he had to cling to'.

Fanny, at this moment, is happy, in spite of everything. She is rid of Mr. Crawford, and is back with her associates at Mansfield Park, where she hopes to be restored in Sir Thomas's opinion. But Sir Thomas is undergoing a serious crisis of awareness: he realizes how deficient he has been in bringing up his daughters.

Mrs. Norris had indulged them; he had been severe, thus teaching them to repress their spirits in his presence, so that their real disposition became unknown to him. And the failure was a moral one:

> He feared that principle, active principle, had been wanting; that they had never been properly taught to govern their inclinations and tempers by that sense of duty which can alone suffice.

Mr. Rushworth divorces Maria, but she parts from Crawford; she hoped for a while he will marry her, but becomes convinced that hope was in vain,

> till the disappointment and wretchedness arising from the conviction rendered her temper so bad, and her feelings for him so like hatred, as to make them for a while each other's punishment.

Says Jane Austen: 'The indignities of stupidity, and the disappointments of selfish passion, can excite little pity.' Everyone becomes everyone else's punishment: Maria, who has destroyed her own character, goes off to live with Mrs. Norris, to this fate.

Sadly, we are not given Edmund's declaration of his love for Fanny. Jane Austen feels she could not describe it:

> let no one presume to give the feelings of a young woman on receiving the assurance of that affection of which she has scarcely allowed herself to entertain a hope.

But Sir Thomas approves: 'Fanny was indeed the daughter that he wanted.' In the family, Susan, her sister, takes her place.

The end fits the moral pattern:

> With so much true merit and true love, and no want of fortune and friends, the happiness of the married cousins must appear as secure as earthly happiness can be . . . their home was the home of affection and comfort.

Mansfield Park must be the 'straightest' novel in the language, and, I believe, completely convincing. Human nature, it is intended to show, can be spoilt by bad influences—consequences of neglect, irresponsibility, egotism, and the culture or atmosphere of false solution. The sensibility can be corrupted, and this matters not because of Christian commandments, but because the consequences are pain, the failure of fulfilment and the destruction of lives. 'Active principle', meaning ethical living, can save us, for the realization of the potentialities of the true self.

The novel lies behind so many great English novels—certainly *Middlemarch, Daniel Deronda, Portrait of a Lady, What Maisie Knew*, and *The Awkward Age*. One important insight in her influence comes from recognition of Jane Austen's penetrating moral concern that 'lightness' and 'liveliness', of an insincere and unprincipled kind, may cause distress and destruction. Today, *Mansfield Park* is felt to be too moral to be art, while Fanny is thought to be too good to be true; yet this novel very largely made the great English novel possible, because of its author's deeply religious moral gravity about authenticity, and her belief that a principled woman is credible.

Some—many students—declare their preference for Emma over Fanny, because she is less 'moral', and makes more mistakes. However, it is important still to recognize that *Emma* too is a strongly moral book, despite its greater degree of comedy. The most active principle, however, in this work is embodied in Mr. Knightley—witness, for instance, the castigation he gives Emma over her insult to Miss Bates. She has, she sees, been 'brutal' and 'cruel'; if we examine the prose carefully, we shall find the same strong words, condemning those lapses which cause pain to others and destroy good relationships.

The same concepts of 'principle' govern the work. Here, one of the major errors over matters of moral principle is Frank Churchill's concealment of his and Jane Fairfax's engagement. This has many serious consequences—it causes pain because people say things they would not have said had they known, and the impulse to conceal impels Frank himself to pay attentions to Emma which—had she not been invulnerable because of her love for Knightley—caused serious and possibly permanent damage. So, it is beyond impropriety, because it could have caused damage to integrity:

> Impropriety! Oh! Mrs. Weston—it is too calm a censure. Much, much beyond impropriety! It has sunk him, I cannot say how much it has sunk him in my opinion. So unlike what a man should be! None of that upright integrity, that strict adherence to truth and principle, that disdain of trick and littleness, which a man should display in every transaction of his life. . . .

Emma is later mollified, and reconciled to Frank Churchill who, it appears, only allowed himself to pay attentions to Emma since he was 'convinced of her indifference'. And, of course, Emma realizes that harm may be caused not only by definite lack of active principle, but by self-indulgence of a vain kind, in imagining possibilities for others, the fulfilment of which is flattering to oneself.

What we are interested in, in Emma, is her shame, and her own moral development through suffering: 'how inconsiderate, how indelicate, how irrational, how unfeeling had been her conduct.' But this, in fact, only makes *Emma* an even more 'moral' book than *Mansfield Park*. Emma is perhaps more attractive to us than Fanny, because she is allowed to have faults, and to grow in self-awareness, in a way with which we are familiar in ourselves, compared with Fanny, who is made to stick almost dogmatically to her principles. But Emma Woodhouse is, after all, a young lady of considerable private means, and also a woman with 'consequence' in her neighbourhood. Fanny's problem is that she is totally dependent upon the family at Mansfield Park for her upbringing and her maintenance: she is by no means independent—and so it is especially painful for her to have to strike out for her principles, even as she is prohibited by loyalty from condemning her cousins or exposing Crawford.

Emma, we may say, is more 'modern' than Fanny, because she is more like an independent woman of today. But the essential theme is the same over her: in the last scenes with Knightley it is clear that what he fears is some lasting damage to her whole life, from Frank Churchill's inauthenticities. And from *Persuasion* we may take it that such damage could mean a daily misery, and sense of utter loss of the potentialities of being. It is this perception which lies at the heart of Jane Austen's art, and nothing is more moving than the way in which, breaking through the barriers of decorum, the lovers in each of her books realize the authenticity of what ought to be for them, and declare it, in final triumph over all the dangers and distractions that might have diverted it or suppressed it for ever. She holds our attention so tenaciously not least because of the implication that the chance of fulfilment may come once and once only, and must be seized for 'life'.

I do not suppose I have said anything original about Jane Austen. I am simply concerned to try to convey my sense that she is deeply moral as an artist in my sense, and that this moral seriousness has an existential quality, of concern over what her heroines make of their lives. In this, she gave a certain crucial significance to the English novel—a theme which those who followed her pursued, even when, like Henry James and Lawrence, they had reservations about her.[8]

NOTES

1. I leave aside the commercial use of false solutions in fiction: see my *The Masks of Hate* on *Goldfinger*. I was interested to see a psychiatrist in *The Times*, Saturday, 6 March 1983, reveal that Ian Fleming was a psychopath. In my book I found his 'solutions' those of a psychopath.

2. Professor John Halpern, author of *The Life of Jane Austen* (Harvester, 1985), who finds her 'cold-hearted', 'cold-blooded', 'sneering', 'bad-tempered', 'snarling', 'cruel', 'nasty', 'neurasthenic', 'crabby', 'judgemental', 'paranoic' and 'malicious'. *Mansfield Park* is her 'most unpleasant novel' and ends in a 'paroxysm of rage'. All her novels have 'botched' endings, using 'the same dreary technique'. See the review by Judith Tomlin in *The Tablet*, 20 April 1985.

3. D. W. Harding, 'Regulated Hatred: An Aspect of the Work of Jane Austen'; *Scrutiny*, VIII, pp. 346–62.

4. The fate of Charlotte Lucas in *Pride and Prejudice*, if one reads it carefully, is quite chilling: 'I am not romantic, you know', she tells Elizabeth Bennett, 'I ask only a comfortable home.' To Elizabeth, she has 'sacrificed every better feeling to worldly advantage'.

5. On Restoration comedy in *Explorations* (1946).

6. The question of young women coming 'out' and the effect on their sensibilities, especially of conversation with married women, is, of course, a central theme in *The Awkward Age*.

7. And George Crabbe, whom Jane Austen admired. Compare the landscape in Crabbe's stories; Pope's *Moral Essay on the Use of Riches* and Holkham and Houghton Halls in Norfolk.

8. Our era has more than reservations, and displays rather a hostility to Jane Austen's kind of sincerity and concern for human welfare. Characteristically, at the time of writing, appears a novel which 'rewrites' *Mansfield Park* in a cynical vein: *Miss Abigail's Part* by Judith Terry (Cape, 1986). It is written from the point of view of Julia Bertram's maid. She records how the sisters compete for the 'fascinating' Henry Crawford, while Tom Bertram 'regards the maids as fair game' and has fathered a child by one of them. The maid becomes the toast of the London stage, no doubt implicitly to ridicule the worries at Mansfield Park about the effects of dramatics: *The Times* described it as a 'pleasant and amusing novel'. The inheritance of the achievement of thought about human life must, it seems, be dragged down into the general level of our deprivation through incomprehension.

2

Authenticity and Sexuality: Henry James's *What Maisie Knew* and *The Awkward Age*

I have recorded my surprise on returning to Jane Austen, to become aware how intensely *moral* are her concerns. This moral concern focusses on whether individuals' lives will be fulfilled or blighted; her grimmest novel is *Persuasion*, in which, her 'bloom' blighted by heart-break, loss and separation, the heroine faces a life which is no life at all.

I was equally surprised, to turn back again to Henry James, to find him picking up this same theme—at times quite clearly under the influence of Jane Austen (sometimes by way of George Eliot) and being as intensely moral. In both, the essential Christian virtues associated with love are extremely powerful— love and 'active principle', the application of a right sense of duty to life, though the application is never crude or simple, and with both is transformed into something very much their own.

The best novel to exemplify James's deep moral concern is *What Maisie Knew*. What the novel in general today has lost by its obsession with mentalized sensuality may be clearly seen if we turn to this, one of the greatest novels about love, lust and human sexual relationships in the English language. There is, of course, not one 'torrid' moment in the novel, nor is there the least vibration of passion. Yet the girl child protagonist is tossed between adults whose relational life is portrayed, subtly and placingly, as sordid, and is seen as deeply immoral in the way it places a painful burden on the child. By this means, the chief characters are shown to be false to themselves. Thus it is not a prudish moral concern. Rather, like Jane Austen's, it attends to the need for 'active principle', so that pain, distress and destruction can be avoided. The point is not that the protagonists are wicked, but that they pursue their satisfactions selfishly, without regard for those decencies which foster personal integrity. All the reader is given is, perhaps, the glimpse of a walking-stick left where it betrays a lie covering slavishness to passion; or a repulsive face whose hardness is related to the virtual purchase of sexual satisfaction; or a glimpse of Ida's bosom which is cut lower to the degree she is pursued in the socialite life of manic promiscuity. The significance of Maisie is that she is exempt (as Mrs. Wix her prim governess is not) from the excitements of (vicarious) involvement in passion; she is concerned only with *what is right*, from the point of view of the child whose primary need is for good relationship, truth, and meaning, and who judges integrity from such real needs.

Maisie, indeed, could be seen to stand for those needs which philosophical anthropology has shown to be primary—divested of those disguises which an obsession with sensuality, prurience or immoralism draws before them. A 'Freudian' interpretation of the book would be wrong, and would raise the question of Maisie's possible 'corruption', such as was once raised in a fruitless correspondence in *Scrutiny*, or of the 'corruption' in Mrs. Wix, which is also irrelevant. Mrs. Wix is confused, but she is not compromised because she is so impressed by Sir Claude. She is not guilty; it is rather that her adherence to the conventional precepts of morality, and to the conventional sense of a child's 'innocence', is so limited as to be ineffective.[1] Maisie's insights go much deeper, because of their naïveté, which is also a purity, and she thus persists as the moral focus of the novel.

Having no fear of passion, what strikes Maisie as the worst failing is the abandonment of integrity in an enslavement to passion. In the background there is also the question of their fear of woman which makes the men so inauthentic. There is a lovely reciprocity between Maisie's pre-pubertal passionlessness,

61

which no one need fear, and the dangerous dynamics in all the mature women including Mrs. Wix.

What Maisie Knew surely enlarges the question of the problem of woman in such a way as to make the insights of philosophical anthropology even more immediately relevant to our consideration of the novel. For in the end integrity and authenticity in personal relationships founder on the fear of woman, which is, in Sir Claude, fear of his own passion.

> 'Yes, I've chosen,' she said to him. 'I'll let her go if you—if you—'
> She faltered: he quickly took her up. 'If I, if I—?'
> 'If you'll give up Mrs. Beale.'
> 'Oh,' he exclaimed; on which she saw how much, how hopelessly he was afraid . . . Mrs. Wix was right. He was afraid of his weakness—of weakness. (Penguin edition, p. 237)

The end of the book is a superb and complex drama, to relish the full subtlety of which one has to read it again and again. The mannerisms of James's prose are there, but the writing has an embodied quality; his imagination has entered into his subjects, and he feels with them superbly; here, 'their faces were grave and tired':

> There, however, on the landing, out of sight of the people below, they collapsed so that they had to sink down altogether for support: they simply seated themselves on the uppermost step while Sir Claude grasped the hand of his stepdaughter with a pressure that at another moment would probably have made her squeal. (p. 238)

The wanderings of Maisie and Sir Claude are done with a powerful immediacy—of 'felt life'. Sir Claude is trying to get her, Maisie, to enable her, to make a 'free' choice, over whether she is prepared to let Mrs. Wix go, and to live with Sir Claude and Mrs. Beale; both are 'free'—but this only means they have made certain agreements with their respective partners to tolerate separation, while it seems unlikely they would be able to get divorced. They are going to live together 'in sin', and they will probably do this in France. The presence of Maisie would give them some kind of respectability and would also help them to justify their relationship giving them a 'footing'; it would be almost a duty:

'. . . She *is* your mother now, Mrs. Beale, by what has happened, and I, in the same way, I'm your father. No one can contradict that, and we can't get out of it. My idea would be a nice little place—somewhere in the South—where she and you would be together and as good as anyone else. And I should be as good, too, don't you see? For I shouldn't live with you—just round the corner, and it would be just the same. My idea would be that it should all be open and frank. *Honi soit qui mal y pense*, don't you know? You're the best thing—you and what we can do for you— that either of us has ever known.' (p.229)

The novel is full of situations in which adults place a heavy burden on the child, but this final burden of bestowing respectability Maisie eventually sees would be too much, too *false*, despite her early acceptance of the logic of her 'mother' and 'father' living together. She is also aware of a flaw behind the argument, for she has divined already that Sir Claude has *not* been telling the truth. He came back in the night, and he *has* been with Mrs. Beale—so, he is (in Mrs. Wix's terms) a 'slave':

'. . . he's just a poor sunk slave', she asserted with sudden energy.
Maisie wondered again. 'A slave?'
'To his passions.' (p. 215)

Sitting in the café having breakfast, Maisie sees that much of his manner to her is, if not a pretence, a pose—inauthentic:

This difference was in his face, in his voice, in every look he gave her and in every movement he gave her and every movement he made. They were not the looks and the movements he really wanted to show, and she could feel as well that they were not those she herself wanted. She had seen him nervous, she had seen everyone she had come in contact with nervous, but she had never seen him so nervous as this. Little by little it gave her a settled terror, a terror that partook of the coldness she had felt just before, at the hotel, to find herself, on his answer about Mrs. Beale, disbelieve him. . . . Why was such a man so often afraid? . . . He could be afraid of himself. (p. 223)

We may not share Mrs. Wix's view of Mrs. Beale, that she is as bad as Mr. Beale's Countess, and that if it were not for Sir Claude she'd 'live off other men'. But we may recall the way she pocketed the pile of sovereigns which the Countess gives Maisie; there is more than a touch of calculated self-interest about Mrs. Beale, in her beauty and the charm and persuasion

63

she exerts. Maisie, certainly, has enough of a glimpse of this, to feel doubtful about casting in her lot with this project, of the two ex-partners of her parents living in a deceptive state of respectability, with her as the mask, in a clandestine liaison.

It is not that it is immoral, but that there are radical inauthenticities in it. Maisie *does* have a moral sense, but it is not like that of Mrs. Wix, who simply adheres to Christian respectability and social conventions. Mrs. Wix is rather like our Mrs. Mary Whitehouse; she has a certainty about what is acceptable and what not. She is sometimes moved towards understanding and compassion, by her 'adoration' of Sir Claude—but this never extends to any possibility of accepting what she regards as immoral or compromising in any way situations of adultery or sinful union.

The whole point of the book, however, is that mere 'immorality' means nothing to Maisie. The dimension of passion, of sexual love, of sensual indulgence and habit undermining the best intentions, and generating treachery to relationship—the 'flesh'—is just not in her consciousness. Maisie is of the latency period, and she can experience neither prurience nor revulsion, neither sexual envy nor disgust, as Mrs. Wix can. In fact, of course, such a purity is really impossible, even in a child; but Maisie is a dramatic device based on an assumption that such a thing could be possible—and this device enables us to attend to what is important in human relationship. In this respect she is like Huckleberry Finn, who observes the world from an assumed naïveté, too, as though seeing it for the first time. In truth, children are aware, 'unconsciously', of sexuality and have experienced sensual sadistic but not really 'sexual' lust,[2] envy, the impulse to empty and annihilate others. But there is also a capacity in the child, as in latency, to disregard the sexual-sensual, and to see experience beyond this in the dimensions of the primary need for relationship and integrity.

So, Maisie's concern is with what is authentic, for her, and for others, especially between themselves. An orphan of divorce, she knows that the human being needs a 'significant other', and that a child needs a mother and father. She judges everything in the human merry-go-round, from the point of view of these needs, and the need to be true to oneself and to others—above all, she has the child's desire that people significant to oneself should be 'good', but her good faith is surrounded by bad; when it proves impossible to deal with the situation, when selfish wills conflict and try to use her against one another, she pretends to be stupid, or is silent—the child's only way of avoiding compromise with inauthenticity.

By this device, James draws our attention in his comedy, to what *authenticity* and *integrity* are. Let us leave aside (the artist says) the dimension of 'passion' and ask (as if from a child's innocent vision) what matters between human beings, what has meaning? Sexual passion, as in many modern novels, may supply a seeming meaning, as with Lawrence, that may usurp the deeper and wider needs for meaning that transcend it; to Lawrence at best it was the sphere that involved 'being'. Philosophical anthropology insists that the primary human need is for *meaning* and that sincere committed personal relationships are a direct means to that meaning, which is somewhat different in its emphasis. Maisie is the focus of an existential concern with this fundamental principle in human life. In this her 'moral sense' is much deeper than Mrs. Wix's, which adheres merely to the ten commandments.

It is inevitable in the end that Maisie should go off with Mrs. Wix, leaving Sir Claude with Mrs. Beale:

> . . . at last, in mid-channel, surrounded by the quiet sea, Mrs. Wix had courage to revert. 'I didn't look back, did you?'
>
> 'Yes. He wasn't there,' said Maisie. 'Not on the balcony?' Maisie waited a moment, then, 'He wasn't there,' she simply said again.
>
> Mrs. Wix was silent a while. 'He went to *her*,' she finally observed.
>
> 'Oh I know!' the child replied. (p. 248)

Mrs. Wix wonders what Maisie knew; to her it is startling to suppose that Maisie accepts that Sir Claude has gone into Mrs. Beale's room, or perhaps to bed with her. But this is not the point, not what Maisie 'knows'. She knows that Sir Claude was not so devoted to her that he would gaze out to sea at her departure in agonized frustration. He and Mrs. Beale were probably having one of their rows. But now the idea of having Maisie as a mask has had to be given up. Sir Claude is simply reconciled to making the best of it in his passionate slavery to

Mrs. Beale; Maisie realizes she has made the right choice, not
to be an instrument, not to be simply a convenience. She has
salvaged herself, out of the last subtle temptation to be
exploited, inauthentically, by selfish and weak adults. Incidentally, she has also triumphed over Mrs. Wix, by displaying a
superior capacity for authentic existential choice, even as Mrs.
Wix had been 'probing', supposing that her long walk with Sir
Claude meant that her moral sense had gone for good. Maisie
displays 'something still deeper than a moral sense' (p. 242)—
as by saying she would go with Sir Claude, 'if he gave up Mrs.
Beale', the 'only right decision', according to his lights, implying he would trust him if only he were not a 'slave' to passion.
By this, Sir Claude realizes 'We *can't* work her in . . . she's
unique. We're not good enough. . . .' Maisie in the row at the
end persists in asking of Mrs. Beale 'Will you give him up?'

But this is an unreal, idealistic, almost rhetorical question—
like wishing he was not a man, and she (Mrs. Beale) was not a
woman with a sexual tie to him. Mrs. Wix is appalled because
she supposes Maisie is addressing herself to their sexual
cohabitation, when the child is really trying to opt for the most
authentic and trustworthy relationship in view—recognizing
that (as Sir Claude says) Mrs. Beale really hates her.

The final recognition is that 'we are not good enough', while
Maisie and Sir Claude, looking in one another's eyes, recognize
that 'their eyes met as the eyes of those who have done for each
other what they can' (p. 248). The novel leaves the matter thus
in suspension: if you take the child's spirit of existential
integrity, no adult can be good enough. All that adults can try
to do is not to betray that source of meaning and values; even *to
try* is itself a value.

In the first part of the book, of course, few of the characters
do try. Ida is totally irresponsible and selfish, and appears with
a succession of rich lovers who will give her a good time until
she comes to loathe them—Sir Claude, Mr. Perriam, Lord Eric,
Mr. Tichbein, the Captain. Beale uses his charm to develop
affairs with a series of striking women—ending up as a paid
gigolo to the physically repulsive Countess.

To the modern reader it has to be laboriously made clear how
firmly *moral* James's concern with Maisie's predicament is. He
speaks of 'misery and a degraded state', and his intention was to

Authenticity and Sexuality

portray the child wringing the chance of happiness, fineness and richness out of 'misbehaviour', 'pain and wrong'. He speaks of 'the selfishness of its [the child's] parents', Beale Farange is described as 'ignoble' and the friend to whom he introduces his daughter as 'deplorable', while Maisie is admitted to be surrounded by 'gross immoralities'. We find it hard to respond adequately to these terms, and to see (as with Jane Austen) that the objection to *falsity* is the *pain* it causes.

James is concerned to sustain Maisie's freshness in an immoral world. She is to be seen as creating 'by the fact of [her] forlornness a relation between [her] step-parents', thereby prompting further misconduct. But because she lives 'with all intensity and perplexity and felicity in [her] terribly mixed little world' she is able to flourish to a degree; 'at the cost of many conventions and proprieties, are decencies, really keeping the torch of virtue alive in an air tending infinitely to smother it.' The comedy is Maisie,

> making confusion worse confounded by drawing some stray fragrance of an ideal across the scent of selfishness, by sowing on barren strands, through the mere fact of presence, the seed of the moral life. (p. 8)

James, despite his own sophistication and elegance, shares nothing of the knowing, ironic detachment of Jane Austen's Crawfords, or his own Mrs. Brookenham. We are left in no doubt as to the selfishness in various degrees of his adults. They, however, are not condemned for offending against the decencies and proprieties—as Mrs. Wix would condemn them—but for offending against integrity, to themselves and others. While Ida and Farange are just coarse and gross, it is perhaps Sir Claude who offends most, despite his good qualities and the way the seeds of moral life are sown in him, by being weak and vacillating, not least to the Maisie he is so fond of. And yet he seems trapped—trapped by his sexual appetite, his fear of his sexual slavery, his fear of Mrs. Beale, and his hopeless original marriage to Ida. He is, truly, a 'victim'—as many adults are; and he cannot be true to Maisie in consequence until, in the end, he allows her to go out of his life with Mrs. Wix. The play on the word 'free' throughout the final drama is simpler; throughout, the more the adults kick over the 'decencies',

67

the less free they become, an insight which the modern world—with its self-deluding attachment to false solutions—finds especially unpalatable, if indeed it is anything other than blankly uncomprehending (none of the ironic subtleties, with the firm moral sense beneath them, would make any sense today, for example, in the pages of *The Times*).

I have invoked *What Maisie Knew* to indicate Henry James's moral strength, because I am trying to suggest that the English novel as a great art depended upon a certain grave existential seriousness. This is not to say that one does not have serious doubts, at times, about James's position, and even about the degree to which he was able to be concerned rather than fascinated by 'wickedness'. One is often doubtful about his 'solutions'.

The Golden Bowl seems to display a profound moral seriousness. Step by step Maggie Verver discovers that she has been the victim of a manipulation by her Prince, who is having an adulterous affair with Charlotte Stanton, a golden girl from his past. In the end she acts, with great patience and concern, to win him back, by the power of love. A good conventional account of the novel, its Christian themes, and of the redemptive power of love, is given by Dorothea Krook: in her study *The Ordeal of Consciousness in Henry James*.

Yet one remains unconvinced; the 'felt life' is not 'there'. The Prince never materializes, as a figure one sees, hears, knows and tangibly feels as a presence—as one 'knows' Sir Claude, or Olive Chancellor. Maggie herself seems an unsympathetic and mousey creature. Reading *The Bostonians* or *What Maisie Knew*, I laugh with delight, and with feelings of pity, sympathy, ironic amusement, with a response to warm humanity. Reading *The Golden Bowl* I am perplexed and puzzled; around Charlotte Standon there is a golden libidinousness, but her marriage to Maggie's father is not somehow realizable—and in the end, to one's distress, one does not care what happens to her, or the shadowy prince, or to Maggie. There is a serious absence of the felt force of sexuality, and of anger. The compelling scene where Maggie is out on a terrace, with everyone else indoors, is full of ominous power; but it ends in what I can only feel to be an impossible episode, given the undercurrents. That is, the characters do not act as they would or should; the passion that

68

should break out does not—and one begins to sense a *roman à thèse* effect, while the interest has shifted to the 'perfection' of the 'art'.

A different doubt arises at the end of *Portrait of a Lady*. I do not feel competent, yet, to write about this master work of the later James, though I read and re-read it with baffled curiosity and fascination. *Portrait of a Lady* is a marvellous novel, and I take the central theme, of Isobel's wilful quest for independence meeting Gilbert Osmond's elegant egotism, idealizing it, and then becoming its victim. I take the point of Isobel at the end feeling guilt over her own part in luring Gilbert into the disastrous union as much as he lured her. And I can see that Lord Warburton and Caspar Goodwood are neither true alternatives. I recognize too James's masterly portrayal, using all that he learnt from Jane Austen and George Eliot, of the way in which human beings 'hook into' one another, and become unable to disentangle themselves (Gwendolen Harleth and Grandcourt are clearly behind *Portrait of a Lady*).

But there are two elements in *Portrait of a Lady* that leave me disturbed. One is Isobel's fear of sexual passion (possibly imported from *Daniel Deronda*)—which does not quite ring true, or serve as a significant element in the whole (Dorothea Krook is illuminating on this). The other is more disastrous, because it seems inauthentic—that is, Isobel's final return to her husband Gilbert Osmond. I take in what Henry James says about her respect for marriage and its meaning. But I feel in that ultimate decision he has applied 'Christian principles', and they falsify. Perhaps I, too, am showing myself to be 'modern' here; but as Isobel learns how Osmond has been Mme. Merle's lover and conspirator, conspiring to marry her for her money, thus totally falsifying the relationship, I am increasingly appalled that she does not find him and the marriage totally loathsome and fit only for rejection. I recognize all the difficulties of property and divorce; but I cannot believe that the woman who is so movingly able to get through to Ralph and recognize their love for one another would go back to Osmond and marriage, even for the sake of Pansy. I believe she would have sought divorce, even if it meant afterwards a life of penury, pain and isolation. I believe she would have been *right* to take that step. I feel that James somehow funked a proper ending to the novel, applying

Christian principles of forgiveness and deference to the recognition of marriage too externally to his subject, and what is missing is the element of *carnal knowledge*, and moral repulsion of being, at that depth. (See note 8.)

Whether or not I am right, it seems to me indicative that I can have doubts. We are not left with such doubts over *What Maisie Knew* or *The Bostonians* (though we may be left in doubts altogether about James, over his *blague* with *The Turn of the Screw*. There is a touch of the *voulu* sometimes with James, as he becomes too pleased with his own power). But what about *The Awkward Age*?

The Awkward Age is related to *What Maisie Knew* by its theme, which here becomes that of 'what Nanda knew', and 'what Little Aggie knew'. It is also related by the contrast between the perspective by which the girl heroine sees 'the world' and what the world is actually like. There are, of course, several shifting perspectives in the book: there is all that is represented by Mr. Longdon and 'Beccles'—a rural world outside the brashness and sophistication of 'London'; but there is also the difference between how Buckingham Crescent regards itself (the characters are always saying 'You're magnificent!' to one another) and the way they actually are and behave—for instance, Harold fills his mother with 'horror' while Vanderbank fills Mr. Longdon from the beginning with fear: 'I think I was rather frightened' (p. 31).[3]

Maisie in *What Maisie Knew* triumphantly remains (because she is pre-puberty), as I have shown, uncomplicatedly unconfused about human passion and its weaknesses. Her view reveals the *inauthenticity* into which adults are drawn, by their compromise by passion and its *selfishness*. Her predicament is poignant because she is a victim of the cruelty and indifference of which slavery to passion is capable.

This position is not possible for Nanda, who is sexually mature, intelligent and perceptive. Indeed one of the 'points' of the book is that Nanda has never been protected from 'knowing' about human passion—she meets married women at Tishy Grendon's, and she reads Van's French novels. She remains quite untroubled and uncorrupted by such influences and stands for an authenticity of intelligence and sensibility that has a moral concern that runs parallel to Maisie's. Only at the end does she reveal the strain of her feelings for Vanderbank (and these are not sufficiently given and placed) when she bursts into tears.

Nanda is nubile and she must be looked after—that is, her future must be taken care of. James picked up this theme from Jane Austen (though we feel that the marriage choice issue is not so critical for the American or London women of James's time).

Leavis declares this novel is a masterpiece, or at least a minor masterpiece; and yet in the end has reservations. He refers to the social comedy and pronounces the novel in its upshot a 'tragedy'. It must, he says, be read with intensity.

It is true that in certain respects, close reading yields much profit to the reader. Close attention, for instance, reveals considerable irony, about the language modes used, about one another, of the 'Mrs. Brook' set. However, it must be said that there are times when the difficulty of reading seems gratuitously imposed by the author for *his* enjoyment of the subtleties of intercourse. Moreover, we may I believe even suspect these subtleties of non-intercourse, of a hedging and baffling failure of people to be 'straight' with one another, to spring from the author's unwillingness to allow them to be as straight as normal human energies and purposes would impel them to be (e.g. the exchange between Mitchy and Mr. Longdon about how Mitchy 'knows'). The mode is a stylized convention; no real human beings could ever be so subtle about nuances; the literary niceties have taken over.

In these tormented exchanges there seems often no compelling reasons for the character to be so tormented. Reading them requires the reader to attend to the subtlety to such words as 'know', and even adverbs or verbs like 'take' or 'had' (not least when James puts them in inverted commas) to such a finessed extent that something momentous seems to be in the air—when, in fact, nothing is, except James's pleasure with his own subtlety. Nothing *hangs*, in terms of choice and action, on the meanings—the significance of the acts and decisions has come to be lost sight of. Of course, in the novel there *are* choices—such as Nanda makes for people, and for herself, and such as

71

Vanderbank makes for himself, obliquely and by default. But the obliquity I mean is a *verbal* bafflement, an obsession with the 'meanings' of words which has in some way become divorced from the springs of action, and of *being*. So the centre of gravity has slid, from the moral (or existential) concern, to the 'art'.

This, I believe, affects our ultimate response to the novel. In what conceivable sense can it be called 'tragic'? This seems to me an extravagant claim, for reasons bound up with the question of definition. What is it the tragedy *of*? Is it one of sexual non-fulfilment? Surely, one can hardly call the failure of sexual fulfilment a 'tragedy'. But we are beginning to run before we can walk; such a complex and subtle novel challenges us to a detailed discussion. Whether the novel is successfully 'authentic' in my terms or not, it is one I find I cannot get away from!

As I have tried to suggest, Nanda bears an obvious relation to Maisie; but Nanda is post-puberty, marriageable, fully sexual in her responses. So are we to take it as her final tragedy that she becomes Mr. Longdon's protégée?

In the end it is not clear what her relationship to Mr. Longdon is to be. She is not going to marry him. Is he 'adopting' her? There is no doubt that she will be *materially* cared for. She does not love Longdon, but she is very fond of him and he *respects* her, at a time when the entourage seems incapable of such old-fashioned respect. What she will not have is any libidinal awakening. She takes the place of her idolized grandmother.

What then is the 'tragedy'? It must be said that, among the haziness of all the relationships, there seems a deficiency of warm-blooded, felt 'life', and firmness of purpose. The novel leaves us with a certain feeling of fastidious, but sterile, old-maidishness. And yet—the more one reads it, the more 'moral' it appears, and the recognition of the destructiveness of in-authenticity is profound.

There are two qualifying things one has to say about the book, however. Its structure is so subtle, complex and astonishingly wrought that there is an odd sense of the author being so pleased with his craft that one wonders whether the 'life' or urgent moral concern have not to some extent bowed to the excited preoccupation with 'technique'. Moreover, the degree to which the characters call one another 'magnificent' (etc.) tends to suggest that perhaps, after all, the author is not very pleased with himself for having invented them, *even when they are 'bad'*: is James somewhat equivocal about his equivalent of the Crawfords?

Dorothea Krook, in *The Ordeal of Consciousness*, picks out two major themes of the novel. One is, of course, the discussion of the way in which young girls are to be 'brought down', from the upper rooms where they are guarded in infancy, to the drawing-room—the way in which they are protected, and then brought 'out'. She distinguishes between the Continental way and the English way which is a compromise. In the event, both ways seem disastrous: Little Aggie once out quickly becomes a 'trollop' (to use Leavis's word), while Nanda, though seemingly un-corrupted by the talk of Tishy Grendon, or even sordid French novels, enters into the bright self-awareness of the Buckingham Crescent talk—but then becomes paralysingly unable to make any kind of relational commitment in that milieu—not least because, in that world, there is no one 'good' enough for her, except Mr. Longdon, who is old enough to be her grandfather. This, it seems to Dorothea Krook (as to Leavis) is the 'tragedy' of the novel.

The dangers of the bright superficial talk of Buckingham Crescent are indicated all the way through, and Vanderbank himself speaks plainly enough about these, from the beginning: 'It will be tremendously interesting to hear how the sort of thing we've fallen into—oh we *have* fallen in!—strikes your fresh uncorrupted ear . . .' (p. 11). Van gives Mrs. Brookenham away, telling Mr. Longdon that she has made out for some time that Nanda is 16 when in fact she is 18 and nearly 19. Mr. Longdon, Van suspects, thinks him nasty for this:

> 'It strikes you also probably as the kind of thing we must be constantly doing; it strikes you that right and left, probably, we keep giving each other away. . . . Yes, 'come to think of it', as they say in America, we do. But what shall I tell you? Practically we all know it and it's as broad as it's long. What's London life after all? It's tit for tat!'
>
> 'Ah but what becomes of friendship?' Mr. Longdon earnestly and pleadingly asked. . . . (p. 17)

It is an important moment, not least because Mr. Longdon grasps Vanderbank's arm and reiterates the word: 'Mr. Longdon maintained the full value of the word.'

Clearly, the origin of the Buckingham Crescent ethos is in Mansfield Park, in the milieu of the Crawfords. James picks up from Jane Austen the vices of the Crawford kind of 'London' set—to talk light-heartedly and amorally about important moral issues, to such a degree that they seem (as they are made to seem in Restoration comedy) as unimportant, besides the 'brilliant talk' itself, and the manic pretence that goes with a certain kind of knowingness. But this knowingness is essentially ignorant because what it does not know is how much its own all-pervading perspective fails to be aware of human depth of being.

In fact, the talk goes with a degree of stupid egotism that causes pain and severe social damage, and severe damage to lives, as moral stupidity does in *Mansfield Park*. Yet at the same time, it has a certain fascination, as it has for Jane Austen—for neither Henry Crawford nor his sister is totally condemned all the way through her novel. In the end, of course, Miss Crawford's failure to display 'modest loathings' is condemned from a specifically Christian position, by Edmund, in a novel intended to deal seriously with Christian themes. But both Henry and Caroline are handsome and intelligent, capable of good acts, and, at various earlier points in the novel, redeemable.

We do not expect a parallel moral firmness from Henry James, of a Christian kind. But we would be foolish to take his position on the Buckingham Crescent set to be that of Mr. Longdon, or that of the negative criticism such as is admitted by Vanderbank, of the milieu and its capacity for destructive gossip. If we took this as the message, that this set both talked destructively and enjoyed it, in their 'golden' complacency, and this made them emotionally impotent, we might fall into the supposition that James himself was ambivalent, that he, too, enjoyed both the clever gossip and the subtle play of endlessly nuanced analysis of which the characters are capable. The complex and subtle structure of his novel might even make us feel that he is willing, for the sake of a 'brilliant' piece of art, to enter into the delights of this linguistic play, around a certain kind of impotence in living: to be, that is, deeply corrupt as an artist. If we did so we might well conclude (as Mrs. Krook does) that Mrs. Brookenham emerges at the end 'likeable and lovable', despite her 'vanity and greed, malice and destructiveness'; but how can she, after she has blighted her own child's life—for her own power-seeking ends? There should be no doubt of James's *placing* of Mrs. Brookenham (which is not to say she is not as interesting as Lady Macbeth).

If there is any fault in James in this novel, it is that he has hidden the deepest flow of his moral concern too subtly, though this may be a criticism of us as readers. For with Henry James, you must remain alert, and when he gives a subtle hint, you must attend to its sharpness, and allow it its full effect. It is not for nothing, for example, that he speaks of Mrs. Brookenham's 'lovely, silly eyes'. Mrs. Krook gets that, and explains the degree of destructiveness in this salon hostess figure. But she seems to remain puzzled about the nature of her relationship with Vanderbank, as does Leavis. She calls it 'ambiguous'. Yet it may be that James's art has become so delicately modulated that we are just failing to see hints?

Everything depends upon whether Vanderbank is literally Mrs. Brookenham's physical lover, despite the phrase, 'We don't even have the excuse of passion.'

In truth, if we examine the novel with great care, and read it well enough, this relationship is not at all ambiguous. The subtle play of 'revealing' dialogue, even at its most confessional, is actually a mode of disguise—it seems to reveal 'all', and to be open, 'sincere' and explicit about everything: but all the time it is hiding the deepest inauthenticities of attitudes, behaviour, and relationships. When we realize this the book becomes more dramatic, but also far more painful—indeed, terrible. And its moral depths become disturbingly apparent: the corruption sinister.

Vanderbank *is* Mrs. Brookenham's lover, and has been for ten years.[4] The relationship contrasts with that between Mr. Longdon and Lady Julia, her mother, because that has been, although unfulfilled, a love which has remained with Longdon totally all his days. Vanderbank does not love, is not 'in love' with Mrs. Brookenham; but he is her slave, a devotee to her 'loveliness' and her charm, her 'brilliance', and her ('silly') power.

We even know when they go to bed. When he first talks to Mr. Longdon, Vanderbank says: '. . . the only thing is that I go to see her every Sunday . . .' (p. 12). 'We don't make enough of Sunday at Beccles . . .', declares Mr. Longdon; but this refers to the socialite scene. But Vanderbank also goes to see Mrs. Brook on another day in the week, it is clear.

This is revealed in a conversation in the presence of Mr. Cashmore, who is it seems both promiscuous and chirpily talkative about his promiscuousness. Mr. Longdon asks about Nanda's ways of spending her time. She is reported to have come to Vanderbank's by herself, at her mother's suggestion, for the first time. Cashmore is flirtatious about it:

> 'I wish she'd bring *me* a pound of tea!' Mr. Cashmore resumed. 'Or ain't I enough of an old woman for her to come and read to me at home?'
> 'Does she habitually visit the workhouse?' Mr. Longdon inquired of Mrs. Brook.
> This lady kept him in a moment's suspense, which another contemplation might, moreover, have detected that Vanderbank in some degree shared.
> 'Every Friday at three.'
> Vanderbank, with a sudden turn, moved straight to one of the windows, and Mr. Cashmore had a happy remembrance. 'Why, this is Friday—she must have gone today. But does she stay so late?' (p. 170)

It turns out that Nanda has also gone to Little Aggie. But nothing in Henry James is padding or redundant. So, what are the implications of that slight pause 'a moment's suspense'? And what does it mean that Vanderbank shares it? And why does he turn to the window? People turn to windows in novels to hide possible feelings which they do not want to be seen in the room. Quite clearly, there is something about Friday afternoons, and the regularity of Nanda's charitable task—which is protracted in various ways, such as by the visit to Little Aggie. It is the tryst hour for Mrs. Brookenham and Vanderbank, and their real meetings are not Sunday at all. In his age, for his public, James could not have made it plainer, that this is her time for adultery.

And from this Friday, let us look back a little in this book: we need, perhaps, to know more about Victorian visiting hours, to get the whole pattern correct. Surely this particular afternoon would have been redolent with feeling, for Mrs. Brookenham and Vanderbank? So, we find them in intimate discourse about the question of Nanda, Mr. Longdon's attitude to Lady Julia, to Mrs. Brook herself, and to her daughter's future. We need to read these dialogues between Vanderbank and Mrs. Brookenham with great care, and examine their tone. They obviously have an intimacy, a degree of shared past experiences, which under-lies their tone; and if we attend, we can find in their words the rhythms and undertones of passion, as we can in the dialogue in George Eliot's *Daniel Deronda*, between Grandcourt and Mrs. Glasher.[5] Of course, once we fully appreciate the relationship between Vanderbank and Mrs. Brook, the scenes take on a deeper irony. Between Mrs. Brookenham and her husband there are blank, dead conversations, in which the poor man is baffled by his wife's clever subtlety ('Oh the things you expect me to feel, my dear' p. 67). With Vanderbank Mrs. Brooken-ham's conversations have many pauses, turnings, implications which could only come between lovers who have been for many years on intimate terms:

> '. . . she asks *me* nothing.'
> 'Nothing?' Vanderbank echoed.
> 'Nothing!'
> He paused again; after which, 'It's very disgusting!' he declared. Then while she took it up as he had taken her word of a moment before, 'It's very preposterous,' he continued.
> Mrs. Brook appeared at a loss. 'Do you mean her helping him?'
> 'It's not of Nanda I'm speaking—it's of him.' [i.e. Cashmore] Vanderbank spoke with a certain impatience. 'His being with her in any sort of direct relation at all. His mixing her up with his other beastly affairs.'
> Mrs. Brook looked intelligent and wan about it, but also perfectly good humoured. 'My dear man, he and his affairs *are* such twaddle!'
> Vanderbank laughed in spite of himself. 'And does that make it any better?'
> Mrs. Brook thought, but presently had a light—she almost smiled with it. 'For *us*.' (p. 155)

Vanderbank here speaks almost as if he were Nanda's father, as if he were responsible for her care, and did not want her to be corrupted by such as the lascivious Mr. Cashmore; but the more he says, the more the question arises, *quis custodiet?* Mrs. Brookenham's view is a Mary Crawford-like one; everything

77

depends upon the quality of the affair. But does it make promiscuity acceptable, for affairs not to be 'twaddle'? Are they only justifiable when they may be intelligently talked about and appreciated? Over the page, they discuss Fanny (Cashmore's wife) for whom a Captain Dent-Douglas waits with a carriage, to run away with her. Why not? Why not let her go?

> 'She's the delight of our life.'
> 'Oh!' Vanderbank sceptically murmured.

There is a tension, then, between Vanderbank's true moral feelings, such as they are, his involvement in Mrs. Brookenham's problems with Nanda, and the brilliant chatter and excitement of the Buckingham Crescent world. Yet, as in the conversations between Gilbert Osmond and Madame Merle, the undercurrent of passionate knowledge mingles with a capacity for calculating and sinister manipulation. And so, at the moment in question (Friday afternoon) they discuss getting Mr. Longdon to 'do something' for Nanda, while showing they rather despise him, in conjunction with references to their intimacy:

> . . . He's a little of an old woman—but all the better for it.' She hung fire but an instant before she pursued: 'What can we make him do for you?'
> Vanderbank at this was very blank. 'Do for me?'
> 'How can any one love you,' she asked, 'without wanting to show it in some way? You know all the ways, dear Van,' she breathed, 'in which *I* want to show it.' (p. 159)

Those accustomed to reading modern novels with their 'torrid' scenes, and echoes of Lawrence's electricity flowing in people's loins, will find it hard to appreciate how much the word 'breathed' here is meant by James to convey, especially on this Friday afternoon. And they will find it hard to grasp how much James means by the juxtaposition here of Mrs. Brook's use of her passionate 'gifts' to Van, to want to turn their bonds into a means of extracting money from Mr. Longdon, turning his fascination with her lover into hard cash to the mutual advantage of them both. (It is very much like the conspiracies between Madame Merle and Osmond.) 'He might have known them, something suddenly fixed in his face appeared to say, but they were not what was, on this speech of hers, most immediately present to him . . .' (p. 159). When we grasp what the relationship fully is, this comment is extremely and grotesquely comic, in which there is a juxtaposition of his enjoyment of her 'loveliness' with her calculation of her relationship with Longdon—her exploitation, even, one must say, of the vestiges of his passion for Lady Julia, which she goes on to discuss.

What they try to present to the world is a relationship at the level of shared cultural and socialite interests. Mr. Longdon takes the relationship at this level; moreover, he has to try to feel positive towards Mrs. Brookenham, although intuitively he distrusts her, even finds her repellent. But when he realizes how difficult it would be to account for the relationship at 'Beccles', it is not because of the adultery:

> Mr. Longdon's face reflected for a minute something he could scarcely have supposed her acute enough to make out, the struggle between his real mistrust of her, founded on the unconscious violence offered by her nature to his every memory of her mother, and his sense on the other hand of the high propriety of his liking her; to which latter force his interest in Vanderbank was a contribution, inasmuch as he was obliged to recognise on the part of the pair an alliance it would have been difficult to explain at Beccles. (p. 164)

Mr. Longdon's goodness and sound moral stance is, to this novel, I believe, what Nelly Dean's is to *Wuthering Heights*: it is an important foundation, but it fails to penetrate to the more deeply disturbing problems of human nature and weakness. But then, of Vanderbank and Mrs. Brookenham, even the Duchess says,

> The situation belongs, I think, to an order I don't understand. I understand either one thing or the other—I understand taking a man up or letting him alone. But I don't really get at Mrs. Brook. . . . (p. 224)

And it is in response to her discussion of the relationship that Mrs. Longdon protests, 'I can absolutely assure you that Mr. Vanderbank entertains no sentiment for Mrs. Brookenham!' This, however, is not a delineation that we must share, for we know better, though, as the Duchess suggests, the relationship does not seem based on the usual kind of 'love' but on a shared 'liveliness'.

The only difficulty, as the Duchess sees it, for Nanda, over

her desire to 'block off everyone except Van' is likely to come
from her mother:

> '. . . but also that that would be stiff.'
> The movement with which Mr. Longdon removed his glasses
> might have denoted a certain fear to participate in too much of
> what the Duchess had known. 'I've not been ignorant that Mrs.
> Brookenham favours Mr. Mitchett.'
> But he was not to be let off with that. 'Then you've been blind,
> I suppose, to her reason for doing so.' He might not have been
> blind, but his vision, at this, scarce showed sharpness, and it
> determined in his interlocutress the shortest of short cuts. 'She
> favours Mr. Mitchett because she wants "old Van" herself.'

We have here a number of complex perspectives all to be
followed at once. We know the Duchess to be both of lax
behaviour, and also to be excited by gossip, so she may be
exaggerating; she also clashes with Mrs. Brookenham and is
perhaps jealous of her. Mr. Longdon is old-fashioned, and
painfully unwilling to hear further startling and scandalous
news about the people he meets in Buckingham Crescent.
Indeed, at times it is as if he only stays in the milieu to protect
Nanda, out of loyalty to the memory of Lady Julia. But we
know, too, or we should if we have read attentively, that between
Van and Mrs. Brookenham it is worse than the Duchess can
invent, or Mr. Longdon could possibly allow himself to believe
(while included in the exchange is the possibility that Mitchy
has been her lover, too).

> He was evidently conscious of looking at her hard.
> 'In what sense—herself?'
> 'Ah you must supply the sense; I can give you only the fact—
> and it's the fact that concerns us. *Voyons*,' she almost impatiently
> broke out; 'don't try to create unnecessary obscurities by being
> unnecessarily modest. Besides, I'm not touching your modesty.
> Supply any sense whatever that may miraculously satisfy your
> fond English imagination: I don't insist in the least on a bad one.
> She does want him herself—that's all I say. '*Pourquoi faire?* you
> ask—or rather, being too shy, don't ask, but would like to if you
> dared or didn't fear I'd be shocked. I can't be shocked, but
> frankly I can't tell you either. . . .' (p. 224)

It is here that Mr. Longdon, in consternation, declares that
Van has no 'affection' for Mrs. Brookenham. And the Duchess

goes on in her mysterious way: but we are not to take hers as the last word:

> . . . He's not in love with her—be comforted! But she's amusing—highly amusing. I do her perfect justice. As your women go, she's rare. If she were French she'd be a *femme d'esprit*. She has invented a *nuance* of her own and she has done it all by herself, for Edward figures in her drawing room as one of those queer extinguishers of fire in the corridors of hotels. He's just a bucket on a peg. . . .

To the duchess, it is all 'intellectual':

> . . . the young men hang round Mrs. Brook, and the clever ones ply her with the uproarious appreciation that keeps her up to the mark. She's in a prodigious fix—she must sacrifice either her daughter or what she once called to me her intellectual habits. Mr. Vanderbank, you've seen for yourself, is one of the most cherished, the most confirmed. . . .

'Three months ago—it couldn't have been any longer kept off—Nanda began definitely to be there and look, by the tea-table, modestly and conveniently abstracted.' Mr. Longdon contradicts her, but the Duchess drives the point home that Nanda presents a 'tiresome difference made by the presence of sweet virginal eighteen.' But what we see is that it is more than that Nanda inhibits the conversation around Mrs. Brookenham; there is always a danger that she will either inhibit, or even come to discover, their sexual intimacy—for, as we have learnt, Nanda has to be sent away to read to old ladies in the workhouse, to allow Vanderbank and Mrs. Brookenham privacy together. The effect of the situation is, as the Duchess points out, that Nanda is in a situation in which any eligible man must suppose that, sooner or later, by talk or being presented with illicit liaisons, Nanda will be spoilt for ever, for the marriage market:

> '. . . If Nanda doesn't get a husband early in the marriage business—'
> 'Well?' said Mr. Longdon, as she appeared to pause with the weight of her idea.
> 'Why, she won't get one late—she won't get one at all. One, I mean, of the kind she'll take. She'll have been in it over-long for *their* taste.' (p. 227)

We may reflect on the irony, that a society which so much enjoyed gossip and even being shocked by *affaires*, was so much aware that the men would respond strongly against any young girl who seemed to have had her innocence corrupted, by being too long 'out' among other women who were married, and in observation of their—so much admired—world.

So, it takes on an even more powerful irony, when Mr. Longdon, as he makes his offer to Vanderbank, declares, 'I want her out of her mother's house'—not least because Vanderbank himself is so deeply 'in' it. Vanderbank laughs, but he has more immediately *coloured*, and jokingly declares, as Mr. Longdon scrutinizes him sharply, 'Oh . . . I'm a mass of corruption!'—one of those 'London' exclamations which are intended to turn any moral condemnation into a joke. Mr. Longdon drives on, to add that he wants Nanda out of her mother's house because she is so strongly against it. This whole scene becomes grotesque, of course, once we know the true relationship between Mrs. Brookenham and Vanderbank. As much as anything, this is the grotesque comedy of Mr. Longdon's naïveté. But as we watch, we know why Vanderbank is so uneasy; Mr. Longdon hints that he has something in his head:

> 'There's nothing that in the circumstances occurs to you as likely I should want to say—' Vanderbank gave a laugh that might have struck an auditor as a trifle uneasy. (p. 230)

By 'an auditor' Henry James means someone who is not so straightforward as Mr. Longdon, someone looking at this human exchange afresh; it could be the reader.

> 'Can you think of nothing at all?'
> 'Do you mean that I've done?'

—earlier Vanderbank has spoken of 'something awful I've done', so his unease is clearly due to guilt; and, of course, he and Mrs. Brookenham are, actually, living in seriously dangerous conditions, always on the brink of discovery. It is with relief, but also with a kind of sense of doom, that Vanderbank learns that Mr. Longdon means Nanda:

> His friend had responded quickly, but for a minute had said nothing more, and the great marble clock that gave the place the air of a club ticked louder in the stillness. The hush between them became the measure of the young man's honesty. . . .

But the whole bitterness of the book lies in the fact that Vanderbank can never be honest because he is compromised. Whatever happens in the story, he can never fulfil the hopes of those who want him to marry Nanda, because the daughter's fate is already decided by Vanderbank's relationship with her mother. It is now inevitable, of course, that he will break his pledge to Mr. Longdon, and tell her about his offer of a *dot* for the bride, because passion is thicker than water. 'I depend on you to keep the fact to yourself'—'Absolutely then and utterly': such bonds are not broken by the mere talkativeness of the Buckingham Crescent set—they are made worthless by the furtive secrecy of sexual relationships which, in this case, are part of the silly, beautiful woman's power and his corrupt possession by her charm.

So, Vanderbank now has to brazen it out, even as Mr. Longdon confronts him with the possibility of what is, in fact, an actuality:

> The response had been prompt, yet Mr. Longdon seemed suddenly to show that he suspected the superficial. 'Unless it's with Mrs. Brook you're in love.' Then on his friend's taking the idea with a mere headshake of negation, a repudiation that might even have astonished by his own lack of surprise. 'Or unless Mrs. Brook's in love with you,' he amended.
>
> Vanderbank had for this any decent gaity. 'Ah that of course may perfectly be!'
>
> 'But *is* it? That's the question.'
>
> He continued light. 'If she had declared her passion shouldn't I rather compromise her—?'

Mr. Longdon is somewhat confused, but repeats the phrase 'Mrs. Brookenham's wanting you—as I've heard it called—herself.'—'That's what you've heard it called?' It could have been a tense moment; but everything can be held at an arm's length by words: 'It's unimaginable. But it doesn't matter. We all call everything—anything. The meaning of it, if you and I put it so, is, well, a modern shade' (p. 241).

There is again a deep resonance of intimacy in the scene that follows a little later, in which Vanderbank reports Mr. Longdon's offer to Mrs. Brookenham. Before he tells her, it emerges that Nanda is to spend some time at Beccles, and Mrs. Brook has urged her to make it as long as possible:

Vanderbank laughed out—as it was even after ten years possible to laugh—at the childlike innocence with which her voice could invest the hardest teachings of life; then with something a trifle nervous in the whole sound and manner he sprang up from his chair. 'What a blessing he is to us all!'

But as it turns out, she is deeply disturbed by his revelation. At last, he says he must get it out, though up to now he has 'funked it'; he scrutinizes her face for her response, and finds himself as so often in the dark.

> That she had turned a little pale was really the one fresh mark. "Funked" it? Why in the world—? His own colour deepened at her accent, which was a sufficient light on his having been stupid. 'Do you mean you've declined the arrangement?'
>
> He only, with a smile somewhat strained, continued for a moment to look at her. . . .

'Do you imagine I want you myself?' she asks. The scene is tense with conflict, and both characters from time to time stoop over a basket of flowers to inhale its fragrance 'with violence'— she emerging with the question. 'What kind of a monster are you trying to make me out?' He has just said that he felt it a duty to 'warn' her that he was Mr. Longdon's chosen candidate— when she, of course, has put her money on another man, Mitchy. The scene has all the tension of watching characters in a conspiracy; but, of course, the dreadfulness of it lies in the recognition that what they are discussing is the disposal of Mrs. Brookenham's daughter, in terms of getting the best *dot*, one of the proposed methods being to marry the girl to her mother's lover, over whom she is here uncomfortably maintaining her power:

> 'What can relieve me of the primary duty of taking precautions,' she wound up, 'when I know as well as that I stand here and look at you—'
>
> 'Yes, what?' he asked as she just paused. 'Why that so far as they count on you they count, my dear Van, on a blank.' Holding him a minute as with the soft low voice of his fate, she sadly but firmly shook her head. 'You won't do it.'
>
> 'Oh!' he almost too loudly protested.
>
> 'You won't do it,' she went on.
>
> 'I *say*!'—he made a joke of it.
>
> 'You won't do it,' she repeated. (p. 261)

In the phrase 'soft low voice of his fate' we have yet another hint that Van is at her mercy, because of passion; she has the Lady Macbeth touch. Call her 'magnificent' as he may, at this point what she exerts over him is the power to make him impotent—and, at the same time, to ruin Nanda's young life. For it is not the talk that destroys Nanda in this novel, but her mother's wilful egotism and sense of sensual power over the man with whom she (the daughter) is in love, and sick as a cat.

In *What Maisie Knew* Henry James manages to make a powerful exploration of the problem of authenticity, of people being true or not true to themselves and their bonds to others. He achieves this by fixing his perspective in Maisie, and so limiting himself to the latency period. None of the adults is good enough for Maisie—or for themselves.

In *The Awkward Age*, however, he is dealing with a girl of 19, and he cannot exclude sexual perspectives. Yet over this area of experience he becomes involved in a fairy tale, a wish-fulfilment. To say as much is not to reject or condemn it; there are fairy-tale qualities in Shakespeare's rendering of Marina in *Pericles*, and woe to him who declares that such goodness is not possible. For what Marina stands for is the capacity of the human spirit to be good—to remain uncorrupted, to resist corruption. And in this she is the embodiment (as symbol) of the redeeming daughter—which kind of creature we also have in Little Dorrit (though she is perhaps Eustasia rather than Marina). This embodiment of the feminine virtues will put up with anything from her father, and pardon all; her innocence and chastity endures and remains loving. There are many such women in Dickens—Estella, Florence Dombey, Agnes.

While these creatures symbolize qualities the artist wishes to find in woman, or has found in woman, there is also a sense in which they represent dynamics within himself. They are what the Jungians would call the positive side of the anima in individuation.

Henry James's preoccupation is with rescuing this creature from corruption. This may be seen as rescuing her from sexuality. The agent of this rescue both in *What Maisie Knew* and *The Awkward Age* is a character of limited sensibility and moral awareness, relying upon an old-fashioned moral system—Mrs. Wix and Mr. Longdon (Mr. Longdon is from time to time described as 'an old woman'). In the fairy story, they represent the Fairy Godmother. This fairy godmother is the magical *deus ex machina* who rescues the heroine from sexuality—and the meaning of the novels, phenomenologically speaking, is that James is wanting to purify the marvellous qualities of woman as *mysterium tremendum* from corruption by sexuality—rescuing her spiritual powers from evil; and this involves rescuing Eve from the Serpent and Adam. The weakness in this project is that its moral scope is limited—because our problems, in both men and women, are of engaging fully with our sexuality, as an aspect of our relational needs. To Henry James sexual relations are too dangerous, and he sees them thus because he had no experience of them; thus, he had no experience of the reparative effects of sexual meeting. To him the sexual life tends to be known from a distance, as a child knows it of his parents, when it is associated by him with fantasies of mutual aggression and the voracious impulse to consume. If, as Harry Guntrip has asserted, Henry James was a schizoid individual, sexuality for him may have been associated with the dangers of love.[6]

So, while *The Awkward Age* is in one sense a tribute to femininity, and a celebration of its mysterious power, it is a tribute which excludes from its grasp the capacity of woman at best to include her finer powers along with sexual passion. Nanda has deep understanding, sympathy and the capacity to be benign; but she is still a virgin at the end of the book and achieves her superiority by renouncing the sexual life ('I shall never marry'). Moreover, there is a hint of her own reluctance to commit herself (as Dorothea Krook points out) which has a touch of that dread of sexual life which Isobel Archer displays. In a milieu in which 'talk' is so largely substituted for genuinely warm-hearted relationships (while also being a screen for promiscuity) Nanda herself, too, tends to be possessed of spoken 'ideas' which do not have as their focus the mainsprings of the emotional life; it is one of these that she wills on to Mitchy, by encouraging him to marry Little Aggie to please her—the most improbable thing in the book. And her own final approach to 'Old Van's' relationships to her mother belongs to the realm of talk—she takes up a posture which shows great understanding, but which also belongs to an idea she has of herself (as 'knowing everything') and of how to deal with the difficult people she has to deal with: a posture which her author admires—but does not, perhaps, sufficiently place as patronizing. He admires it because it shows how superior Nanda is to the men; but does he really see the limitations of such a capacity, confined as it is to a detachment from the realities of the sexual, and involvement in that dimension of bodily emotion?

And yet he shows himself aware that Nanda, who loves Van, has a real life in the body and being, in which she suffers the pain of an authentic yearning. The moment is a deeply moving one:

> It burst from her, flaring up, in a queer quaver that ended in something queerer still—in her abrupt collapse, on the spot, into the nearest chair, where she choked with a torrent of tears. Her buried face could only after a moment give way to the flood, and she sobbed in a passion as sharp and brief as the flurry of a wild thing for an instant uncaged; her old friend meantime keeping his place in the silence broken by her sound and distantly—across the room—closing her eyes to her helplessness and her shame. (p. 479)

Why, however, 'her shame'? Mr. Longdon, too, is crying (she wails, 'I don't know why you mind!'); but the word seems revealing. She is seen to be helpless in the grip of her passionate yearning, and it is painful for her to have her love for Vanderbank revealed, as not being under her control: but 'shame'? I suppose she is ashamed of her tears; but one cannot but detect a slight tone of distaste, felt in the author's *alter ego* Mr. Longdon, that a young girl should yearn for a fully sexual love so bitterly? Yet she, of course, is relieved that she is being adopted by a man who is beyond offering her a sexual life: clearly, Mr. Longdon is supposed to be 'beyond sex'. She says to Longdon in that last interview, 'I'm glad that you're not a young man' (p. 476). We are supposed to take this to mean that young men are egotistic and difficult; but it also means that Nanda herself does not want to encounter the sexual life, and perhaps really dreads it. There are aspects here of the fairy tale; Henry James needs to fantasize a pure femininity which would be glad to be adopted by him, and led away into a sexless Eden—indeed would prefer it. Mr. Longdon calls her 'child' ('It would be easier for me . . . if you didn't, my poor child, so wonderfully love him', p. 479), and again we have a fantasy of the daughter feeding the father through the bars of his prison with her breasts, such as we have in *Little Dorrit*. It is a yearning for a pure love relationship that has no genital component, and none of the associated dangers.

This father–daughter relationship is far superior to the corrupting relationships of her own age-group. Mr. Longdon may wonder 'if between my age and hers, that is, any real contact is possible'; the novel conveys the impression that what he offers is more peaceful, secure and less dangerous than normal relationships. He does not like it that Nanda and Aggie are friends; and, indeed, throughout the book, he is set on a process of getting her away from her mother's house and all the attendant dangers that surround her, as he sees it. (He also, of course, wants to merge her into the venerated image of her grandmother.)

The chief danger is Vanderbank's elegant egotism, combined with his superficial and facile attitude to existence—and his charm. He wants his 'fun', as he says, and Nanda has too serious a conscience for him, as Mrs. Krook points out. There is a significant exchange between Mr. Longdon and Mitchy, over 'the fact that we still like him'. Even Nanda does not want him to miss a future—the future Mr. Longdon offers, if he marries her.

> Mr. Longdon stared. 'Do *you* still like him?'
> 'If I didn't how should I mind—?'
> But on the utterance of it Mitchy fairly pulled up.
> His companion, after another look, laid a mild hand on his shoulder. 'What is it you mind?'
> 'From *him*? Oh, nothing!' He could trust himself again. 'There are people like that—great cases of privilege.'
> 'He is one!' Mr. Longdon mused. 'There it is. They go through life somehow guaranteed. They can't help pleasing.'
> 'Ah,' Mr. Longdon murmured, 'if it hadn't been for that—!'
> 'They hold, they keep every one,' Mitchy went on. 'It's the sacred terror.' (p. 429)

In both Vanderbank and Mrs. Brook there operates a charming, egotistical spell on everyone round them—so that they are not only pardoned, but the milieu actually conspires, as it were, to be 'pleased' by them. But this makes it terrible for Nanda. 'Poor Nanda' has been the subject of Van's not 'risking it', not committing himself to her, despite the temptation, and her love; he does not like her.

> '. . . It was then already too late.' Mitchy asserted with emphasis. 'Too late. She was spoiled for him.'
> If Mr. Longdon had to take it he took it at least quietly, only saying after a time: 'And her mother *isn't*.' (p. 439)

It is a revealing exchange; but what does it mean? We have looked at the question of young girls losing their attraction for men in this milieu, because—once 'out'—they have quickly gained in knowledge of the complexities and dangers of marriage and the sexual life. But this can hardly be the difficulty for Van over Nanda. It is rather that Nanda's realistic and fervent sincerity, real sincerity, makes Vanderbank afraid—and he is afraid because he is her mother's lover. Mr. Longdon's remark is profoundly ironic—more ironic than he knows, because he does not seem to be able to admit that Vanderbank *is* Mrs. Brookenham's lover. But certainly he can see that Van's unwillingness to go in for Nanda despite all the inducements is itself a consequence of his close involvement with a very spoilt and spoiling woman—so Van has no excuse at all for finding Nanda 'corrupted' by 'society'.

Vanderbank's essential corruption is exposed in the first chapter in Book Tenth: 'Nanda', pp. 435ff. It would be hilarious if it were not so painful. This is not the moment of failure, of course: that has taken place on a seat in Mitchy's garden, when there is that feeling in the air that something should be said which is never said. Vanderbank has finally come to 'let Nanda down', kindly; he has come to be kind, and he prattles on about her flowers and her books, and how he has not brought her flowers. But the marvellously depicted flow of his silly talk reveals an inward terror, while Nanda greets it by being 'as literal as he was facetious'. It is a wonderful tribute to feminine wisdom; at last she stems the flow with 'What in the world, Mr. Van, are you afraid of?' (p. 446).

At this, there is the longest look ever exchanged between these two: one of those looks 'which after they have come and gone are felt not only to have changed relations but absolutely to have cleared the air' (p. 446). It is a show-down; and Vanderbank confesses 'The thing is, you see, that I haven't a conscience. I only want my fun.' Nanda declares that she wants *her* fun, too, but this is 'the real thing'; she means she wants to feel happy in the happiness of others. What is at the bottom of her summons to Van is a long talk she has had 'with mother'.

> 'Oh yes,' Van returned with brightly blushing interest. 'The fun,' he laughed, 'that's to be got out of "mother".' (p. 447)

The blush, the attempt to turn it off (as so often) into a joke, is yet another hint at Van's position as her mother's lover; so, too, is Nanda's delicacy: '. . . of course it's rather difficult . . . for me to tell you exactly what I mean. . . .' Oh, Van doesn't find it a bit difficult: 'You've got your mother on your mind. That's very much what I mean by your conscience' (p. 447). It is subtly ironic: here is a woman who is in love with her mother's lover urging him (against her own inclinations) to go back to her; he, on his part, is pretending that his lack of commitment to Nanda is explained by his reaction to her extreme concern about his mother's happiness, which is not true. His embarrassment, which has kept him away from Buckingham Crescent, is over the problem of Mrs. Brookenham's ambition, in which he is involved, to get the fortune out of Mr. Longdon for him, by marrying her daughter. Yet when she explains that her mother did not put her up to it, she is saying all this off her own bat, he can exclaim, 'You're an adorable family!' But yet Nanda reveals herself as to some extent contaminated: 'You said a while ago that we must never be—you and I—anything but frank and natural. . . .' And so she urges Van not to give her mother up.

> Do stick to her. What I really wanted to say to you—to bring it straight out—is that I don't believe you thoroughly know how awfully she likes you. I hope my saying such a thing doesn't affect you as 'immodest'. One never knows—but I don't much care if it does. I suppose it *would* be immodest if I were to say that I verily believe she's in love with you. Not, for that matter, that father would mind—he wouldn't mind, as he says, a tuppeny rap, So'—she extraordinarily kept it up—'you're welcome to any good the information may have for you: though that, I daresay, does sound hideous. No matter—if I produce any effect on you. That's the only thing I want. When I think of her downstairs there so often nowadays practically alone, I feel as if I could scarcely bear it. She's so fearfully young. (p. 449)

As Van says, responding, 'you're indeed, as she herself used to say, the modern daughter.' Here we have to take great care to see what James exactly means. Again, much depends on whether Nanda is aware of the actual physical relationship between her mother and Van. I believe she is aware (but without any real sensual knowledge of sexuality) and that in treating it in such a 'frank' way she is showing herself to be corrupted by the Buckingham Crescent ethos. Nanda's urgings are deeply immoral and immodest, and while we may prefer her knowingness here to that of Little Aggie, it is a grotesque corruption of authenticity in a young woman to urge the man she loves to return to an adulterous relationship with her mother; Buckingham Crescent's 'frank and natural' openness has led to this essential falsity.

> ... I don't know what's the matter between you. ... You're more to her than anyone *ever* was. ... She said once . . . that you had done more for her than anyone, because it was you who had really brought her out. ... (p. 450)

Nanda speaks, grotesquely here, in the language of Buckingham Crescent, and her mother's ethos. Vanderbank responds in an equally grotesque manner, reinforced in his egotistical self-regard:

> ... I'm bound to say I don't know quite what I did—one does those things, no doubt, with a fine unconsciousness . . . But I assure you I accept all the consequences and all the responsibilities. ... (p. 450)

—but Van has been shown to accept none. Yet he goes on to speak of 'she and her so unwittingly faithless one'

> The great thing is that—bless both your hearts!—one doesn't, one simply *can't* if one would, give your mother up . . . there she is, like the moon or the Marble Arch. (p. 450)

But it is, of course, Nanda's misery that he can't give her mother up: 'She's a fixed star. ... She's youth. She's *my* youth—she *was* mine. ...' 'And then she's so lovely', cries Nanda.—'Awfully pretty!'—the come-down echoes Van's ghastly insincerity at the beginning of the scene; and so we see Nanda, thrusting him back into the superficial, brilliant world of her mother's play-life, acknowledging his essential triviality, prattling

91

on about '. . . one's appreciation of the charming things. . . . she
has surprises . . . she has little ways. . . .' 'Well, I'm glad you do
like her,' Nanda gravely replied. 'And Van gushes about her
sacrifice, 'it's quite as charming as it's amusing.'

Vanderbank wants her to put in a good word for him with
Mr. Longdon, in hope he can think of him as less than a brute.
But to us, surely, Vanderbank must seem, and is meant to
seem, a selfish dilettante? '. . . make out somehow or other that
I'm *not* a beast . . .' (p. 454).

As so often, in novels and the world, the man is immature,
self-indulgent, superficial and insensitive. By contrast the
woman is rooted in the reality of her emotions, to which she
gives authentic recognition, while, in her wise realism, she is
causing herself severe pain by renunciation. At the same time
Nanda is shown as severely limited. She, like Maisie, wants her
mother to have a stable relationship with a lover, out of some
childish fantasy, even though it is adulterous and promiscuous—
and so unlikely to bring anyone happiness.

In the subsequent scene with Mitchy, she tells him, with
parallel wisdom, that 'Aggie is only trying to find out what sort
of person she is.' But Nanda's relationship with Mitchy seems
less convincing; it does not seem any solution for Aggie to be
getting on closer terms with Mrs. Brook, while Mitchy's hope
for the *salon* seems unjustified:

> the salon will shift and change, but the institution itself, as
> resting on a deep human need, has a long course yet to run and a
> good work yet to do. *We* shan't last, but your mother will and as
> Aggie is happily very young she's therefore provided for. . . .

Nanda responds to Mitchy's enquiries about her future with
Mr. Longdon with 'a sort of solemnity of tenderness', and her
voice trembles; she refuses to allow Mitchy to kiss her hand,
telling him 'you're wild'. What did James mean to tell us by this
scene? That Mitchy offered Nanda genuine whole-hearted
sexual love, and that she renounces that, too, albeit with regret?
That Nanda has an admirable wisdom even in that? Aggie,
Nanda says, is not like her.

> 'Like you?'
> 'Why I get the benefit of the fact that there was never a time
> when I didn't know *something* or other, and that I became more

and more aware, as I grew older, of a hundred little chinks of
daylight.'
    Mitchy stared. 'You're stupendous, my dear!' (p. 469)

But is Nanda's 'knowing' so stupendous? After all, it has only
led to her present misery, her compromise with Buckingham
Crescent *moeurs*, and her renunciation of her nubility?
    She is, of course, put on the Lady Julia pedestal. She belongs
to a superior plane than her mother's; when Mrs. Brookenham
asks 'Does he make up to you?' Nanda feels 'her mother had
suddenly become vulgar.' 'He makes one enjoy being liked so
much—liked better, I do think, than I've ever been liked by
anyone . . . (p. 286). Yes, she would marry Mr. Longdon, and is
utterly sincere about him; but these benefits seem possible only
in the absence of sex.
    The fatal division between Nanda and Vanderbank actually
comes at a moment when they are discussing women, as they
used to be, and as they are 'now'. The conversation passes on to
one about Harold's borrowing (that occasional coarse reminder
of the less pleasant side of reality, and of egotism). It is at this
moment that Nanda represents a realism about woman and
human nature that Vanderbank cannot stand; this is why he
cannot relate to her. Psychologically, perhaps, we can see that
his *affaire* with Mrs. Brookenham, with its 'civilised' pretence
(that 'we do not even have the excuse of passion'), is in him a
mark of an incapacity to relate fully to a woman, in a committed
way.
    Of the discussion of 'girls' Van says, 'You've gone into it with
him?'

> 'As far as a man and a woman can together.'
> . . .
> There fell between them on this a silence of some minutes,
> after which it would probably not have been possible for either to
> say if their eyes had met while it lasted. . . .

She then challenges him by alluding to his sensitivity; but
perhaps we see it as her intuitive sense of his delicate position?

> Well, you really haven't any natural 'cheek'—not like *some* of
> them. You're in yourself as uneasy, if anything's said and every-
> one giggles or makes some face, as Mr. Longdon and if Lord
> Petherton hadn't once told me that a man hates almost as much

to be called modest as a woman does, I'd say that very often in London now you must pass some bad moments. (p. 304)

This response provokes embarrassment, 'or at least' *stupefaction* in Vanderbank. His response must have been complex. He is not used to being talked to like this by a woman, despite the Buckingham Crescent pretence of openness. To be so open is dangerous to a man involved in his kind of clandestine love affair, not least because of this being with her mother. Perhaps what she has noticed is not his 'modesty' so much as his sensitiveness over the problem of his relationship to that mother?

But she goes on, in her frankness and innocence, to urge upon him a separateness from the Buckingham Crescent ethos that is not true.

> 'It's the tone and current and the effect of all the others that push you along. . . . If such things are contagious, as everyone says, you prove it perhaps as much as anyone. But you don't begin . . . or you can't at least originally have begun. . . .

It is not only seeming to impose on him an impossible innocence, but it implies by protesting his innocence that (unknown to her) he is deeply corrupt. This is why, in her open sincerity, he cannot relate to her, not even at this critical moment:

> So she appeared to put it to him, with something in her lucidity that would have been infinitely touching: a strange, grave, calm consciousness of their common doom and of what in especial in it would be worst for herself. He sprang up indeed after an instant as if he had been infinitely touched. . . .

He takes on the air of a man 'in suspense about himself'.

> The most initiated observer of all would have been poor Mr. Longdon, in that case destined, however, to be also the worst defeated, with the sign of his tension a smothered 'Ah if he doesn't do it now!' Well, Vanderbank didn't do it 'now', and the odd, slow, irrelevant sigh he gave out might have sufficed as the record of his recovery from a peril lasting just long enough to be measured. (p. 305)

An observer 'would have hung on his lips': but the word 'peril' indicates the problem. In the face of a real, tangible woman, Vanderbank is impotent.

Van is her mother's property; oddly she does not recognize

the fact when quite early on in the book she covets his cigarette
case, which has clearly been given him by her mother.

> She rubbed her cheek an instant with the polished silver and
> again the next moment turned over the case. 'This is the kind of
> one I should like.'
>   Her companion glanced down at it. 'Why it holds twenty.'
>   'Well I want one that holds twenty.'
>   Vanderbank only threw out his smoke. 'I want so to give you
> something,' he said at last, 'that, in my relief at lighting on an
> object that will do, I will, if you don't look out, give you either
> that or a pipe.'
>   'Do you mean this particular one?'
>   'I've had it for years—but even that one if you like it.'
>   She kept it—continued to finger it. 'And by whom was it given
> you?'
>   At this he turned to her smiling. 'You think I've forgotten that
> too?'
>   'Certainly you must have forgotten, to be willing to give it
> away again.'
>   'But how do you know it was a present?'
>   'Such things always are—people don't buy them for themselves.'
>   She had now relinquished the object, laying it upon the bench,
> and Vanderbank took it up. 'It's origin's lost in the night of
> time—it has no history except that I've used it. But I assure you
> that I do want to give you something. I've never given you
> anything.'
>   She was silent a little. 'The exhibition you're making,' she
> seriously sighed at last, 'of your inconstancy and superficiality!
> All the relics of you that I've treasured and that I supposed all
> the time to have meant something!' (p. 184)

'I use gold paper', he says, the gold paper of the mind; 'Don't
talk, my dear child, as if you don't really know me for the best
friend you have in the world.'

Vanderbank reveals himself as deeply insincere. The little
moment is highly symbolic. The cigarette case has surely been
given him by Mrs. Brookenham (though James does not tell us
that), and we may interpret it, in a psychoanalytical way, in
terms of its symbolism of intimacy: a phallic tribute. Nanda
enjoys it against her cheek. He would like to give it to her. She
supposes he cannot tell her who gave it to him because he does
not remember the donor. But he cannot tell her it was her

mother, because he cannot give the same phallic tribute to the daughter. So, his remark about being her best friend is both genuine, as he speaks as a kind of father, and yet treacherous, as he can never be a real friend as a lover could be, because (as the cigarette case indicates) his heart belongs to Mumma.

Criticisms have been levelled at James, for his very subtlety in this book, and for its elaborate and delicate structure. But every time we examine the complex and subtle meaning, we find a deeper sense of the doom that overtakes those in this 'London' world of duplicity and 'sincere' insincere talk about the duplicities. James obviously enjoyed writing the duplicitous and doubly duplicitous dialogue, with its masks of 'you're magnificent' and exclamations about the 'adorable' family in which there are such deep divisions and hostilities. He portrays a distressing degree of agony under the loquacious surface. But there is another misery beneath even that—his own dread of sexuality: the combination of admiration for woman, celebration of her mysterious wisdom of being and his fear of her which sometimes jumps out into a catty hostility—see him, for instance, on Tishy Grendon's décolleté ('it might have taken the last November gale to account for the completeness with which, in some quarters, she had shed her leaves' (p. 345)) or Carrie Donner's make-up—and his own catastrophic impotence, which impels him to want to rescue woman from the world.

What seems to have gone wrong with Henry James is a kind of defensive self-satisfaction. I call it defensive because it seems to me to hide a central emptiness, and a vacancy where there might have been experience of passion. I put it that way, having heard from Leavis that James was a 'eunuch', and having read that H. Guntrip thought him schizoid; between these views it seems that James was a man without sexual experience who found the engagement with human reality a problem—and who lived increasingly in a world of words.

But as a great artist in his best work James picks up from Jane Austen the theme of *authenticity*, and from George Eliot the theme of *significant moral choice*. In *What Maisie Knew* these themes are pursued superbly, and can be, because we are confined, as I have tried to show, to the latency period, and so deflected from direct confrontation with adult sexual passion. Yet the passion is there: Miss Overmore is driven by it, Sir

Claude is compromised by it, brought to his knees by it—
together they fail Maisie, and must fail her, in order to fulfil
their own foremost needs. We know they are not good enough
for her, but in this knowledge we know we are never in the end
'good enough' for a child, because there will always be a clash
between the child's idealism and the much more complex
dynamics of adult sexual need.

The child in us, or in anyone, must be shocked by the antics
to which adults will resort, to satisfy their need for meaningful
sexual fulfilment: awkward meetings, locked doors, rendezvous,
subterfuges, lies, wallowings in bed and bath; the gamekeeper's
hut, the inn or hotel, the carriage, the private room, the yacht.
In *What Maisie Knew* it seems that the horrors are adultery,
promiscuity, infidelity. They are, but even more of a horror is
the fact that adults are driven at all to deny and defy bonds and
obligations, to satisfy passion. The perspectives of Mrs. Wix
will not encompass this; the author is however fascinated by it.
Yet he has no experience, and while he is able to use Maisie to
view the menace to bonds and obligations, he is at the same
time as bewildered as she is.

For the same reason, while he is aware of the sinister way in
which a Madame Merle exploits passion, and in which an
Isabel Archer is seduced out of her independent self-reliance by
sexual charm, he cannot realize imaginatively the repugnance
which ought to impel his heroine—unless his purpose is to show
her, too, bound by the habits of sexual passion, which she
rationalizes as a sense of duty and deference to the meaning of
marriage. As so often, he cannot allow his heroines to pursue
sexual fulfilment beyond a certain point, and gloats on their
non-fulfilment or their pain.

This is what I mean by self-indulgence. I believe that Mr.
Longdon in *The Awkward Age* is close to James—neat, well
dressed, handsome, with a sunny smile, intelligent, perceptive,
and a man of principle (though he is of 'Beccles' and by no
means as sophisticated and worldly as James). But it is also
clear that Mr. Longdon is impotent, or, at any rate, that he is
not 'sexually active', not impelled by passion; he is devoted only
to past passion, and so is no 'threat' to Nanda. He could even be
seen to embody a distaste such as Isabel Archer displays for
sexuality, and which James distantly reveals at times. Mr.

Longdon does not offer her marriage; he offers her a sanctuary, to live in his house, enjoy his care, and his wealth, 'for ever'. But we have only to look back at the marriage of Dr. Strong and Annie in *David Copperfield* to remind ourselves that there could be a marriage between people of this disparity in years; but that there could be dangers—dangers of the woman's passionate needs yearning naturally for a mate of her own age.

But James makes Nanda 'knowing' to such an extent, so much part of the Buckingham Crescent milieu, that she actually prefers to love where love is impossible; she has become so critically self-conscious, and yet also so conscience-impelled, that she cannot make herself loved by anyone except in the way she becomes a ghost of Lady Julia, for Mr. Longdon, who offers her a sexless care, in endowing her with all the aura of the woman who had 'everything', but whom Mr. Longdon never married. This is not a Cinderella dream, but it is rather like the kind of Euphrasia[7] dream we have in *Little Dorrit*, the dream of the daughter who will feed the father with her breasts when he is in prison: that is, it is a dream of a daughter become an idealized and non-sexual mother.

Leavis calls *The Awkward Age* a 'tragedy'; but how can one call it a tragedy, when a girl of 19 goes to live ('for ever') with a man of (?)65, in care but not in sexual relationship? In fifteen years' time, when he dies, she will be only 34 and extremely wealthy; in the interim, what might not happen to her? To ask such questions is to dispel the dream; we may even ask, what might turn out for Nanda in (say) the world of Edith Wharton, who knows so much more about woman and passion?

'Tragedy' is quite the wrong word, and if we reject it, and point out the failure to know passion in the book, it shrinks; it is clever, witty, ironic, and highly moral, but only within the depiction of a certain area of *moeurs*—of people (it must be said) of limited interest. Their moral failures are exposed, but they do not matter as much as (say) those of Lydgate or Gwendolen Harleth—they are less 'our' problems—though they have a relevance to us and will have, as long as there are people like the Crawfords and a 'London' which breeds fashionable destructiveness. But there is a limit to our interest in the way these people frustrate themselves. Certainly they are not of tragic status, nor do they rise sufficiently above triviality to engage with the ultimate problems urged upon us by death.

Longdon has lived with his sister ('we were sorry for each other and it somehow suited us'). She has died two years ago. When he tells this to Vanderbank he tries to read into it 'all the unsaid', 'quite tenderly'. Longdon had once, briefly, been in love with Vanderbank's mother; but 'there was nothing after Lady Julia'—he 'hasn't got over her yet'. The memory comes back to him with 'a faint sweetness'; Mr. Longdon and his love for a lost Lady Julia is intensely idealized—it is (as it were) the love for what might have been and never was or could be, such as James himself could only have known. There is a slight edge under the surface:

> I think she rather liked the state to which she had reduced me, though she didn't, you know, at least presume on it. . . . though Lady Julia insisted I ought to marry she wouldn't really have liked it much if I had. (p. 28)

Vanderbank suspects Mr. Longdon considers he was made for better things. 'Help me to them, Mr. Longdon; help me to them, and I don't know what I won't do for you!' Then after all, says Longdon, 'you're *not* past saving!' But the problem is the extent to which Vanderbank is compromised—and here I am not sure James himself made up his mind.

I had not expected to be as interested in Henry James as I have become since returning to teaching in 1981. I had always had doubts about those highly attuned followers of literary criticism who finished up, as it were, with only a few of the later works of Henry James, the only novels able to satisfy their high criteria for the novel.

Re-reading *The Bostonians* made me laugh aloud, and was so robust, so Dickensianly robust, and yet so acute in a Jane Austen way, that I came to feel that James must be given a central place in the art of the novel. I have often returned to *What Maisie Knew*, for its discriminating and ironically comic engagement with a human problem, with a certain grave delight; and I am always surprised on re-reading again to find it so passionately *moral*.

I believe that James at his best is an example of how great

literary art, as in the novel when it is a serious creative medium, is always deeply moral, in the existentialist sense—in its attention to the truths of being and the possibilities of authentic self-fulfilment. I hope I have made my appreciation of James as a great artist plain in the above discussions of his work. But something does go wrong with Henry James, and it is clear to most critics that things go seriously out of focus—and there is a decline of 'life' in the novels.

It is in the discussion of 'life' that we often find Leavis's criticism least satisfactory. He was concerned, obviously, about that certain falling off in the powers of Henry James. We have in *The Bostonians*, in *What Maisie Knew* and in *The Portrait of a Lady* both vivid realization and a firm 'morality'—albeit the 'enacted' morality of the artist. In *The Wings of a Dove* and *The Awkward Age* we have an eteliolation of the technique and a certain mistiness over moral issues. (Or perhaps rather we have a problem of penetrating to the firm ground, even if it is there; our problem is whether it is there or not. Leavis's word in supervisions was 'cobwebby'.)

This has something to do with the phenomenological powers of the artist in question. He could no longer write as successfully as he once did. But in what way can we connect this with 'life'? It is difficult to relate this to the artist's life. The writer sits at his desk. It is for each day a dull and exacting routine, even at best, even when the imagination is being most excitedly applied. (We may remember Stanley Spencer who complained of all the work involved in painting in each leaf and each brick in a wall, which he called 'knitting'.) If there is some failure or deficiency, this must surely be seen as an aspect of a highly complex process of mind and feelings: a subtle psychological process. And it is a philosophical problem—a problem of the relationship between the man's philosophy of being and his capacity to collaborate with the unconscious. It cannot be exactly accounted for. The art consists as many have recorded of giving oneself over as if to some 'other power'. It is a strange collaboration between the knowing mind and deeper areas of intuition, spirit and creative imagination.

When he comes to the question of 'life', Leavis is too simple in his consideration of this problem. Over Henry James's later period he says:

It had already been plain that the hypertrophy of technique, the overdoing, was correlated with a malnutrition. James paid the penalty of living too much as a novelist, and not richly enough as a man. (*Scrutiny*, Spring, 1948, Vol. XV, No. 2, 102)

Such connections are impossible to make with any relevance to the quality and context of creative work. There have been plenty of artists who did not engage in 'public' or 'normal' life (Gerard Manley Hopkins, Emily Dickinson) but who did not decline in quality, and plenty of people who lead a normal life whose creative or critical faculties are mean, dead or atrophied. In Leavis's attitude there does seem to be a requirement, which is almost religious, that the artist must pursue a certain 'pure' kind of existence; and in the background, I suspect, is his distaste of 'Bloomsbury': a life of leisure made possible by money, with an indulgence in cultural pursuits almost as a kind of fashion-following, combined with experiments in various forms of sexual freedom—the kind of thing that used to go on at Garsington.

Leavis goes on, making it worse:

> He paid the price, too, of his upbringing—of never having been allowed to take rest in any community, so that, for all his intense interest in civilisation, he never developed any sense of society as a system of functions and responsibilities.

But this, surely, could be said of Lawrence, that he never took root in any community, not, at least, after his marriage? And yet surely Leavis would uphold him as someone who had a deep sense of functions and responsibilities, in his art?

But here again, the position simply appears ridiculous whenever one applies it to a specific case—say, to Debussy or even Keats. What kind of life must the artists be engaged in, in everyday life, for success? The impulse to prescribe this is not unlike the kind of injunctions offered to artists in communist countries—that they should identify with the proletariat, and so forth. It is puritanical, and implicitly demands of the artist a certain kind of religious discipline and devotion. Certainly, the Bloomsbury kind of socialite life could become inimical, and Leavis hints that Henry James fell into something like that:

> And he spent his life, when he was not at house-parties of a merely social kind (he was unaware, it would seem, of the Victorian country-house at its functional best), dining and writing.

'Dining' and 'house parties' often seem to have been for Leavis highly suspect and corrupting activities; note, too, that merely *social* house-parties are implicitly condemned—a *functional* social life would be different. Anything purposeful, devoted to domestic economy and family welfare is beneficial; simply enjoying oneself in company is likely to lead to spiritual malnutrition—that is, it is *sinful*, to the puritan mind.

There may be more truth in Leavis's next remark: 'The deep consciousness that he had no public and no hope of real critical attention would confirm the dispositions tending to life-impoverishment in his art'—but in what way? What it is possible to assume is an undercurrent of hopelessness, in compensation for which a writer might immerse himself in his own created world, like Sorabji. But even to begin to think about this leads one back to Henry James's quality of sensibility—the kind of man he was. It is inconceivable that by (say) lighting bonfires or seeking sexual or emotional relationships, Henry James could have restored his art's vitality. It does not in the least follow that an absence of critical response would 'confirm' dispositions 'tending to life-impoverishment in the art'—which phrase in any case begs the question, for a lack of vivid realization is not necessarily to be characterized as 'life-impoverishment'. 'Life' may be a necessary word, but it is important to distinguish its uses. To say 'this picture is lifeless' uses the word 'life' in a different way from how we use it when we say, 'Jill seemed a bit lifeless yesterday.' One use refers to a complex living organism, the other refers to *symbolism* and its effectiveness; of course, the symbolism is a manifestation of the phenomena of a consciousness, and so it is a lifeless consciousness which is likely to generate lifeless symbolism.

Confusion is worse confounded when Leavis goes on to say of James:

> It is in this late period that the inherited symbolism assumed control, and we can see why this should be so; it moves into the place once occupied in force by the system of interests belonging to the novelist as novelist—the system of interests derived from the most vital experience. We can see too that in coming so to power it both increases, and disguises from James, the separation of his art from life.

The system of symbolism, in short, doesn't represent the

102

structure of interests behind his operative sensibility; it doesn't begin with his creativeness.

The 'symbolism' Leavis is speaking of here is that analysed by Quentin Anderson who sees the later works as belonging to a 'single poem embracing the history of mankind' (Leavis speaks of a 'blend of Swedenborg and Fourier'). Leavis is saying that the trouble with the later works is that they do not spring from James's essential creativity as the early masterpieces do.

The problem, surely, is a complex one of belief, of the artist's 'philosophy of being', and the psychological complex in which this position is held. James seems to try to follow Christian principles in his works. But, as so often, there is another mythology—that of the schizoid man, whose life was sexless and whose sensibility was thereby deprived of first-hand experience of the force within one's being of the snares and joys of passion.

One problem of belief is that of the attribution of the origins of evil. James obviously detests irresponsible promiscuity, because of its selfishness and the pain and destructiveness it caused. But does evil arise (as in D. H. Lawrence's *St. Mawr*) from some kind of 'tide' in the world, or in modern civilization? Or is it a dynamic which arises out of frustration in the human soul? Or must we see 'evil' as a natural consequence of some human failing—solutions to the problem of life going 'wrong'?

Here it is important to note that many of James's novels are about non-fulfilment (*Washington Square*, *The Awkward Age*) and others are about attempts by women to save others—as the governess 'saves' the children in *The Turn of the Screw* (or tries to), Maggie Verver 'saves' the Prince, Mr. Longdon 'saves' Nanda, and so on. These savings represent the power of love; but I want to express certain doubts about the convincingness of this theme.

I used to dislike Leavis's phrase 'Henry James was a eunuch', but in re-reading him, I have come to feel that his detachment from sexual experience, in his dealings with love, is the most important thing about him. It was this that led to his eventual haziness, surely. While it enables him to concentrate, as in *What Maisie Knew*, on the deeper question of integrity, being true to oneself, and being authentic in personal relationships, it led him to be vague and confused at times, as over Nanda.

Here the strangest revelation of James's weaknesses is to be found in his thriller *blague, The Turn of the Screw.* What *is* the threat to the children in *The Turn of the Screw?* It is clear that Peter Quint and Miss Jessel had some kind of illicit sexual relationship. I can see that their 'diabolical' influence might tend to corrupt the children's relationship with adults and the world at large—and that they might be drawn into a horrible consorting with demons. But I cannot believe that Miles was drawn into *sexual acts* with the dead servants, or that Miles's wickedness at school was anything to do with homosexuality.

It seems characteristic that American critics would come to believe this. In (Freudian) America the obsession with sexual symbolism (or the 'meanings' of perversion) is itself a false solution to the problem of existential meaning. It is this that Rollo May exposed, in *Love and Will.*

But with James, the difficulty throughout this work is that, although he can see the falsifications which addiction to sexual passion can lead to, he cannot himself know what sexual passion is, and cannot see how love can be fulfilled in relationship in a 'whole' way. He sees sexuality very much as a child in the latency period, and so either comic and repulsive (like Beale's being kept by the hideous 'Countess', or Ida's low-cut bosom) or ultimately menacing (as to the children in *The Turn of the Screw* where the ghostly combined parents threaten annihilation and death). Sexual corruption does not threaten perverted immoral acts, but rather menaces with annihilation (or, to use the Freudian term, castration). In *The Turn of the Screw* it seems almost as if exposure to the adult world (of the combined parents in sex) is itself dangerous—threatening corruption and nothingness.

I have argued that Henry James is intensely 'moral', and I believe this moral concern, at best, when it attends to authenticity, is the basis of his great art.

Only there seem to me two weaknesses about his position which are likely to be disastrous.

On the one hand, as I have suggested, he reverts too obviously to 'received' Christian values. It is possible to believe that Maggie Verver would have been better off having a showdown with Charlotte Stanton; Maisie might have been happier with

Sir Claude and Mrs. Beale; Isabel Archer would have been better off divorced.[8]

But on the other hand, there also seems a serious weakness, in James's conceptions of what badness and wickedness might be. Egotism, cruelty, vanity, are all qualities which he shows to be corrupting. But there is often a hint of something worse— something 'evil'; and yet we would be hard put to it to say exactly what it might be.

It is clear that in *What Maisie Knew* both Beale and Ida are promiscuous, having affairs with people they pick up. Moreover, while Ida's men are often bankers and rich men, Beale is 'paid' to be the lover of the rich and ugly 'Countess'. In *The Golden Bowl* Charlotte Stanton marries the older Mr. Verver, so as to make it possible to be in a situation in which she can continue her adulterous affair with the Prince. (Verver, it seems clear, is impotent.) In *Portrait of a Lady*, Madame Merle, who has been Osmund's lover, urges him to marry Isabel, so that he can provide for their illegitimate child, Pansy; there is no suggestion that the relationship between Mme. Merle and Osmund continues. In *The Awkward Age* it seems as if Vanderberg is Mrs. Brookenham's lover, but the worst aspect of the Brookenham set is their destructive talk, which pretends to be so 'open' and free but in fact is esoteric and inhibitive on genuine emotional life and hides corruption, including sexual compromise.

However, there are often dark hints at something more awful, in James's depiction of his evils; and this may be associated with his depiction of Isabel Archer as being afraid of sexual passion— an aspect of the novel noted by Dorothea Krook.

Is this *James's* fear? There are moments in James when there seems to be a dreadfulness about sex, and (as a corollary) an awkwardness. Perhaps it is this which lies beneath the odd difficulties some critics have had with Mrs. Wix. Her husband is singularly absent from her stories about Clara Mathilda; was Mrs. Wix simply seduced? At one point, she suddenly gives Sir Claude a great slap; and there are times when her response is not coarse or guilty, but strangely libidinous, in an odd and disturbing way. To the strange effect of this her repugnant faded feminine and unprepossessing aspect contributes something grotesque.

But perhaps the most revealing glimpses are to be found in

the ghost story, *The Turn of the Screw*. The question must surely
arise in our minds: what was it the two ghosts are trying to do to
the children? In a sense, to steal and possess their souls, as
diabolic manifestations of 'evil'. But because they had been
lovers in life, there is a dark hint of some deeper form of
corruption. The governess wonders whether Miles is a thief; but
nothing like that seems 'bad' enough to justify the dread which
Quint and Miss Jessel inspire.

In the end, Miles dies, from the ordeal of being rescued from
the ghosts. We may read in the fantasy, I believe, a particular
symbolism from the world of dreams. The ghosts are the
'combined parents': that is, they are the mother and father
united in sexual congress, in a form conceived of as being *like
eating*, and therefore liable to bring annihilation. *The Turn of the
Screw* is thus a castration fantasy, in which the undercurrent of
dread is a fear of being driven out of existence, not least by
hungry *looks*.

We can move back from this insight, to the other works. The
Quint-Jessel combination seems to threaten the children in a
very deep way; if they are exposed to adult sexuality, they will
be corrupted and will go out of existence (and Miles does).
Maisie manages to preserve a beautiful invulnerability to adult
sexuality, by being protected in her latency; what she 'knows' is
the kind of 'active principle' which seeks integrity and authenticity; what she does not know is what adults do in bed. Nanda
is protected, or rather her own intelligence protects her, in
much the same way. And here it is noteworthy that so many of
James's heroines are either frustrated of fulfilment, or differ
from their unfortunate liaisons: Verena Tarrent is going to
suffer; Isabel suffers (though she does not, from being in love
with the *crippled* Ralph); Maggie suffers, Nanda is not going to
marry; and so on. They have, it would seem, to be *saved* from
adult libidinousness; and so from its *deathly* effects, as James
feels them to be, at the unconscious level.

And here an important distinction needs to be made. Adult
sexuality can at best have a continuing tenderness; the strange,
voracious, impelled act which is sex can be transmuted into an
affirmation of the beloved, by love, by the meeting of beings.
Those who do not know this (like children) must always see it as
strange, bizarre and voracious, as the sexuality of the castrating

mother or the combined parents. And this, I believe, is how James saw it; sexual love to him was *without reparative power*, because he had never experienced the power of sexual joy to generate the capacity in us to tolerate and come to terms with all the negative and destructive elements in the love-partner and to find grace even in the coarsest aspects of body-life. Dread of sexual love (and of sexually libidinous woman) is an important and central theme in our literature, not least the greatest—as (for instance) in Shakespeare. Henry James had no chance of coming to terms with the problems of the unconscious fantasy life underlying sexual experience, and so he could not ultimately explore the (moral) problems of being which he set out to confront. He could not find that sexual love has a healing reparative power as well as a threatening and corrupting influence, and that this development of love is inhibited by attempts at 'purity', and may be frustrated by mere 'rescue'.

NOTES

1. Her underlying Freudian jealousy of Sir Claude, however, it must be said, *is* indicated by the slap she gives him.
2. W. R. D. Fairbairn made the important recommendation that it would be better to use the word 'sensual' rather than 'sexual' for the child's intense experiences of oral and other bodily forms of passion.
3. References are to the Macmillan hardback edition (1930).
4. The gritty intimacy between Mrs. Brook and Mr. Cashmore, and hints in their conversation, especially on pp. 150–57, make me feel it is likely they have been lovers in the past, too. See especially Chapter I in Book Fourth.
5. So, 'we do not even have the excuse of passion' means 'we are not coarse slaves to our drives' or 'we have a sophisticated well-organised sexual life.'
6. *Schizoid Phenomena, Object Relations and the Self*, pp. 98 ff. Guntrip refers to *Henry James*, by Michael Swan, Booker, London, 1952.
7. Euphrasia, daughter of King Evander of Syracuse, fed him while he was in prison with the milk of her breasts.
8. I think it is possible that James based his conclusions in *Portrait of a Lady*, when Isabel renounces divorce, on Daniel Deronda's attitudes to Gwendolen Harleth's consideration of separation from Grandcourt, when she decides this would be intolerable. Isabel, of course, says, 'I can't publish my mistake . . . I'd rather die.' But I find James's emphasis on 'certain obligations . . . involved in the very fact of marriage . . . quite independent of the quantity of enjoyment extracted from it' an index to a certain falsity in the conclusion.

107

3

The Touch of Nihilism in E. M. Forster's *A Passage to India*

In one of her last essays, Mrs. Q. D. Leavis declared that the pervasive irony in the writings of the Bloomsbury Group was 'merely self-protective' and 'an assertion of superiority': 'it is a give-away, even in Forster's best novel *A Passage to India.*' This seems to be a judgement of the character of the people in the Bloomsbury atmosphere, and of the ethos of the milieu. I think it would have been more effective had the Leavises examined the philosophical roots of the Bloomsbury attitude to life.

As with Bertrand Russell, it was a Humanist position which based itself essentially on positivism, on a materialistic mechanistic view of the Cosmos and man, from which many present-day attitudes derive, the sense of the 'futility' of man's life, and the view that man's life is an 'accident' and so forth.[1] This attitude to life Leavis found repugnant, but, as I believe we see in his arguments about Tragedy, he seems simply to have recorded his repugnance, and then rejected the posture on the grounds of a dubious psychology. Such people, he suggested, were incapable of a true tragic response, because they were enclosed too much in 'the ego'. A much better solution would have been to examine the falsity of the philosophical position itself.

In *A Passage to India* the problem is surely not so much an air of Bloomsbury 'superiority' as the display of a playful or ironic disdain for any kind of belief, on grounds parallel to those

108

adopted by Russell, in his attitude to the universe. The trouble is that this virtually cuts the ground away from under the feet of the art itself.

I found myself teaching *A Passage to India* again, recently, while pondering the problem of whether it was so, that writers in our time can 'find nothing to believe in'. I was startled to find such an undercurrent of nihilism in E. M. Forster. I had always remembered *A Passage to India* for its liberal humanism, its firm belief in rational attempts to break through racial prejudice, beyond the conventions of chauvinism and corrupt power. Fielding, the educational principal, tries to be rational. Despite his weaknesses and mistakes, and despite the emotionalism and pliability of Dr. Aziz, they do, in a sense, 'connect'. From time to time, encounter between them is possible, despite the dreadful events of the book: Aziz's wrongful accusation, his imprisonment, and the tendency on both sides, Indian self-determination and British Colonial power, to use the occasion to threaten one another, submerging reason in the process.

Forster's ironic analysis of the British imperial middle class is superb—and painful. On the one hand there is its state Christianity, inculcated in the public school ('Ronny's religion was of the sterilized Public School brand which never goes bad, even in the tropics'). On the other hand is their herd instinct which is only too willing to allow reason to be submerged. Nothing enraged Anglo-India more

> than the lantern of reason if it is exhibited for one moment after its extinction is decreed. All over Chandrapore that day the Europeans were putting aside their normal personalities and sinking themselves in their community. Pity, wrath, heroism, filled them, but the power of putting two and two together was annihilated. (p. 162)[2]

Forster delineates a 'collective infection' in the Anglo-Indian community, based on noble feelings of a kind, to protect our 'women and children' from outrage, which yet develops on paranoid lines until it threatens anarchy and chaos—as between the white mob's impulse to teach the brown men a 'lesson' and the brown mob's impulse to overthrow their colonial masters. This superb aspect of the novel is immediately relevant of course to problems in Zimbabwe and South Africa today, where the same dreadful cycles of conflict are being followed.

However, the question arises—in the name of what, ultimately, do we care about human and social values? Miss Quested, for example, develops in character throughout the book, not least because of the suffering that comes to her because of her (subjective) falsification of a situation. Whether or not anyone assaulted her sexually in the cave, it could not have been Dr. Aziz, because he did not follow her in there. This is the two-plus-two fact of the case. It is not certain, either, that anyone did assault her at all; Mrs. Moore had (for instance) experienced a deeply disturbing contact a little earlier in a cave by bumping into a baby! Miss Quested had just asked Dr. Aziz if, as a Mohammedan, he had more than one wife—and as she stumbled more and more deeply into this unfortunate (and, to him, insulting) mess of a conversation, something—call it sex—reared its ugly head. Perhaps what she encountered in the cave were her own darker serpents? This is an area of experience where two plus two is no answer; what does Forster believe here?

If we read the novel with attention to this level, we may see the cactus thorns in Miss Quested's flesh after the incident as inevitable consequences of a hysterical denial of her own nature in an outburst of terror and dread. But there is a deeper symbol: the Marabar *striking its gong*. What does the gong of the Marabar signify? This question is obviously central to the novel as dramatic poem.

We see how Mrs. Moore and Miss Quested react to the Marabar Caves. But the question I found myself asking was: how does *reason* stand up to the Marabar? How does Forster's kind of liberal humanism and stoicism stand up to them?

Let us turn back from this diagnosis of what Blake called 'Newton's sleep' as seen by philosophical anthropology, and look at the universe as it appears to E. M. Forster. There is no doubt that Forster's universe is that of positivistic science; it is, in Marjorie Grene's words, 'the Cartesian-Newtonian world which was, in the last analysis, a world without life' (*The Knower and the Known*, p. 14). This lifeless universe is also death, and both are manifest in the Marabar Caves. The Marabar Caves are a symbol in *A Passage to India*—but what they symbolize, or rather the effect of them as a symbol of the positivistic universe, makes it impossible to believe in anything. We may here note a sentence in the homosexual novel *Maurice* which we shall see in its context in a moment: 'Since Cambridge I believe in nothing.' The effect of the caves is meant to be devastatingly nihilistic not only on the characters, but also on us, and it is surprising to find this dynamic in Forster. We even remain in the end uncertain whether or not he gives way to scepticism, as Leavis seems to believe he did, with Mrs. Moore. If he does, it is as if Mahler were to end his Ninth Symphony, on the passage *Wie ein schwerer Kondukt* (first movement, score p. 49, bar 327ff.), 'like a heavy funeral procession', with its dreadful drumstrokes and anguished cadences.

Forster's humanism is a spirit of sympathy between human beings that is upheld in the face of the bleak surroundings in which men find themselves. Forster's man is not in the world and part of it, but set against it. The universe is alien fire and slime however beautiful the sunset. Of Fielding he says,

> the world, he believed, is a globe of men who are trying to reach one another and can best do so by the help of goodwill plus culture and intelligence. (p. 62)

But Forster was apparently not a materialist. In one passage in *Maurice* he makes it plain that he believes the achievements of man transcend him:

> . . . he was doing a fine thing—proving on how little the soul can exist. Fed neither by Heaven nor by earth he was going forward, a lamp that would have blown out, were materialism true. . . . struggles like his are the supreme achievements of humanity, and surpass any legends about Heaven. (*Maurice*, p. 127)

'I do not believe in Heaven', says Fielding, 'but I believe honesty gets us there.' However much man may transcend himself and achieve heaven in this humanistic sense, however, there is for Forster no actual heaven in another world. This world is all we have—yet Forster's universe is alien, while man merely, as it were, crawls out of the slime, makes a futile if beautiful gesture, and then reverts to it. It is not a matter of 'dust to dust and ashes to ashes'; it is rather that death and the indifferent cosmos reduce to nothing the very possibility of meaning: 'in all things men have moved blindly, have evolved

out of slime to dissolve into it when this accident of consequences is over . . .' (*Maurice*, p. 104).

I shall return to this passage again, but these phrases are
enough to reveal the impact upon Forster of evolutionary theory
with its emphasis on chance, and the reductive effect of
Darwinism. Man is not an achievement of life's unfolding,
towards consciousness and responsibility, the *animal symbolicum*,
in a new dimension of existence, born to be open to the world,
and responsible to far horizons because of his upright posture.
He is an accident of the slime, out of which he has blindly
crawled. His consciousness is simply a terrible burden—a point
of view which is encountered everywhere in modern thought
and art; Forster perhaps found it in Bertrand Russell?[3]

The backcloth to this crawl from the slime is what is revealed
by 'geology' and astronomy. Maurice listens to his dying
grandfather, who has a pseudo-religious theory of the universe:

> It was that a meteor swarm impinged on the rings of Saturn, and
> chipped pieces off them and fell into the sun. Now Mr. Grace
> located the wicked in the outer planets of our system, and since
> he believed in eternal damnation had been troubled how to
> extricate them. The new theory explained this. They were
> chipped off and reabsorbed into the good! Courteous and grave,
> the young man listened until a fear seized him that this tosh
> might be true. The fear was momentary, yet started one of those
> rearrangements that affect the whole character. It left him with a
> conviction that his grandfather was convinced. One more human
> being had come alive. He had accomplished an act of creation,
> and as he did so, Death turned her head away. 'It's a great thing
> to believe as you do,' he said very sadly. 'Since Cambridge I
> believe in nothing—except in a sort of darkness,' (*Maurice*,
> p. 123)

Maurice, I believe, is very close to Forster himself, and the
passage is very revealing. Forster would have liked to believe in
something more than humanistic transcendence to set against
materialism. But it seemed that science had shown that any
such kind of belief was 'tosh'. Of course the grandfather's theory
is tosh. Yet to Maurice for a moment the tosh seems magnificent
because it is believed, because grandfather is convinced. This
conviction is an act of creation, and Death turns her head away.
By implication, however, this gesture is only to build a

sandcastle, which will eventually be swept away, since evidently Death only turns her head momentarily in pity. Creativity can do no more than this—and eventually death and nothingness will extinguish even all such achievement of conviction; this seems to be Forster's belief.

Mahler's greatness, I believe, in his last great works, was to meet the possibility that death and nothingness could extinguish all meaning, but then to wrestle with this nihilistic menace—and achieve a triumph, enacting meaning as he doggedly strove to find it. He achieves the sense of *Dasein*—of 'being there', of having meaningfully existed. So, he can achieve gratitude for having existed, and embody a transcending sense of continuity in his music. This he does by a conviction that it is possible to find meaning in love, and that this is bound up with loving the world: 'O world of endless loving!' is a characteristic outburst in *Das Lied von der Erde*.

Mahler's world of the endless circle of the blue horizon (*Ewig!*) is not the world of 'objective' science. Mahler finds 'the category of life' as modern mechanism does not. However, here, the philosophy of science is now catching up with the creative achievement—led by biology with its discoveries of 'centricity' and such concepts as *Weltbeziehung durch Innerlichkeit* ('relation to the environment from inwardness'), from Portmann, Goldstein and Plessner. Biology is beginning to find order in Nature and some kind of 'innovative principle', while even its techniques of knowing demand a recognition of subjectivity, and so of consciousness; so that, as Marjorie Grene says, there is something else in the universe other than matter-in-motion—there is knowing mind. This in turn requires a reconsideration of what knowing *is*. Even a strict empirical biologist like Pantin finds that there are creative elements even in knowing biological facts because this involves the recognition of individuals; he discusses the implications of telling students to 'bring in any worms that sneer at you'—because this is how one finds oneself identifying and classifying species by subjective, aesthetic, tacit disciplines. (See *The Recognition of Species*, C. F. A. Pantin, M.A., Sc.D., F.R.S., *Science Progress* (October, 1954), p. 87.) The relationship between human perception and the world of life is far more complex than we yet fully realize, and the nature of the life we know is far more mysterious, too. The very fact that life is here at all is something about which science has nothing to say. But most of the recognition of this has emerged recently, and there was no source for Forster for a rejection of the burden of the Galilean-Newtonian universe, and it is unlikely that he ever heard the rumblings of dissatisfaction coming across the North Sea from Dilthey, Bretano, Husserl and others.[4] And, of course, the Bloomsbury ethos to which he belonged was deeply influenced by the Viennese school of logical positivism, and by the bleak realism of a humanistic belief in 'the rational', in the positivist universe. But where in this scheme of things—a 'matter in motion' universe, operating like a machine, containing nothing that could not be found and explained by empirical investigation, logic, and reason—can we put man's achievement of transcendence, his unconsciousness or *id*, his vision, his madness, even? Where is there room for the ghosts that haunt him, his yearnings for meaning, his religious impulses, his dread of something 'beyond', inexplicable, that any creative writer cannot but be aware of?

These ghosts leap out, in *A Passage to India*: the hyena that dashed into the Nawab's car; the figure that wrestles with Miss Quested in the cave; and, of course, the 'something snub-nosed' that threatens Mrs. Moore. And where Miss Quested and Aziz are concerned, this snub-nosed menace, which reminds us that fact and reason are not all there is to existence, is associated with love and sexuality.

Here, I believe, we have to bring together Forster's homosexuality, and his philosophical problem. In *Maurice* he tells us that homosexuality comes to be felt by the protagonist to be 'authentic' for him. The psychotherapist, I believe, hears a different story; to opt for homosexuality may be a solution but behind it there sometimes lurks a poignant desire for a more authentic fulfilment of potential.[5] But certainly insofar as homosexuality comes to seem authentic to Maurice, it comes into such conflict with middle-class conventional values as to generate an anguish of conscience—in which it is Christianity that has to go, because of its cruelty and its threat to the only way the man can live. But if an individual is forced to give up Christianity, to choose homosexuality—what can he believe? For a time, perhaps, a Cambridge-King's kind of Hellenism; but this, too, collapses in the person of Clive. So (as we have seen in the passage above) even all that is meant by 'Greece' becomes just another sandcastle. The fate of Maurice's grandfather is related to this problem.

Maurice's grandfather's God lived inside the sun. His faith was based on a rejection of 'the tasteful accounts of the unseen handed out by the churches'; but meanwhile 'the hellenist had got on with him.' Because of his dissatisfaction with Christianity, and middle-class taboos about homosexuality, Maurice feels drawn to Greece. But Greece in *Maurice* the novel also comes itself to be associated with sterility and death. At one point Clive, Maurice's first lover, is sitting in the theatre of Dionysus, having written to Maurice to announce his engagement to a woman, since he has become 'normal'. He has gods, the Greek gods, but they are not real:

> He saw barren plains running down to the sea. . . . Here dwell his gods—Pallas Athene. . . . She understood all men, though motherless and a virgin. He had been coming to thank her for years because she lifted him out of the mire.
>
> But he only saw dying light and a dead land. He uttered no prayer, believed in no deity and knew that the past was devoid of meaning like the present, and a refuge for cowards. (*Maurice*, p. 104)

To take to Hellenism, or its myths, is simply a retreat into pure sandcastles from the bleak realism of modern science. In a short story, *The Machine Stops*, Forster depicts a character in a flying machine who draws a curtain over the window as it flies over Greece: 'No ideas there,' she murmurs, and this is ironic (about the triumph of technology). But in *Maurice*, Clive comes to feel that Greece *is* dead and sterile, and that the Greek gods are as dead as the Christian ones. One feels the inner experience here is close to something Forster himself had experienced:

> He descended to the theatre wearily. Who could help anything? not only in sex, but in all things men have moved blindly, have evolved out of slime to dissolve into it when this accident of consequences is over. *Me phynai ton hapanta nikai logon*[6] sighed the actors in this very place two thousand years before. Even that remark, though further from vanity than most, was vain. (*Maurice*, p. 104)

115

Man's appearance on earth by the blind processes of Darwinian evolution was an accident. By similar blind processes one becomes a homosexual. But Clive has become 'normal'; in either case, one enters darkness after darkness. Whatever one is, it were better never to have been born; death is a mere dissolution into the slime. It is vain even to say that one had better never to have been born (certainly vain to say one had better never to have been born than born a homosexual); vainer still (the implication is) to believe that there is anything to believe in, to believe that life can have a meaning which does not dissolve with one's death. *No-one can help anything.* Here is an ultimately nihilistic position, and it dogs Forster more than is usually admitted. It overcomes Mrs. Moore in *A Passage to India,* and confuses Fielding. It could be argued that in *Maurice* Clive's is a moment of sorrow, over his rejection of the protagonist; but it is actually a moment at which Clive had decided to *marry*—and not only to save Penge, the house which is to become his when he dies.

Forster's predicament seems to have given him an almost cosmic dread of sex as an aspect of fate's (the universe's) darkness. As Maurice develops in adolescence Forster speaks of maturity as a 'darkness': 'Then darkness rolled up again, the darkness that is primeval but not eternal, and yields to its own painful dawn' (p. 20). Again, the emergence of man out of slime is associated with darkness and the dawn of sexuality. In childhood, on going home from school, Maurice experiences a dreadful fantasy of skulls in his bedroom, rather akin to the fantasies of Adela in the Marabar Caves (it happens because the gardener's boy George whose company he enjoyed has been sacked, and the nightmare is an unconscious manifestation of homosexuality). When he becomes an adolescent, Forster speaks of 'The valley of the shadow of Life'; and throughout *Maurice* sexuality seems a dreadful experience—a sense not relieved by the embarrassing drama at the end, in which a kind of coarse game-keeper-manservant figure, who even tries to blackmail Maurice at one point, is depicted as being a suitable partner for him in physical homosexuality. As we shall see, even Forster admits faking this 'solution' to the problem of darkness and sexuality.

Forster's inability to find anything to believe in, then, is

116

rooted in his homosexuality. Out of this arises his scorn of
Christianity. 'Those who base their conduct upon what they are
rather than what they ought to be, must always throw it up in
the end' (*Maurice*, p. 60). In this we have Forster's emphasis on
intellectual and moral honesty, the best face of Humanism. But
it also seemed to him that when one gave up Christianity,
because one chose to be a homosexual, one also gave up any
hope of believing in anything—even ancient Greece, or even
that one could create meaning in love or by imaginative acts.

All that we can do, then, is to try to 'reach one another'
before we sink back into the slime of non-meaning. The medium
for this nihilistic general philosophy in Forster's Indian novel
is Mrs. Moore. Are her thoughts about life, death and the
universe simply in character? Or are they but a vehicle for
Forster to utter his *Weltanschauung*?

Leavis thought that Mrs. Moore is simply employed as an
opportunity to put over a dose of the Bloomsbury ethos.
'Standard enlightenment', he declares, 'is an essentially
destructive complexity' (*Nor Shall my Sword*, p. 226). And he
quoted the crucial phrases: 'pathos, piety, courage—they exist,
but are identical, and so is filth. Everything exists, nothing has
value.' Leavis comments.

> It might be retorted that this is dramatic. But it isn't, for Mrs.
> Moore herself, the elderly woman of the Marabar Cave, doesn't
> exist—except as a contrived opportunity for Edward Morgan
> Forster to make, without the embarrassment of avowed personal
> utterance, what seems to him an impressive statement of his
> genuine Bloomsbury lack of creative conviction. (p. 226)

This, says Leavis, is taken 'without disturbance'. Yet Mrs.
Moore's own response to the voice of the Marabar is disturbing.
It is not true to say she does not exist; Leavis is being unfair.
She encounters Aziz in the mosque early in the book, and in a
strange way she 'meets' him across the gulf. She becomes
something he loves; to the mob around the courtroom, a hint
that she believes Aziz innocent, turns her into the goddess
Esmiss Esmoor, to whom offerings are made in saucers. The
symbolic irony of this is that simple minds are capable of
making an object of belief out of an ageing and rather ill woman
who has lost her faith, and who virually dies because of it. Even

at Forster's level of 'meeting' between human beings, she becomes broken down: 'her christian tenderness had gone' (p. 194). She becomes morally and spiritually impotent:

> Why can't this be done and that be done in my way and they be done and I at peace? Why has anything to be done, I cannot see. Why all this marriage, marriage? . . . The human race would have become a single person centuries ago if marriage was any use. And all this rubbish about love, love in a church, love in a cave, as if there is the least difference, and I held up from my business over such trifles. (p. 197)

Mrs. Moore becomes petulant, irritable, destructive, negative, and dies from a kind of psychosomatic response to the voice of the Marabar ('My body, my miserable body,' she sighed, 'Why isn't it strong? Oh, why can't I walk away and be gone?'). It is quite clear that Forster *places* her, as one whose psychological disintegration, and nihilistic attitudes at last, are the consequence of an appalling experience in a cave which arouses philosophical problems she cannot cope with. Seeking a sense of love and meaning in India, in 'life' indeed ('Pretty dear', said Mrs. Moore to the wasp), she is defeated by her encounter with the bleakest manifestation of a universe that (according to the dogmas of Western paradigms) only *is*, and in which life has no place. This she cannot tolerate. She wants to be at one with the universe; the voice of the Marabar (which, in a sense, of course, 'says' what Forster makes it say) renders this impossible. One can only be over against the universe, for the universe is death. Forster may be held responsible for what seems to be in the end the irresistible view that the universe is death and nothingness; but I believe Leavis is wrong to see Mrs. Moore as merely a mouthpiece for Forster's Bloomsbury enlightenment. If she were that, she would hardly be allowed to lose her hold on life completely as a consequence of her own philosophy. And, of course, her philosophy changes, disastrously, to destructiveness when she is defeated by the cave.

What I think Forster *can* be held responsible for is his own inability to see any other response to the Marabar but defeat. Perhaps that is not quite the whole truth either; the effect of the Caves is, after all, to bring out a certain heroism in Miss Quested and Fielding, and even capacities for strength of

integrity and forgiveness in Aziz. But these do not, I think, for
Forster, establish a *Dasein*-quality. The symbolic theme throughout the novel is the enormousness of the Caves, which Fielding
sees from the verandah; they obliterate everything: 'he saw the
fists and fingers of the Marabar swell until they included the
whole sky' (p. 242). This phrase (at the end of Chapter 25)
comes at a significant moment, when Fielding is tempted by
what seems now (in the light of psychoanalysis and· phenomenology) a perfectly acceptable insight:

> fatigued by the merciless and enormous day, he lost his usual
> sane view of human intercourse, and felt that we exist not in
> ourselves, but in terms of each other's minds—a notion for which
> logic offers no support and which had attacked him only once
> before, the evening after the catastrophe . . . (p. 242)

—then follows the above phrase. The Marabar Caves, then,
threaten 'reason', 'logic' and 'sanity'. But the disturbing notion
which they thrust on Fielding is in a sense acceptable; we do
exist in that we are *creatively reflected* by others, in that we know
ourselves by being aware of the perception others have of us.
And while some, like Sartre, see this only as threatening, it can
be, through love and 'meeting', an enriching source of con-
firmation of our being: 'From man to man the heavenly bread of
self being is passed', as Martin Buber puts it. If the 'sane view
of human intercourse' fails to embrace this, then it needs to
extend itself beyond sanity and reason (which is, of course,
what R. D. Laing at best has helped us do as in *The Divided
Self*). Forster, however, sees this intersubjectivity in terms of a
Cambridge analytical philosophy which plays (as in *The Longest
Journey*) with the trick of making the cow cease to exist when you
are not there to see it—a mere logical amusement to undermine
the sense of being-in-the-world.

While the Marabar Caves are threatening, they also seem, at
this moment, capable of being challenging in a useful way—if,
for example, they were to encourage Fielding to include more of
the subjective in his paradigm. But one feature of them is that
they mock love (and so generate in Mrs. Moore the cynicism she
shows in the passage above). This mockery of love is described in
a very significant passage, in which the appalling caves seem to
have a beauty and even sensuous quality that should enable one

to love them; one ought to be able to love the world (just as one should be glad of finding oneself in the mind of the other). But when one kisses the Newtonian universe, everything dies:

> There is little to see, and no eye to see it, until the visitor arrives for his five minutes, and strikes a match. Immediately another flame rises in the depths of the rock and moves towards the surface like an imprisoned spirit: the walls of the chamber have been most marvellously polished. The two flames approach and strive to unite, but cannot, because one of them breathes air, the other stone. A mirror inlaid with lovely colours divides the lovers, delicate stars of pink and grey interpose, exquisite nebulae, shadings fainter than the tail of a comet or the midday noon, all the evanescent life of the granite, only here visible. Fists and finger thrust above the advancing soil—here at last is their skin, finer than any covering acquired by the animals, smoother than windless water, more voluptuous than love. The radiance increases, the flames touch one another, kiss, expire. The cave is dark again, like all the caves. (p. 124)

Surely, in this we find a yearning to love the world, deeply frustrated, as Mahler's similar yearning is not? Forster is perplexed by the existence of natural forms where there is no eye to see them.

In the next paragraph we read that there are chambers that have no entrances:

> Chambers never unsealed since the arrival of the gods. Local report declares that these exceed in number those that can be visited, as the dead exceed the living—four hundred of them, four thousand or million. Nothing is inside them, they were sealed up before the creation of pestilence or treasure; if mankind grew curious and excavated, nothing, nothing would be added to the sum of good or evil (p. 125)[7]

On the previous page he says of the caves, 'Nothing, nothing attaches to them, and their reputation—for they have one—does not depend on human speech.'

The word 'nothing' is repeated four times on these pages; nothingness is attached to the caves. They seem to be factitious; they have all the qualities of an artefact, spherical, polished. But they are not artefacts. Their existence owes nothing to human speech or knowing. So why bother with them—why expect them to bear in any way on problems of 'good and evil', however many there are? To put the question in perspective we may turn to the first page of Michael Polanyi's *Personal Knowledge*:

> . . . if we decided to examine the universe objectively in the sense of paying equal attention to portions of equal mass, this would result in a lifelong preoccupation with interstellar dust, relieved only at brief intervals by a survey of incandescent masses of hydrogen—*not in a thousand million lifetimes would the time come to give man even a second's notice.* (p. 3, my italics)

No one looks at the universe in this day, declares Polanyi, whatever lip-service is paid to 'objectivity'.

> For, as human beings, we must inevitably see the universe from a centre lying within ourselves and speak about it in terms of a human language shaped by the exigencies of human intercourse. Any attempt vigorously to eliminate our human perspective from our picture of the world must lead to absurdity. (p. 3)

What Forster is doing therefore is invoking a large chunk of matter, shaped by chance, from the world of 'objective' science, from the idealized objectivity of scientific paradigm, to threaten us with absurdity. In the face of that universe (as Marjorie Grene declares) the only response *is* absurdity and despair. *But we do not have to accept that universe.*

So, the Marabar Caves represent something different from death; like the chromatic, disintegrative 'hate' theme in Mahler's Ninth, they represent the failure of meaning, of all hope of finding a meaning in one's life, or gratitude for having existed. For this reason, Mrs. Moore ends by being quite unable (as above) to feel any gladness about love or marriage, or the future generation (' "less attention should be paid to my future daughter-in-law and more to me, there is no sorrow like my sorrow", although when the attention was paid she rejected it irritably', p. 203). In truth, Mrs. Moore suffers a terrible fate and hers is a catastrophe one cannot even call tragic, since her earlier values perish with her and nothing triumphs over her obscure end, brought on by the heat, as the ship sails south before entering the Suez Canal, her body being buried at sea somewhere in the Indian Ocean.

Leavis's hatred of Bloomsbury confuses him, I believe, over Mrs. Moore. She does exist; but something is wrong, and what that is can only be found by philosophical investigation of the kind Leavis always disallowed. The author does use Mrs. Moore to make choric pronouncements on the relationship, between the self and the world, and it is these which require our attention, as we enquire after the ultimate basis of Forster's values:

> She had come to that state where the horror of the universe and its smallness are both visible at the same time—the twilight of the double vision in which so many elderly people are involved. If this world is not to our taste, well, at all events there is Heaven, Hell, Annihilation—one or other of those large things, that hugs scenic background of stars, fires, blue or black air. All heroic endeavour, and all that is known as art, assumes that there's such a background, just as all practical endeavours, when the world is to our taste, assumes that the world is all. But in the twilight of the double vision, a spiritual muddledown is set up for which no high-sounding words can be found; we can neither act nor refrain from action, we can neither ignore nor respect Infinity. (p. 202)

Mrs. Moore has seen beauty—'the moon, caught in the shawl of night with all the other stars'—and aspired towards transcendent meaning: 'To be at one within a universe! So dignified and simple.' But while she was 'turning up some new card from the diminishing pack', 'the Marabar struck its gong.'

What we have to say, I believe, is that Forster goes rather beyond showing a procrastinating middle-aged woman losing her faith because of a disturbing experience in a foreign country. He wants to use the Marabar symbol and its effect on her to *threaten our hold on meaning*. We are perfectly prepared, of course, to believe that the echo 'began to undermine her hold on life'. We can even believe it is she who, exasperated with Adela, associates her own unbelief in Miss Quested with her unbelief in Christianity and even morality (though this speech seems terribly forced (it is more like a dig by a fanatical humanist):

> Oh why is everything still my duty? when shall I be free from your fuss? Was he in the cave and were you in the cave and on and on . . . and Unto us a Son is born, unto us a Child is given . . . and am I good and is he bad and are we saved? . . . *and ending everything the echo*. (p. 200, my italics)

But in the next chapter the author tells us not what she sees in the caves, but what *he* sees there:

What had spoken to her in that scoured-out cavity of the granite? What dwelt in the first of the caves? Something very old and very small. Before time, it was before space also. Something snub-nosed, incapable of generosity—the undying worm itself. Since hearing its voice, she had not entertained one large thought, she was actually envious of Adela. All this fuss over a frightened girl! Nothing had happened, 'and if it had,' she found herself thinking with the cynicism of a withered priestess, 'if it had, there are worse evils than love.' The unspeakable attempt presented itself to her as love: in a cave, in a church—Boum, it amounts to the same. . . . (p. 203)

The disturbing thing about this is the sudden glimpse we gain of a person's state of collapse of their moral structures—and it is not only Mrs. Moore's, but Forster's. It is like that moment with Clive: 'Who could help anything?' The passage is a strange mixture of insight and confusion. Mrs. Moore does, for reasons I have indicated, become incapable of gratitude because of the failure of meaning; so, she can only become envious. But it is asking too much to expect us to believe that a sexual assault in a cave could be seen by Mrs. Moore as 'love'—even under the influence of the Marabar gong.

Something is speaking out from Forster: and that is clear in the opening sentences. What is this 'boum'? If it were death, the novel could rise to it, despite the sordid collapse of poor Mrs. Moore. But it is, on examination, something almost occult—a death principle, or even something worse, right at the heart of the 'matter in motion' universe. Throughout, Forster seems to uphold the rational, sound common sense, the humanistic truth, and even the capacity of man to transcend himself beyond materialism. But when the darkness rolls up from the shadow of sexuality, and the effect is not only to undermine beliefs, but rather the whole capacity to find meaning in the universe, by creative disciplines: 'Visions are supposed to entail profundity, but—wait till you get one, dear reader: The abyss may also be petty, the serpent of eternity made of maggots . . .' (p. 203).

Actually, at this point, there is a certain note which makes it difficult for us to take Forster seriously. It is something like Max Stirner's 'creative frivolity' which is a dynamic of his egoistical nihilism. Not death, but a sick vision of a collapse of meaning (like Callot's engravings which influenced Mahler) leads him

123

for a moment to cast doubt even on human vision; if we exercise our powers of vision, we may simply develop that view of the maggoty meanness of the universe—its 'horror' and its 'smallness'. But this is not adequate as an ultimate picture of the mystery and torment of existence, the marvel that we are here at all, to 'meet', to perceive, to throw over the universe the only meanings it has.

Reading *Maurice* and *A Passage to India* one is led, I suggest, into the anguish of a man who could not solve the problems of being a homosexual, and of not being a Christian: a man believing in man, but not being able to see how—apart from such manifest qualities wrung from worms-food as courage and integrity—one could believe in anything, not 'anything else' but *anything*, since (as in Mrs. Moore) even courage and integrity could disintegrate, if the Marabar strikes its gong at the right moment, at any time.

The perplexity can be followed in Fielding. He, surely, is the character in *A Passage to India* closest to Forster himself (at one point, for instance, like Forster, he wears Indian costume). But there is one revealing phrase used of Fielding: 'Fielding was a black, frank atheist'. What, one wonders, is the force of that 'black'? Does it not have the same effect as the passage about Mrs. Moore's vision that urges absurdity on us? In Fielding this predicament is poignantly given us, as in the same passage from which the above phrase comes:

> Facts are facts, and everyone would learn of Mrs. Moore's death in the morning. But it struck him that people are not really dead until they are felt to be dead. As long as there is some mis-understanding about them, they possess a sort of immortality. An experience of his own confirmed this. Many years ago he had lost a great friend, a woman, who believed in the Christian heaven, and assured him that after the changes and chances of mortal life they would meet in it again. Fielding was a black, frank atheist, but he respected every opinion his friend held: to do this is essential in friendship. And it seemed to him for a time that the dead awaited him, and when the illusion faded it left behind it an emptiness that was almost guilt: 'This is really the end,' he thought, 'and I gave her the final blow.' He had tried to kill Mrs. Moore this evening . . . but she still eluded him. . . . Presently the moon arose—the exhausted crescent that precedes

the sun—and shortly after men and oxen began their interminable labour, as the gracious interlude which he had tried to curtail came to its natural conclusion. (pp. 247–48)

I, too, would put the belief in an afterlife down as tosh. I am not of course questioning Forster's rejection of the idea of another world. I am trying to draw attention to the way he presents the alternatives. There is only (he posits) a choice between 'illusion' (as of the dead going on living in an afterlife), or the drowning of all meaning in 'reality'. To the non-believer there can be (Forster seems to suggest) only the 'black' blankness of atheism, the interminable processes of life under the sun, and *futile* 'interminable labour'. India simply reminds one of the reality of natural processes which are those delineated by positivist science, and so even the achievement of 'meeting' or 'connecting' can be itself only an ephemeral gain. It cannot be the basis of an ethic: but in this predicament (which is the predicament of Carthesian dualism) *what can?*

In discussing Forster, Leavis quotes D. H. Lawrence: 'E.M.F. does see people and only people ad nauseam.' But even when he upholds relationships between people we find a degree of ambivalence in Forster. Because of his lack of confidence that meaning can be found and because of a failure to be able to find confidence in 'creative reflection' (a failure which extends to the universe) there is a deep distrust of 'loving we-hood'; *liebende Wirheit* cannot triumph over the essential blankness of Forster's universe.

Not even Fielding can uphold, against the fists and fingers of the 'real', any triumphant sense of how man can achieve a 'being in the presence of the other', a sense of having meaningfully existed because one has loved, *because* one has been creatively *seen* and has existed in the minds of others.

In Mrs. Moore's mind, for example, 'too much fuss has been made over marriage': 'centuries of carnal embracement, yet man is no nearer to understanding man' (p. 134). Forster displays a kind of puzzlement about what love might be. Aziz finds love, but only after, in the arranged relationship, he has begot his first child in 'animality':

The change began after its birth. He was won by her love for him, by a loyalty that implied something more than submission,

125

and by her efforts to educate herself against that lifting of the purdah that would come . . . Sensuous enjoyment—well, even if he had had it, it would have dulled in a year, and he had gained something instead, which seemed to increase the longer they lived together. She became the mother of a son . . . and in giving him a second son she died. Then he realised what he had lost, and that no woman would ever take her place: a friend would come nearer to her than another woman. She had gone, there was no one like her, and what is that uniqueness but love. (p. 55)

There follows a genuinely serious discussion of Aziz's meditation on the after-life and belief. But the love Aziz finds is made to appear incidental to belief.

Forster may be said to *know about love* in its relationship to values and meaning, in the sense of the uniqueness it yields. But he does not advance beyond his sense of irreplaceableness, to the triumphant sense of meaning in being that love can yield: a sense of the meaning it yielded, for example, to Mahler. He is always somewhat patronizing and lightly ironic while from time to time, in *A Passage to India*, we even glimpse (as in Sylvia Plath), the blank face of the mother—a blankness Forster is surely trying to overcome by the lovely passage about the reflections in the walls of the cave above? He lacks conviction as if he had never known love and the possibilities of love. Among the English, certainly, love is presented as a very low-key experience. Certainly, there is no embodiment in *A Passage to India* of a love that can create such transcendent meaning that it could overcome the primary reality of the rocks, and yield an indestructible sense of the *Dasein*. Perhaps Forster's own love of Italy might suggest some possibility of the kind, or the strange love between Gino and Ralph in *Where Angels Fear to Tread*—a suppressed (or not very suppressed) form of homosexuality. But where does Forster ever convey the triumph of meaning in love? The best he can do, as in *The Longest Journey*, is to idealize 'brutality' as in the animal-like Stephen, and to falsify a happiness he did not believe in, in *Maurice*; love between Leonard Bast and Margaret Schlegel is really unbelievable.

In *A Passage to India*, in the absence of any recognition of possible sources of meaning in 'having a presence in the being of the other', creative perception itself must be frustrated in the end, while the Indian landscape mostly challenges all attempts to find it benign. As the characters approach the Marabar, perception fails:

> Life went on as usual, but had no consequences, that is to say, sounds did not echo or thoughts develop. Everything seemed cut off at its root, and therefore infected with illusion. . . . (p. 139)

India is worth studying, because it is from this atmosphere that the delusions of Miss Quested, and the horrible wave of nihilism that attacks Mrs. Moore, emerge: '. . . when she looked through Ronny's field glasses, she found it wasn't a snake. . . . Nothing was explained, and yet there was no romance.' In the Marabar experience, the world is virtually stripped of meaning itself: 'The plain quietly disappeared, peeled off, so to speak, and nothing was to be seen on either side but the granite very dead and quiet . . .' (p. 139).

To Forster, strangely, perception here seems entirely passive, and so, to enter the Marabar is to enter nothingness: 'The small black hole gaped where their varied forms and colours had momentarily functioned. . . .' Inside, the echo is the voice of the fists and fingers of the void:

> 'Boum' is the sound as far as the human alphabet can express it, or 'bo-oum', or 'oh-boum',—utterly dull. Hope, politeness, the blowing of a nose, the squeak of a boot, all produce 'boum'. . . . later no-one could romanticize the Marabar because it robbed infinity and eternity of their vastness, the only quality that accommodates them to mankind (pp. 139 and 147)

There may be, it is true, episodes in life when the immediate pressure of a sordid and brutal reminder of our mortality strips us of the capacity to uphold a sense of meaning. What Forster perhaps means by 'infinity' and 'eternity' here is those capacities in us for a sense of tragedy that triumphs over nothingness and death; as we have seen, it is this capacity which Mrs. Moore loses. At deep moments of suffering by a graveside or in a torment of grief, the 'facts of the world' may strip one of one's capacities for personal belief. But they do not strip the whole of human consciousness forever of its capacity to throw meaning over the universe, unless the struggle is wilfully given up. We know (especially if we know and love creativity) that the human spirit can achieve meanings of a

Dasein ('being there') substantiality, which nothing can ever eradicate, once the meanings have been created. With Forster, it would seem, the struggle is given up with a kind of spiteful bitterness:

> She tried to go on . . . reminding herself . . . that the despair creeping over her was merely her despair, her personal weakness, and that if ever she got a sunstroke and went mad the rest of the world would go on. . . .

But we are not allowed to see the problem as merely hers. Forster seems to wish to allow us no possible way out. And so, as throughout the book he ridicules religion, as the futile throwing of red powder, the ringing of gongs, the masks and boats and rituals, and the singing of Professor Godbole that goes with his moral impotence. When Mrs. Moore meets 'reality':

> suddenly, at the edge of her mind, Religion appeared, poor little talkative Christianity, and she knew that all its divine words from 'let there be light' to 'It is finished' only amounted to 'boum'.

The Marabar Caves are thus the philosophical-poetic centre for all Forster's irony: 'The Ganges happens not to be holy here' (p. 9). 'God who saves the King, will surely support the police' (p. 206); 'all sorrow was annihilated' (p. 263). Reading *A Passage to India* again, I was shocked by the mockery directed at all ritual and belief, not that it would have mattered so much had we not been left with that clarion call to nihilism: 'everything exists: nothing has value.' For the effect, overall, is to ridicule all man's cultural achievements—though Forster himself by no means gave them up. Anything said in the Marabar Cave, however profound, however *poetic*, would seem garbled mumbo-jumbo; in its light does everything become sandcastles, even King's Chapel and its music, and the College with it civilized traditions?

One could read the best parts of *A Passage to India* about human courage and the integrity of reason, in that cave, and all one would get would be 'bo-oum'! But what capitulation is this? And with 'poor little talkative Christianity', do we throw out, as boum-talk, Bach's *St. Matthew Passion*, the cathedral, Bruckner and Messiaen, and the *Book of Job*? Forster did not; but this is virtually what he declares in his novel, that nothing has value in the face of slime and the echo: the squeak of one's boots, 'Hope', spiritual disciplines, everything is equal; the echo undermines every hold on life, as it undermined Mrs. Moore's. Where does Forster himself declare for any other view?

Of course, Forster tried to have it both ways—at once seeming to suggest that she feels this only during a moment when she is fatigued, but then showing that it did not go away when she made allowances for the fatigue:

> coming at a moment when she chanced to be fatigued, it had managed to murmur, 'Pathos, piety, courage—they exist. Everything exists, nothing has value.' If one had spoken vileness in that place, or *quoted lofty poetry*, the comment would have been the same—'bo-boum'. If one had spoken with the tongues of angels and pleaded for all the unhappiness and misunderstanding in the world, past, present and to come, for all the misery men must undergo whatever their opinion and position, and however much they dodge or bluff—it would would be the same, the serpent would descend and return to the ceiling. (p. 146, my italics)

We do not really experience in the novel a relief from this nihilistic position. He means that once religion begins to examine its tenets in the light of reason and science it comes in danger of losing the capacity to believe in anything. But this may also be applied to Forster himself as creative artist. If one forfeits, in the name of a simplified form of 'frank' enlightened rational humanism, all sense of the categories of life, levels of being, of the special powers of consciousness, recognition of order, value and the need for teleological explanations in the universe, *and* the power of consciousness to express and attribute meaning to the universe, one *may* indeed be left with nothing. Everything depends, of course, on whether we forfeit the belief that meaning can be achieved as Mrs. Moore did. Where, in *A Passage to India*, does Forster show us how to avoid her terrible fate? It is true that Forster is positive when he says 'the song for the future must transcend greed'. But if we are to find a basis for this moral development in man, for this better social and interhuman future, we must also find a song that can transcend the brutal reality of the fists and fingers of the Marabar, and express a more adequate concept of love as a source of meaning than anything developed in Forster's novels.

I am not arguing that the overall effect of Forster's art is nihilistic. I am arguing that he was seriously touched by it. Some things he evidently believed in passionately—intellectual honesty, and a sense of natural passionate 'life' such as he often evokes around 'Italy'. But there is a pressure of nihilism in his work, arising from a belief that to be intellectually honest one must see the material universe and death as realities which cannot be overcome by any creative gesture, a view of existence which I suggest has been challenged by philosophers who have argued that it is based on inadequate concepts of *how we know*— and so on inadequate concepts of the truth about homosexuality, about that dreadful darkness, of yearning for an authenticity which can never be achieved. We may feel the deep poignancy. But we must reject the extrapolation of this into a general philosophy. Even if we admit Heidegger's 'being-unto-death', it *is* possible to achieve meanings which can endure, and our imaginative constructions *do* have a validity. Only a misconception of the nature of knowing, and of the universe, makes it seem that they do not. While Forster could not know of the philosophical revolution which argues thus, we can, I believe, even from his best work, reject his nihilistic refusal of all ultimate meaning as no 'realism' but something of a sentimental indulgence. The roots of this are exposed by *Maurice* to be in the agonies and confusions of his homosexuality—this condition of life made him feel *abandonné* (in Sartre's sense) in a bleak universe in which opportunities for genuine creative achievement, even in the name of 'connecting', were really futile.

Forster's position is only one more example of that failure of creative conviction that plagues so much of twentieth-century literature, written under the daunting shadow of the false myths of an idealized objectivity, whose effects are more nihilistic than we often admit—despite the radical fallacies in which they are rooted.

NOTES

1. 'Scepticism may be painful, and may be barren, but at least it is honest. . .', *The Scientific Outlook*, p. 104.
2. Page references are to the Penguin editions.

3. 'The loneliness of the human soul is unendurable' (1, 146): 'I have been merely oppressed by the weariness and tedium and vanity of things lately; nothing stirs me, nothing seems worth doing or worth having done', letter to Gilbert Murray, 21 March 1903. See Andrew Brink, 'Bertrand Russell, The Angry Pacifist', *Journal of Psychohistory*, vol. 12, No. 9.
4. See Marjorie Grene, *Approaches to a Philosophical Biology*, Basic Books: and the present author's *Evolution and the Humanities* and *Education and Philosophical Anthropology*.
5. See Masud Khan, *Alienation in Perversion* and Robert Stoller on gender in his various works. Those who politicize homosexuality reject such interpretations and sometimes even attempt to suppress debate. But the question is an open one and must remain open, surely?
6. 'Not to be born is best', *Oedipus Coloneus*, 1224–225.
7. As Karl Stern points out, the earth is Mother Earth. Jungians would interpret Forster's caves as wombs. In the light of Winnicott's theories of 'creative reflection' on the mother's part the above passage suggests a dreadful failure of reflective response behind Forster's feeling about the walls of the caves in the rock, and his references to death and 'nothing' associated with them—to be related to his nihilistic feelings about the universe of matter (mater).

4

Endorsing Inauthenticity: Alan Sillitoe's *Saturday Night and Sunday Morning*

As we approach the modern novel, let me record a kind of difficulty I experience from time to time, when I turn to read a novel recommended not merely in casual interest by a colleague or friend, but by a syllabus. When a novel is taught, of course, it must seem both to teacher and student that the choice endorses it—and so to some extent its 'message', or 'upshot', about life.

I had never read Alan Sillitoe, though I knew he was taught as 'socialist' literature in some English departments. I picked up a paperback to read on a train journey, feeling I should read the novel because it is taught in schools. It is believed that Sillitoe provides an introduction to working-class people, and offers realism about urban industrial life. What kind of model of human nature did he offer? And how did his portrayal of working people compare with Lawrence's? (My touchstone here would be the tragic dignity of miners portrayed in *Odour of Chrysanthemums*.)

The cover of my paperback[1] indicates one problem of the literary critical approach to such a book. There is a voyeuristic still from the film, showing the hero Arthur Seaton in bed naked with his mate's wife. This kind of thing is to be expected, at a time when scenes from Lawrence's novels, with some justification it must be admitted, are filmed and shown on television, including explicit sexuality. But the blurb is also indicative: 'A novel of today with a freshness and raw fury that makes *Room at the Top* look like a vicarage tea-party', *Daily Telegraph*. What is indicative is this journalistic note of a deepening progress in sensational portrayals of human 'reality', in the process of 'liberation'. 'Thirty years have passed since Lawrence's pro-letarian hero [in *Lady Chatterley's Lover*] shook the bookshops. Now, from the Lawrence country, comes a new author with a hero who might have startled Lawrence himself', the *Sunday Express* is quoted as commenting. The implication is that authors and publishers are striving to outdo one another in outrageousness: and this, of course, has been a gift for the commercial publisher.

> Here is a first novel of explosive impact which has been praised to the skies on both sides of the Atlantic—a raw and uninhibited story of a working-class district in Nottingham and the people who live, love, laugh and fight there.

'Brilliant', the *New Yorker* is quoted as saying; 'if he never writes anything more, he has assured himself a place in the history of the English novel.' Somehow, all these claims ring hollow. There is an unmistakable implication that life among the 'working class' is raw, that the book is 'strong', and that it is a work by an 'important' author. The dismal reality is that this kind of promotion works, and Sillitoe was elevated thus into the establishment of commended modern literature.

Yet when we examine his prose, it turns out to be a very inferior imitation of the Lawrence mode; it has none of Lawrence's vitality, but, more importantly, none of Lawrence's tenderness and sympathy towards his creatures. It conveys, by contrast, the 'brutal' model, the sense that to be a brute is to be a *real man*. The self-assumption of the hero on these lines is not placed; it is endorsed: human beings are 'like this'.

> The bartender placed a pint before him. He paid one-and-eightpence and drank it almost in a single gulp. His strength magically returned, and he shouted for another, thinking: the thirteenth. Unlucky for some, but we'll see how it turns out. He received the pint and drank a little more slowly, but half way through it, the temptation to be sick became a necessity that beat insistently against the back of his throat. He fought it off and struggled to light a cigarette. (p. 10)

It is not only that there is no artistic 'placing', far from it—but that the falsities of the drinker's self-delusion, about the way he pursues his manic false sense of strength, are themselves offered for approval. The 'stream of consciousness' mode is used to involve the reader in identifying with the hero. There is no sensitive insight into a human soul in its vacillation between true and false. The false is shown to be strong, and the posture is defended by 'irony': 'unlucky for some, but we'll see how it turns out.'

We might compare with this moment Lawrence's rich portrayal of George in his first novel, *The White Peacock*: at one moment enjoying the vigour of his own bodily work in mowing, but later declining into alcoholism, and then flying into destructive rages, terrorizing his family, and ending in resigned self-denial and the relinquishing of life. We are appalled; but our hearts are wrung, not least by the sympathetic insight of the novelist. There is no doubt in Lawrence's mind that George's alcoholic bouts are a sign of a deeply disturbed view of the world. They have drama of a deadly kind, but our attitude to him, following that of the author, is that of compassion, in which we see the dreadful falsity of his self-loathing:

> He turned to me, his dark eyes alive with horror and despair.
> 'I shall soon be out of everybody's way!' he said. . . .

But however deep George sinks, he retains that nobility with which Lawrence imbues his characters. There is nothing of this quality about Arthur Seaton; with him we are simply invited to approve his false solutions—he's a helluva fella:

> Smoke caught in his windpipe, and he had just time enough to push his way through the crush—nudging his elbow into standing people who unknowingly blocked his way, half choked by smoke now issuing from mouth and nostrils, feeling strangely taken up by a fierce power that he could not control—before he gave way to the temptation that had stood by him since falling down the stairs, and emitted a belching roar over a middle-aged man sitting with a woman on one of the green leather seats.

'A fierce power that he could not control' is 'Lawrentian' language; yet this is used to give us a scene in which the coarseness of the hero is meant to involve us in fascination with a blackguard. It is rather like the way the popular press presents villains, pretending to condemn them when the real reason for the presentation is to arouse prurient excitement:

'Look what yer've done, yer young bleeder', the woman was shouting at him. 'Spewed all over Alf's bes' suit. And all you do is jus' stand there. . . . Go on, apologise.'

There follows a moment in which we may glimpse Sillitoe's real contempt for working-class people:

> From her constant use of the word apologise it seemed as if she had either just learned its meaning—perhaps after a transmission breakdown on television—or as if she had first learned to say it by spelling it out with coloured bricks at school forty years ago.
>
> 'Apologise,' she cried, her maniacal face tight against him. 'Go on, apologise.'
>
> The beast inside Arthur's stomach gripped him again, and suddenly, mercilessly, before he could stop it or move out of the way, or warn anybody that it was coming, it leapt out of his mouth with an appalling growl.
>
> She was astonished. Through the haze her face clarified. . . . Arthur saw teeth between open lips, narrowed eyes, claws raised. She was a tigress. . . .

Note the way in which we are drawn to feel superior to a woman who attempts to invoke social values and decency and how this is intended to enhance her ironic degradation by the strong 'beast' in Arthur; it seems almost as if the ('tigress') woman gets what she deserves.

In Tolstoy, Conrad or Lawrence, such an episode would have been presented as an appalling human degradation; compare, for example, the episode in which Rasumov beats the drunken peasant Ziemianich in *Under Western Eyes*, in which the futile brutality of the act, and the paralysed response, represents the predicament of the protagonist on the one hand, in his moral trap, and the petrified torpor of the peasantry on the other. With Sillitoe we are encouraged to enjoy the sense his man has, of a 'merciless' beast inside him, and to find comic his ruthless attack on others, with no repugnance and less insight. It seems like a new 'realism' which 'unmasks' us as we are; but it is a long way from truth. We know from our own experience that to be as drunk as this would leave us poisoned, racked with pain and depressed. Nothing of this, in the Sillitoe fantasy; the incident is followed by no ill consequences, guilt, lowness of spirit, or alienation from others as with David Copperfield drunk confronting Agnes, or as it would have been in Gorki or Dostoevsky, or would indeed be in real life. Arthur goes at once to call on Brenda, his workmate's wife, and all is pleasant around him:

> It was a mild autumn night, a wind playing the occasional sharp sound of someone slamming a door or closing a window. . . . He was blissfully happy, for he did not have the uncomfortable feeling of wanting to be sick any more, though at the same time he had retained enough alcohol to stay both high-spirited and sleepy. He made the curious experiment of speaking out loud to see whether or not he could hear his own voice.
>
> 'Couldn't care less, couldn't care less, couldn't care less'—in answer to questions that came into his mind regarding sleeping with a woman who had a husband and two kids, getting blind drunk on seven gins and umpteen pints, falling down a flight of stairs, and being sick over a man and a woman. Bliss and guilt joined forces in such a way that they caused no trouble but merely sunk his mind into a welcome nonchalance. . . .

The portrayal of experience is utterly unreal, but the intention becomes clear: 'wickedly' (in the terms of the popular press) to idolize the lout, and to involve us in the 'naughty' approval of loutishness. There is to be no suspicion that such behaviour is false or wrong, or that we need feel any concern either for Arthur, or for those he violates. It is simply a question of 'being sick over a man and a woman', and we laugh (Oh, he's a one!) we adopt his 'couldn't care less', as an acceptable stance towards the world (the affinity with the amoral aggressive stance of the 'pop' idol should be clear).[2]

A man who is so drunk that he believes that the cold pavement is bed, as Arthur has just been, is always repulsive— maddening to deal with, volatile in mood, smelly, cringing and physically repulsive. Whenever he arrives at his woman, Arthur is always sweetly received; she colludes with his fantasy, one might say:

> '. . . let's be quiet as we go in, or we'll wake the kids.'
>
> Got to be careful, he said to himself. Nosy neighbour'll tell Jack. He lifted the band of hair from her coat collar and kissed her neck. She turned to him petulantly: 'Can't you wait till we get upstairs?'
>
> 'No,' he admitted, with a mock-gloating laugh. . . .

136

They creep 'like two thieves' into the living-room. The moment is utterly unreal, the man does not totter; he is amiable and potent.

But in reality, what kind of woman would be so willing for her lover, when he comes in from a drunken bout, having fallen downstairs, no doubt splashed with vomit? He even gloats on being unattractive, with 'his short disordered hair sticking out like the bristles of a blond porcupine, and the mark of an old pimple healing on his cheek'. It is all part of the corrupt indulgence in a certain kind of aggressive fantasy—to which it seems important that the man should be repulsive, and that the woman—indeed all women—should yet love him and be instantly and always a passive servant to his needs. So, she is all tenderness: ' "Don't let's stay down here long, Arthur," she said softly.' A man who has drunk as much as Arthur, after such a night, would almost certainly be impotent, and his main ambition would simply be to sleep, stupefied. In any real situation the woman's main concern would be to get the boor out of the house, in case he sank into a drunken sleep from which he could not be aroused before her husband's return. Not in Sillitoe's fantasy; Arthur is alert and potent, utterly welcome:

> He released her, and, knowing every corner of the house and acting as if it belonged to him, stripped off his coat and shirt and went into the scullery to wash the tiredness from his eyes. Once in bed, they would not go to sleep at once: he wanted to be fresh for an hour before floating endlessly down into the warm bed beside Brenda's soft body.

Nauseating to any responsive reader is the essential untruthfulness, the calculation, the corrupting effect, of celebrating this hero in his sordid escapades—with deliberate coarseness, immediately followed by the use of the 'Lawrentian' language of tenderness ('floating endlessly', 'soft body').

The woman, significantly, is always responsive and loving, like a patient mother. She can be treated in any way, with indifference, coarseness, selfishness, unfeeling brutality; she is always willing, tender and ready.

Of course, there are coarse people in the world, and people do commit adultery and have sexual relationships which are casual, untender, and even brutal. But, in the light of psychoanalytical studies and all we know from philosophical anthropology, to say nothing of great novels, such acts must always be seen as having a meaning, since they too arise from deep inward needs, and thus need to be seen from a point of view of compassionate understanding. Lawrence's greatness as an artist is in his recognition of these needs, at best. No such criteria are applicable to Sillitoe; indeed, it is a disadvantage in a critic to be seeking honest insights from his work, and it is this which appals one as one reads. It would be futile here to invoke extensive psychological insights, or to point out that in invoking these it does not really matter whether people are 'working class' or not. The novel here is not of a level of serious art which makes such a debate relevant. What Sillitoe represents is the calculated manipulation of the description of experience, not in the pursuit of truth or art as in Lawrence, but of the validation of inauthenticity, as by the implication that one forfeits nothing by indulging one's lust, egoism or destructiveness.

When Arthur is waiting from Brenda to come off a bus, to meet him at the club, the author's concern is not to imagine what might be going on in such a young man's mind, but to provide us with a certain opportunity to identify with a fantasy figure, whose toughness represents a successful suppression of his human sensitivity and responsibility.

The writing may be called a kind of lame dehydrated Lawrence; both the 'tenderness' and the 'roughness' are false:

> He went out to meet her, taking hold of her and drawing her into the shadows. 'Hello, duck,' he said, kissing her on the cheek. 'How are you?'
>
> . . . .
>
> He knew he was hurting her, squeezing her wrist as he led her deeper into the wood, but it did not occur to him to relax his hold. Trees and bushes crowding around in the darkness made him melancholy. One minute he thought he was holding her wrist tightly because he was in a hurry to find a good dry place; then he felt it was because there was something about her and the whole situation that made him want to hurt her, something to do with the way she was deceiving Jack. Even though he, now leading her to a spot that suddenly came into his mind, would soon be enjoying it, he thought: 'Women are all the same. If they do it to their husbands they would do it to you, if you gave them half a chance.' (p. 42)

138

I call it lame Lawrence because, as we can see in *The White Peacock*, or *Kangaroo*, one of Lawrence's gifts was to be aware of the hostility that often underlies man–woman relationships, not least when people are exerting their will on one another, sexually. Sillitoe is dimly aware of the hostility implicit in Arthur's adulterous intentions on Jack's wife, but, characteristically, he turns it away into ironic contempt and complacency. The touch of sadism is not seen with insight as an aspect of the aggression and hate that lies behind the ambivalence of love. It is simply a spice to the sexual depiction, an ingredient in the product. He 'would soon be enjoying it', and the only dynamic in Arthur with which we are to identify is brutal self-interest. What we do not find, to enjoy, is any mutual tenderness, wrung from ambivalence.

The place is blunt and sordid:

> The ground was hard and dry. They walked over a hump clear of bushes, the roof of a concealed tunnel burrowed into the earth and strengthened with pit-props, an air-raid shelter for the sawmill men during the war.

She asks him if he won't be cold:

> Hearing her so solicitous, he could hardly wait for what was to come. He laughed out loud. 'No fear. This is nothing to what we had to put up with in the Army. And I hadn't got you with me to keep me warm, duck!'

Even though he can 'hardly wait', he has a thread of contemptuous hostility running in his mind: 'Women are all the same. If they do it to their husbands they would do it to you if you gave them half a chance.'

Yet despite the sordid outdoor spot, the egocentricity of Arthur, his underlying hostility, the risk, the adulterous nature of the assignment—all make for ecstasy, and Sillitoe uses the Lawrentian language for this bliss:

> She put her arms around him, and allowed him to unbutton her coat. He smelled again the smell of a woman whose excitement at doing something she considered not quite right was but one step from the hasty abandonment of making love. He felt the hardness of the imitation pearl brooch against her blouse, and then the buttons themselves, and they lay down on the spot where he had carefully placed his overcoat. They forgot the cold soil and

139

towering trees, and lost themselves in a warm passion in the comfortable silence of a primeval vegetation, a void wherein no one could discover your secrets, or kill the delight that a man and a woman generate between them in an overcoat in the darkness. (p. 43)

It is all fake. The spot in reality surely must have been one in which the 'secret' is all too likely to be discovered. The smell of 'primeval vegetation' seems more likely to be the smell of oil or stagnant puddles: to be anything but 'comfortable'—and with them clothed, in the cold, haunted by fear of discovery, how could sexual love here be 'delight'? Such phrases as 'the comfortable silence of a wood at night' (meaning the wood of passion) are empty, because nothing is realized—for the episode is clearly manufactured with an eye to the film industry rather than to the truth about human love.

Ersatz as it may be, the book still has a 'philosophy', an 'attitude to existence'. It is this that is so disturbing about the descent of English literature both into triviality and into the *Weltanschauung* of Andy Kapp and the *Sunday People*:

> when the day's work is over, Arthur is off to the pubs, raving for adventure. He is a warrior of the bottle and the bedroom—his slogan is 'If it's going, it's for me'—for his aim is to cheat the world before it can cheat him. . . .

This has a strong appeal to the tendency in us all to fall into moral inversion; we will deny our inner emptiness and weakness, and the threats that the world offers to our sense of meaninglessness will be a paranoid one; we will survive by cheating before we are cheated. It is this that gives *Saturday Night and Sunday Morning* its popular appeal and its 'socialist' label—Arthur is a 'victim' of a 'society'. The gross travesty of 'working-class life', deficient in human sympathy and understanding, is given the spurious vindication that what is being depicted is the life of an underdog whose viciousness is excusable and whose hate is 'politically' commendable as 'protest'.

In the end, Arthur is 'hooked', and goes fishing. This is the 'Sunday morning' time of reckoning, the time for facing up to life. The gesture at commitment, it must be said, is slight. And Arthur, at the end, shows himself to be a true son of the working class (it is asserted) by his paranoid view of society; to a fish he says 'don't grumble when you feel that point sticking in your chops'):

> trouble for me it'll be, fighting every day until I die. Why do they make soldiers out of us when we're fighting up to the hilt as it is? Fighting with mothers and wives, landlords and gaffers, coppers, army, government. If it's not one thing it's another, apart from the work we have to do and the way we spend our wages. There's bound to be trouble in store for me every day of my life, because trouble it's always been and always will be. Born drunk and married blind, misbegotten into a strange and crazy world, dragged-up through the dole and into the war with a gas-mask on your clock, and the sirens rattling into you every night while you rot with scabies in an air-raid shelter. Slung into khaki at eighteen, and when they let you out, you sweat again in a factory, grabbing for an extra pint, doing women at the weekend and getting to know whose husbands are on the night-shift, working with rotten guts and an aching spine, and nothing for it but money to drag you back there every Monday morning. (p. 191)

It is this kind of indulgence in self-pity, offered as realism about working people's lives, that apparently makes Sillitoe's work seem 'socialist literature' to English departments that want to be 'up to date'. One feels like telling Arthur that the 'trouble' he talks about he has brought largely on himself (as George brings his downfall on himself in *The White Peacock*—but accepts it with resignation). The writing is fast and loose—war-time sirens did not 'rattle' into one, nor as far as I know, did anyone rot with scabies in air-raid shelters. But the whimpering view of the situation of a working man is pathetically inept (by contrast we may invoke the dignity of an Adam Bede that Lawrence obviously found sympathetic to his own presentation of the miners he knew in childhood).

In the end Arthur is laughing all the same; oh, he's been a one, cocking his snook at the world:

> Well, it's a good life and a good world, all said and done, if you don't weaken if you know that the big wide world hasn't heard from you yet, no, not by a long way, though it won't be long now.
> The float bobbed more violently than before and, with a grin on his face, he had better wind in the reel. (End of novel)

He has just said to the fish that it was curtains for the next one: 'he wanted fish to take home, either to cook in the pan or feed to the cat. It's trouble for you and trouble for me. . . .' The implication is that life has been such a trial for Arthur, that he has been entitled to exert his selfish loutishness on it. He will kill a fish to show the world where it gets off! He is entitled *not to be weak*, and to exert his kind of aggressive 'strength' ('doing women'). This machismo behaviour has paid off: 'it's a good life and a good world, all said and done. . .'—that is, we are to close the book with a sense that Arthur has won against life, not least by his drunkenness, the deceits and adulteries, the trampling on women's emotions, the abortion, the beatings-up, the persistent coarseness and abominable egotism.

Insofar as it is appropriate to talk of a 'philosophy' here, it implies vindication of a deliberate *cultural* brutality. This, indeed, is what 'Arthur' means at the end when he is made to say 'the big wide world hasn't heard from you yet . . . though it won't be long now'; he means himself, and the author means himself, too. Soon, the world will have a new 'anti-hero':

> He rubbed his hand over the rough features of his face, upwards over thick lips, grey eyes, low forehead, short fair hair. . . . Forgetting the stilled float in the water he stopped to urinate against the bushes. . . . (p. 190)

Sillitoe's association of working-class people with urination, vomit, blood, sweat and gin is, like his watered-down Lawrence, watered-down Orwell. His *nostalgie de la boue* (or *de la merde*) lacks conviction: 'like the corporal in the Army who said it was marvellous the things you thought as you sat on the lavatory . . .' (p. 189). 'Realism' today must have its feet firmly on the cloacal, and this is what the blurbs offer us as 'fresh'. A useful exercise is to ask what else would be in the scene, and why the eye is drawn so perversely to the stained, the ugly, the depressing, and what this tells us about the writer's attitude to his creatures and to experience. In Orwell, of course, this element becomes increasingly wilful as his novels progress. In novels like *Keep the Aspidistra Flying*, his hero Gordon Comstock seeks to 'sink . . . Down, down into the ghost-kingdom, the shadowy world where shame, effort, decency do not exist'. This anti-hero is so boring, actually, that one does not care where he goes, but Orwell seems to want to offer this impulse as a way of escaping from the world of bourgeois values into a world of 'meaningless mechanical work', to come home to a 'frowsty bed', to be dirty, to show 'sulkiness a *je m'en fou* in the face of the world' (pp. 711–12, Penguin Complete Novels Edition). It is perhaps from this original mode that the English novel of today has taken its clue, as if this is the way to 'protest' against 'society'; yet, of course, the effect is simply to deepen the dehumanization already thrust on us by a mechanistic civilization. Orwell, himself a product of Eton and the Burma Police, seemed to want to show his solidarity with the working class, and, below them, in *les bas fonds*, with *les plongeurs*, by his slumming. But there is clearly a strong, masochistic, self-destructive element in this, and his world of sordid rooms, excreta-smeared streets and vomit is unrelieved by any human generosity or hope.

There is also something essentially adolescent about it, and this has communicated itself to the English novel—as if Orwell could never complete the process and come out on the other side of that period of reckless confrontation and prostration in protest that the adolescent normally goes through. (While in Jura, Orwell took his whole family out on the sea, near the famous Corrievrechan whirlpool, knowing that the tides were such as to make the spot dangerous; of course they were wrecked, and nearly all drowned—and this self-destructive tendency was characteristic of the man.)

In Orwell's *Coming Up for Air*, an earlier novel with an equally unprepossessing hero, there is an element which relieves it a little: a nostalgia for the exploits of childhood, especially fishing. The complaint in that novel is that the world of the child's natural relationship with nature, as in fishing, has been spoilt. It seems likely that the fishing theme in *Saturday Night and Sunday Morning* owes something to this. What Arthur thinks about, as he is fishing, is 'freedom'—which he takes to be 'not being caught'—as if he too would prefer to live in an eternal adolescence in which responsibilities may be escaped: 'Everyone in the world was caught, somehow, one way or another. . . . To be caught was death to a fish. For a man perhaps it would not be too bad:

Without knowing what you were doing you had chewed off more than you could bite and had to stick with the same piece of bait

143

for the rest of your life . . . He laughed to think that he was full of bait already, half-digested slop that had certainly given him a share of trouble, one way or another. (p. 189)

The 'half-digested slop' is his intention to marry Doreen in three months. There is in this novel no better concept of relationship between man and woman than the grudging admission that perhaps to be 'caught' could be 'the beginning of something better in life', swallowing a slop for bait—for, after all, 'If you went through life refusing all the bait dangled before you, that would be no life at all.' Again, the analogy with Andy Kapp seems appropriate. Far from offering any fresh sense of human equality, or any resistance in the name of being, to the degradations of industrial life, such a novel merely reinforces the brutal old prejudices.

Arthur is shown walking away from the 'obstinacy' of two women who had no use for him.

> Not that he minded them drinking his stout. He expected it from Nottingham women who, he told himself were cheeky-daft, and thought so much of themselves that they would drink your ale whether they liked your company or not. Whores, all of them. Never again. They'd had all they were going to get from him. Brenda wasn't worth the trouble he had been through to keep her. As if it made any difference whether he had written to her or not. It was only an excuse to make trouble. Most likely, when he went away, she had been glad to see the back of him, and had passed the whole fortnight doing the dirty on him, not to mention on poor old Jack. (p. 126)

Arthur is one to think of 'poor old Jack'! And now the hate behind the easy, 'comfortable', ecstasies flows:

> Instead of boozing in the Match she should be at home looking after her two kids, the poor little sods. If ever I get married, he thought, and have a wife that carries on like Brenda and Winnie carry on, I'll give her the biggest pasting any woman ever had. I'd kill her. My wife'll have to look after any kids I fill her with,[3] keep the house spotless. And if she's good at that I might let her go to the pictures now and again and take her out for a drink on Saturday. But if I thought she was carrying on behind my back she'd be sent back to her mother with two black eyes before she knew what's happening. By God she would. (p. 126)

To depict a man's inner thoughts in such blunt prose is to take his brutal mouthings in the pub as the whole of his consciousness. And if we allow its 'realism', how is it possible then to find him so admirable in his stance towards 'society' as a hero?

I suppose it could be argued that Sillitoe is making the point that the industrial world makes people like Arthur feel simply a bundle of functions—and so their attitude to sex becomes mechanical.

> He pondered a great deal on Brenda and Winnie as he spun and thrust and pulled at the life of his lathe. Like the tool and stops before him he played off one woman against the other, taking Winnie to the Langham and Brenda to the Rose. . . . He did not see Doreen often, because his weeks and weekends were divided between Brenda and Winnie. . . . the pleasure and danger of having two married women had been too sweet to resist. (p. 135)

The truth, however, is otherwise. When a man divides his attention between a number of women, without feeling a loyalty to anyone, it is because there is something seriously wrong with his emotional life. To behave as Arthur did, sleeping with one woman, making the appointment with another to see him the next night, then casually picking up a third, is to behave in a psychopathological way—or, at least, to display an impotence in one's emotional and relational life. As Stoller points out,[4] there is a great deal of hostility in such behaviour.

> He decided that his chances of spending the night with her would be better if they didn't take a bus. This supposition that a bright ending was after all possible for his tumultuous day seemed reasonable when she squeezed his forearm affectionately . . . promising now the odours of a woman's body and bedroom to crown the end of a mobile and passionate day.[5] . . . His opinion of Nottingham women had changed slightly. Of course they were gold-diggers, he told himself, but more often than not they were of the right stuff, and you could usually get what you wanted if you were careful and went out of your way sufficiently to pick the right sort of woman. (p. 134)

For women to be 'of the right stuff' is for them to satisfy the lust of Arthur Seaton; relationships to them are a matter of 'careful' calculation, and manipulations of behaviour, so that you get what you want. This nihilistic egoism is the central philosophy of the new cult of loutishness portrayed for its own sake, without insight, since insight would require grounds for itself in human concern.

In such an ethos the sense of meaning and value—love, certainly—is no longer even seen. There can be no reconciliation between this world and that of *Scenes from Clerical Life*, say, or *Portrait of a Lady*. These, I suppose, to the 'radical' English teacher, admirers of Sillitoe, are 'bourgeois'. But at least in bourgeois art we find a high value set on humanness and its meaning. The new brutal trivialities have destroyed this, and they suppose this marks some new advance into a 'liberation', or a 'democratization'.

An important relevant point here is made by Mrs. Q. D. Leavis in her essay already referred to, *The Englishness of the English Novel*. The English novel became a great art form because its characters, especially its women characters, were heretical—that is, they were prepared to challenge existing established moral and social codes, when the integrity of the self was threatened, when authenticity was menaced. This Mrs. Leavis attributes to the Protestant tradition, but it is also a product of the creative impulse to find the truth of life as it is—to find *being*: 'what throbs fast and full, though hidden, what the blood rushes through, what is the unseen seat of life and the sentient target of death'—this remarkable existential statement is from Charlotte Brontë.

Thus the greatness of the English novel lies in the positive moral life and sense of personal responsibility that gave significance and interest to the histories of the protagonists in this form of serious art. This has been replaced in the modern novel by moral stupidity, or cultivated immorality, and the idolization of personal irresponsibility, as in Arthur Seaton. Because of this, the novel has inevitably sunk into insignificance and triviality.

Referring to an incident in Stendhal, Mrs. Leavis says of a character who does not at a critical moment make a moral reflection:

> But not to be subject to self-scrutiny in such circumstances is surely to be sub-human, and the fact that such a situation would have been impossible for an English novelist [in the past] to

146

record admiringly is one proof that our novelists had a more mature and civilised tradition than the French to work in.

Yes—but the phrase in brackets 'in the past' is necessary; today the commercial novelist does present such moral turpitude admiringly, and can present a character like Arthur Seaton, sub-human in his total incapacity for self-scrutiny, as admirable.

The decline is a mark not only of the nature of the novel; it is all part of a widespread decline in moral awareness, a blight of consciousness, a loss of the sense of values. To take up Mrs. Leavis's point about the Protestant ethic and the integrity of the individual conscience: if our culture is debased in this way, and assuming that the novel does have an effect on attitudes and behaviour, what is lost is of importance to society; for what is lost is the free play of conscience and the essentially radical impulse to choose and act from the centre of one's own being. What is damaged by the cult of loutishness is our very existential freedom itself.

To Alan Sillitoe, as we can see by an occasional slip of the pen, personal responsibility, in the sense of commitment of being to being, is deadly; existential freedom is death. At the end of the book there is a sudden lapse into conventional relationship. In conventional myths of sexual mores, a woman who does not give herself away easily wins in the end. This is what happens here (and it shows that the novel really belongs to magazine literature).

Doreen is the girl who makes Arthur take his hands away in the cinema, and she 'nets' Arthur in the end by these very means. It is interesting to note that when she does yield in the end the author describes it as being 'drawn by a *deathly* and irresistible passion, they lay down together in the bottom of a hedge' (p. 180, my italics). They have been looking into the water, and, by this Lawrentian symbolism, Sillitoe obviously means to imply a coming to terms with reality.

But the word slips out; there is, in the background, a feeling that to exploit people and the world as Arthur did is 'freedom'; to commit oneself is 'deathly'. It is, in one sense, just a Lawrentian word, but Lawrence would have used it to imply a mutual stranglehold, a loss of the world, a recognition of the problem of hate which is always bound up with love. Sillitoe

147

reveals by it his attachment to Arthur's anarchic anarchism, and his dread of love, his flight from reality itself.

Towards the end of Chapter 15 Arthur and Doreen declare their love and refer to the occasion: 'I shan't forget that walk we did that Sunday', she said quietly, taking his hand, 'when we looked into the water near Cossal and then went into the fields.' There follows another consciously 'Lawrentian' paragraph:

> They sat as if the weight of the world had in this minute been lifted from them both and left them dumb with surprise. But this lasted only for the moment. Arthur held her murderously tight, as if to vanquish her spirit even in the first short contest. But she responded to him, as if she would break him first. It was stalemate, and they sought relief from the great decision they had brought on themselves. He spoke to her softly, and she nodded her head to his words without knowing what they meant. Neither did Arthur know what he was saying: both transmission and reception were drowned, and they broke through to the opened furrows of the earth. (p. 188)

As we have seen, Arthur reverts to being a grinning egotist at the end; there is no radical change in him, while Doreen is unsympathetically presented as a girl involved in the conventional dreams of magazine romance: 'What's more, he was good-looking, was tall, thin, had fair hair. What girl wouldn't be happy with a man like that?' (p. 139; Doreen is not far away from Joyce's Gerty MacDowell). She is too unsympathetically presented to bear the burden of the gravity Sillitoe seeks to impose on her. It is too much to expect us to attribute to this couple, among all the beer and cigarettes and fumbling in the dark, the grave earthy attributes of the Lawrentian sexual conflict, even if the language gestures at his kind of dealings with love's depths. The 'dumbness', the 'deathly and irresistible passion' the 'murderous tightness' are merely borrowed terms.

It is in Lawrence that people speak without knowing what they mean, and in their sexuality 'break through to the furrows of the earth'. But with characters as coarsely drawn as Arthur and Doreen, it is impossible to redeem them by suddenly lapsing into this borrowed mode; the reference to 'earth', when we remember *The Rainbow*, is here grotesquely pathetic.

Sillitoe's attempts at Lawrentian eroticism ('lime trees were coming to life by the laneside, tiny erectile buds emerging to enjoy the spring . . .') simply do not go with the simple gross anarchism he associates with Arthur: 'there was still the vast crushing power of government against which to lean his white-skinned bony shoulder, a thousand of its laws to be ignored and therefore broken. . . .' Arthur is not the rebel he takes himself for and his author takes him. He is *of* the factory world, as a product of its dehumanization: 'But listen, this lathe is my everlasting pal because it gets me thinking. . . .' What he means by 'thinking' is to react with aggression and lust: 'is that a machine gun?'

> Der-der-der-der-der-der-der . . . I hope I'm not here to see it, but I know I will be. I'm a bloody billy-goat trying to screw the world, and no wonder I am, because it's trying to do the same to me. (p. 177)

Nothing in Arthur's 'condition' obliges him to 'screw the world', since, from all appearances, his world is a free one. He hardly behaves like a crushed victim of society, though he may be seen as a victim of its amoral hedonism. At one point he is shown deliberately not to know the difference, in his impulse to 'screw the world', between right and wrong:

> 'Where shall we go then, Arthur?' He did not know. In more ways than one it was a big question. Action, he thought. That's more my line. So he shed his morbidity in a second and steered her along the right-angled line of the hedge. Wheat hid them from view, and he kicked out at it, wanted to flatten it.
>   'It's wrong,' she said. 'You shouldn't trample it like that.'
>   'What's wrong? I enjoy doing it. Besides, what does it matter?'
>   'Just as I said,' she replied, faintly smiling. 'You don't know the difference between right and wrong.'
>   'No I don't. And I don't want anybody to start teaching me either.'
>   'I suppose you've got the right idea. This is a good place,' she said, looking into a smooth hollow at the bottom of the hedge. 'I do love you, Arthur,' she added. They sat down and kissed each other passionately. (p. 118)

This is the message that comes over from the commercial novel.

A real woman under such circumstances would not say 'you've got the right idea'—certainly not one who knew, as Brenda

149

should, what this lecher is capable of. Sillitoe's woman says 'This is a good place' and 'I do love you'; she is the controllable woman of a masturbation fantasy, submissive, ultimately, to man's contemptuous exploitation (with his hostility running self-defensively in his head meanwhile).

Arthur's future escapades with Brenda are idolized in such a vein, and taken to be justified by his self-pity at his alleged social deprivation.

> Life went on like an assegai into the blue, with dim memories of the dole and schooldays behind, and a dimmer feeling of death in front, a present life punctuated by meetings with Brenda on certain beautiful evenings when the streets were warm and noisy and the clouds did a moonlit-flit over the rooftops. They made love in parlour or bedroom and felt the ocean of suburb falling asleep outside their minuscule coracle of untouchable hope and bliss.
> (p. 111)

This minuscule 'coracle of hope and bliss' floats through an abortion by gin and hot bath which works (without any ill effects) and is abruptly dismissed, in which sordid scene even 'The ample lower portions' of Brenda's body are described as visible in the bath. Even in the middle of her anguish in this brutal episode, she declares 'You're a good-hearted lad, Arthur.' She is groaning and closing her eyes from the heat, drinking herself into a stupor, to destroy her foetus, but still calls her lout 'good-hearted': could wish-fulfilment stretch further? Afterwards, Arthur cannot

> throw off the vivid and *blood-like* scene of Brenda's white body reclining in the bath, and Em'ler's idiot face passing glass after glass of gin, until Brenda was hopeless and helpless in her swill-tippling and unable to speak or recognise anyone in the room.
> (p. 80—my italics)

How was it 'blood-like'? The word is revealing: it gives just that touch of spicy sensation which the kitsch commercial work needs. It is such touches in the language that reveal the corrupt purpose.

It is not long before Arthur is back in his randy condition again, nothing daunted: 'her breasts, large and out of proportion in size to the rest of her body, pushed the folds of her purple jumper forward. You touch me, they said, and see what a smack you get. Mounds of mischief' (p. 81). The juxtaposition of such coarse relish with the misery of the abortion scene is outrageous. It conveys a mean indifference to human sensitivity and to the consequences of our actions: an indifference to violation and pain, in relation to moral issues. It is this confusion of authenticity, in the sense of recognizing integrity, which is now commonplace in the English 'novel'.

The above vision makes Arthur reflect on Winnie's and Brenda's origins, the sisters.

> A bit of funny business went on in the family twenty-odd years ago. Some gypsy selling clothes pegs got hold of the mother and gave her what for, I'm sure, when she offered him a cup of tea. You've only got to look at her eyes and them high cheeks and that coal-black hair and the beaky little nose. A nice change though from a bread-pudding face with spotted dick eyes and ginger-pink tabs. . . . (p. 82.)

In such a brief aside Sillitoe reveals his sad attitude to working-class people. They do it like stoats: if the father has a face like a bread-pudding, they will have a go with a clothes-peg gypsy. It is all as crude as that, life at this level. It is sad that stories of 'common life' should have sunk to this level, in the country of Dickens and Lawrence. The real problem is one of a decline of attitudes to human existence, and here, I am afraid, there have been disasters at the highest level. The ensuing monologue here, is as grotesque a travesty of the lives of ordinary people as T. S. Eliot's 'HURRY UP PLEASE IT'S TIME' in *The Waste Land*: 'No, duck, the sooner he's home the better, then he can look after you as a bloke should.' Of course it is not long before Arthur has 'a triumphant night with Winnie' (he is nothing if not potent), followed by being beaten up by her soldier husband and a swaddie colleague—this violent scene another gift to the cinema industry. But Brenda has no suspicion of Arthur's infidelity, and all is happiness 'in the minuscule coracle of untouchable hope and bliss'. In what sense could it be hope, and 'untouchable', when the marauding adulterer has to leave at midnight to avoid being seen by husband Jack, 'as he came in cold and ill-tempered from the night shift'.[2]

Reading *Saturday Night and Sunday Morning* was for me a depressing experience, not so much because it is an ugly, commonplace story, but because it has been accepted and is taught in the 'canon'; ask a group of foreign visitors at a British Council Course what they have read, and they will chant 'Amis, Sillitoe . . .' in the same voice with which they mention Forster or Lawrence—though some are puzzled. We only need to compare (say) *Odour of Chrysanthemums* to assert that working people are not like that, and that art can portray ordinary people with dignity and understanding, not least in our century.

Far from representing a defence of the human being from the coarsening effects of industrialization, the new 'realism' celebrates dehumanization as 'robust'. Arthur finds he is fetching contraceptives, for the foreman.

> 'Three packets!' he shouted out. 'The dirty bogger! He's got a fancy-woman! Nine times a week!' So the news broke in the shop . . . if Robboe were not in the shop he would yell back at the top of his voice, 'I'm going downtown to get Robboe's rubbers!' in his broad, deliberately brutalized Robin Hood accent that brought screams of laughter from the women, and guffaws from the men. (p. 34)

Is it necessary to comment? The people of 'Lawrence's country' have been reduced, in the name of 'realism', to 'dirty boggers', the novel to this. What I would wish to draw attention to is the way in which we take in a *concept of ourselves* from our culture. From such coarse farce we learn to despise ourselves. Of course, in the era of Tom Sharpe, things have become a hundred times worse.

So, the people of a nation with a great tradition in the novel have become disinherited. And being disinherited, they are deprived of access to creative fiction; for as sensibility is corrupted, not least by such successful brutalities, so the pathways become closed. Who would publish *The White Peacock* today? Certainly, *The Rainbow* would seem far too serious, too poetic, too hopeful about human nature, too emphatic as to its dignity and worth, after so many Sillitoes. The loutishness which this novel offers is thus a contribution, among many hundreds, to the destruction of one of the major art forms in our civilization. With such works, we have a moral and cultural inversion of a particularly sinister kind, in which the cult of inauthenticity comes to be elevated to predominance, thus supplanting a cultural mode which offered formerly an opportunity for every reader to contemplate the true possibilities of his being.

NOTES

1. Pan Books (1958).
2. But it should also be clear that this kind of stance, so often offered in our time as 'working class', is actually one imposed on the people by middle-class intellectuals like journalists and television producers and commercial authors.
3. The man's 'right' to 'fill' a woman with 'kids' is asserted more than once in *Saturday Night and Sunday Morning*, without being placed for its atrocious brutality.
4. See again Robert Stoller, *Perversion, the Erotic Form of Hatred.*
5. Note in the quotation above (from p. 43) the reference to 'the smell of a woman who was doing something she considered not quite right'. Here again there is a subtle and slightly perverted emphasis on this, with an underlying hostility.

5

Falsity in the Modern Novel

I began this study by invoking the findings of philosophical anthropology in the literary criticism of the novel. Turning from such disciplines as existential psychoanalysis and *Daseins-analysis*, I found that those works I consider to be great English novels are deeply moral, in the widest sense. They attend to questions of the fulfilment of the true self, and the relationship between the I-Thou and the meaning of life.

Elsewhere[1] I have suggested that something went seriously wrong after D. H. Lawrence, and that how this was may be indicated by *Mr. Noon*. In that novel there is a profound confusion, and a split between the deeper feelings in the sensibility of the author, and the things he wants to believe about relationship, at the explicit level. This is one significant characteristic of the 'modern novel': confusion about where the answer to our present-day existential yearning may lie. We urgently need a sense of trueness and meaning, but we do not know where to look. I believe that after *The Rainbow* Lawrence fell more and more into false solutions, and the question is how such a disaster could come about. I have tried to show in Alan Sillitoe's novel how the Lawrence 'mode' is employed to vindicate a dynamic of egotism, in which the reader is subtly involved, by a use of language that is in the service of an indulgence in a kind of brutality, in contempt for woman and the needs of being.

I am pursuing here a theme I have already investigated in *Lost Bearings in English Poetry*. In the light of the work of Karl Stern, the rejection of 'the feminine' in symbolic culture may be seen as a manifestation of a feeling of being alien to the universe, and also of being afraid of being human—certainly afraid of the deeper claims of being, since 'the feminine' is that which creates being. In my previous work I quote Saul Bellow from *Mr. Sammler's Planet*:

> As long as there is no ethical life and everything is poured so barbarously and recklessly into personal gesture this must be endured. . . . There is a peculiar longing for non-being. . . . why should they be human? . . . The individual . . . seems to want a divorce from all the states he knows. . . .

Saul Bellow is one of the novelists of today one respects, not least because he records the essential failure of ethical life in our time. And if we read such a work as Ian Hamilton's biography of Robert Lowell, we can see how this longing for non-being overtakes the literary sensibility; Lowell seems to have died out of a kind of death-wish, but his pupils Sylvia Plath and Anne Sexton both committed suicide, as did his own teacher Randell Jarrell and his friends Theodore Roethke and John Berryman. This is surely a very fearful dynamic in the world of modern literature?

We have to distinguish, however, carefully, between a number of things. There is the prevalent sense of a failure of all traditional states of being, and a sense of meaninglessness, in some serious people who write books. Even here there need to be discriminations, as between the antipathy of a writer like Henry Miller to civilization, which seems ambiguous (not least now his manuscripts are selling for hundreds of thousands), and that of Sartre's Saint Genet, who clearly erected a whole moral system on the inversion of values, and the principle 'Evil be thou my Good' of the deeply schizoid individual. Despite Genet's evident sincerity in this, what shall we say of a man who endorsed the morality of the Baader-Meinhof gang (one of whose members wrote in his diary 'Twenty-four hours of HATE each day'), and even attempted at one stage to vindicate the cruelty of the Gestapo? Here, with the 'serious' writer of moral inversion, who based his sense of identity on being a thief and a sexual pervert, we need to make careful discriminations between schizoid and non-schizoid modes of existence, to try to seek, as I have done with Sylvia Plath, the flaws in the psychic logic, as the psychotherapist does.

155

In other areas the problem is more perplexing. As I shall try to suggest, there are those who 'adopt' certain modes and attitudes, which seem to require forms of offence to truth and being, and they seek to justify their positions on the grounds of a certain 'model' of human nature and philosophy of life. This tends to be related to Freudian 'unmasking', with instinct theory and a kind of organic mechanism in the background. The moment has come, through the developments of existential and *Daseins*-analytical psychotherapy, and through philosophical anthropology, when this model can no longer be sustained. How will the attachment of our literary writers, like (say) Ted Hughes, to the bleak 'scientific' view of existence look, when it is shown to be untenable?

But then, again, of course, these insights do not fully explain the weekly output of 'modern novels' which are acclaimed in the pages of *The Times* and other journals. What interests me here is a certain kind of dissociation between normal morality and decency and the grossness of the culture of commercial promotion. For instance, one may find a novel discussed in a review in *The Times* in such terms:

> When he takes an African mistress she gives him a dose of the clap. . . . the Deputy Commissioner's daughter finally decides to succumb to his overweight charms. . . . ('Don't touch it!' he shrieked violently, as though to an innocent child about to pet an adder. . . .)

There are hints of an obscene episode, and yet commendations ('Amis with a touch of Tom Sharpe')—but what one is left with is a mental image of a woman about to touch a syphilitic penis, offered in a tone which implies that this kind of 'comedy' is perfectly unobjectionable and amusing. (At this moment, the author was an honoured guest at the college table.) This, it is implied, is the kind of 'novel' the fashion-following educated person ought to be reading.

Charming faces look out from the publicity photographs, as in *The Times* at the time of writing, as one goes off to teach *Middlemarch*, which is also a 'novel'. The text tells one about the plots: 'a disfigured and divorced professor of politics, who lusts after a student girl and dominates her, then mutilates and kills her. . . .' The author makes us 'enter the fierce, logical

156

predatory mind of the intelligent beast. . . . remorseless prose. . . . ugly killer. . . . sordid story. . . . destruction of the Beauty who is titillated by his deformity. . . .' Another novel in the same review is about a woman keeping a culture in her freezer: 'the beast and culture awaken, Naomi has her first orgasm, and the world springs to fecund life. . . .' The next 'deals in dark matters with the rape of a mother by her son. . . . depth of feeling . . .'.

In supervision, a student presents an essay which deals with one novel which is certainly suitable, but compares it with another concoction which I read with dismay; it begins with a negro girl child being raped, and progresses through the now accepted fashionable pattern of militant 'feminist' depiction of man as worthless, treacherous, a rapist, the possibilities of a lesbian solution, and the rest, in a rather sickly sentimental-ironic style derived from Salinger. Later, in this somewhat puzzled week, I realize that this novel has been systematically presented through the newspapers and journals, because a huge sum of money has been invested in its promotion, as the film made out of it is about to be launched. It was even a favourite for a leading film prize, but failed to make it. So, both I and my student are victims of an expensive commercial promotion, and the so-called 'important theme' of the novel is no more than an *ersatz* invention for the purposes of marketing a product.

Yet, clearly, as one finds whenever it is possible to find out anything about the publishing trade, the grotesque and gross novels by the smiling lady novelists, who grin over their exploitations of mental rage, probably sell only a few hundred and sometimes not at all. At the same time, the expectations created in the readership, respectable suburban dwellers, staggering out of the local library weekly with a pile of such grim tales, manifest against anything genuine ever reaching print. The decisions about what is published are often made by young people trained at the new universities where such literature has been solemnly discussed and acclaimed, and there are virtually no outlets for any other form of literature outside the 'London literary world', which controls all the sources of information and criticism.

There is thus both a genuine problem and a spurious one which belongs to sociology rather than criticism. The serious question is that which is raised by the fact that, as Rollo May puts it, 'the best of the novels and dramas and paintings of our day are those which present to us the tremendous meaning in the fact of meaninglessness'. He says that

> in presenting the *ostensible* lack of the greatness in man and his actions, or the lack of meaning, these works . . . are confronting exactly what *is* tragic in our day, namely the complete confusion, banality, ambiguity, and vacuum of ethical standards and the consequent inability to act or . . . the paralysing fear of one's own tenderness. . . . (*Love and Will*, p. 110)

May is thinking of such works as *Waiting for Godot* and Beckett's novels, and O'Neill's *The Iceman Cometh*. He sees these as representing the most tragic thing of all, 'the ultimate attitude, "It doesn't matter".' 'The ultimate tragic condition in a negative sense is the apathy, the adamant, rigid, "cool", which refuses to admit the genuinely tragic.' These works reveal, he believes, as an existentialist psychotherapist, what is wrong with love and will in our day. He sees them as manifesting the schizoid characteristics of our life, not least in great cities like New York. In works like *Who's Afraid of Virginia Woolf?* and *Godot* he sees the expression of modern man's 'inability to act' (though there may be 'expectation') or a rabid denial of love that expresses an inability to come to terms with whatever love and tenderness may be offered—and these are exactly the problems he encounters in his work in therapy.

I would like, however, to dwell on certain significant words in Rollo May's discussion: 'the fact of meaninglessness' and '*ostensible* . . .'. Behind his view there is a certain modern metaphysic, and the word 'ostensible' reveals that May admits the possibility that this philosophy of existence may be erroneous. It is around this matter that our debate must concentrate. There is a modern dogma, rooted in Darwinian mechanism and in matter-in-motion materialism, that life in the world came into existence by 'accident' and that evolution happens by 'chance' mutations, led forth into development by a ruthless struggle for survival. Only physical entities and forces are real, so any illusion man has, of his capacity to determine his fate, is a mere form of false comfort. He is essentially a mechanism, whose existence is determined by the random processes of physical operation, and doomed by the laws of Entropy to ultimate decay. His life is meaningless, and so there can be no real grounds for values, meanings, choices. Even if, on existential grounds, man seeks to define himself, this desperate act itself has no essential validity and is futile.

This view of existence, however, is not 'fact'. It is all based on hypotheses which are now felt by many to be extremely doubtful. Evolution, the coming into being of life, and consciousness cannot be explained as the products of chance. Philosophers of science talk of 'achievement', and the impossibility of explaining life in the world without recognizing some kind of 'formative principle'. Human consciousness and culture may be seen as significant achievements of this principle, and this suggests we have a particular rôle as the only 'knowers' in the universe, the only feature of the cosmos which gives it meaning. This in turn may oblige us to attend to the responsibility to which F. R. Leavis gave the name *'Ahnung'*—the 'inkling' which should impel us to attend to inner and outer truth and to exercise our conscience at a very deep level. In short, there is today the possibility of a philosophy of being, upon which real values could be developed and the capacity for real choices based. (See the present author's *Evolution and the Humanities*, the work of Michael Polanyi and Marjorie Grene, and especially *New Knowledge in Human Values*, ed. Abraham Maslow (1959).)

That is, there is no need to accept that the view of the world as meaningless and human existence as futile, which predominates in so much of our culture, is inescapable. This, then, raises the question as to why such a pessimistic and nihilistic philosophy of life predominates. If one reads the work and lives of certain writers, such as Robert Lowell, Theodore Roethke, Sylvia Plath, Saul Bellow and Ted Hughes, one can see sensitive and thoughtful individuals seemingly unable to exercise any positive sense of life's potentialities and meanings, in the face of a philosophy of existence which seems to make any such effort seem futile. Of course, this has been a problem for a long time: Peter Mudford in *The Art of Celebration* records how such authors as Tolstoy were daunted by feelings of meaninglessness, and indicates aspects of the problem in writers such as Conrad, W. B. Yeats, and Thomas Hardy. To some, like

Hardy, the whole universe has seemed a vast 'mistake'. I explored this problem in *Lost Bearings in English Poetry*, in relation to poetry today.

The view of existence to which I refer, and to which Rollo May directs his attention, is, of course, as May makes clear, *schizoid*. This is a valuable word which does not, however, mean 'split', but rather indicates a sense of emptiness. The experience of the schizoid state has been superbly delineated by therapists like R. D. Laing, W. R. D. Fairbairn, Harry Guntrip, and May himself. It results from an inadequate experience in infancy, of those processes in the I-Thou between mother and infant, which give a sense of the substantiality of the self, the capacity to relate to the 'Thou', and thus to the world—to reality, by the 'living principle' as Leavis called it. Our creative engagement with the world, with a world felt to be real and meaningful, develops out of the primary I-Thou relationship, in which the mother offers 'creative reflection' to the emerging child, so that when he looks into her face, or into her mind, what he sees is his true emerging self. It is indicative that so many important modern writers in the world of today are individuals in which these processes quite evidently failed—Sylvia Plath, Jean Genet, Jean-Paul Sartre, Samuel Beckett, for example.

The view of the world which sees it as bleak, futile, meaningless and valueless, is however a specifically *schizoid* view. As Karl Stern indicates in *The Flight from Woman*, there is here a correspondence between the pathological experience of self and world by those who have been seriously failed by woman-as-mother, and a philosophy of existence in which 'Mother Earth' is felt to be alien or hostile. But there is another aspect of this problem, which emerges from the studies of Fairbairn; because love has failed the schizoid, he seeks to develop a morality based on *hate*, because this is for one thing *safer* (love having proved dangerous), while, for another, it can yield satisfactions when love cannot. In this last dynamic of consciousness, a fierce *immoral motive* develops—because the schizoid individual cannot find any satisfaction in love, he will give himself up to the joys of hating, to get what he can out of that. Thus, he declares, '*Evil be thou my good.*' There can be a kind of heroism in this, and it was for this kind of hate-solution, and the intensity of his immoral morality, that Jean-Paul Sartre made Genet into a martyr. The implications are of the kind discussed by Michael Polanyi in his chapter on Nihilism in *Knowing and Being*; it leads to a fervent moral passion directed into destructiveness

A little of this pathological moral inversion might be absorbed by our civilization. The danger is that it has come to predominate and, in association with the dogma of a meaningless universe, has led to a new situation in which every stage in a deepening inversion of morality in works of art has been heralded as a new liberation. At the same time, open discussion of the essential problems underlying these developments has come to be suppressed. As Polanyi put it, such fanatical immoralism can soon become *immanent*, and so beyond the reach of discourse and criticism.

Yet the benefit, as Rollo May indicates, in schizoid expression, lies in the way it provides access to the *escape* from apathy and the vacuum. Actually, I believe May is wrong in one important respect. A sense of alienation, impotence, dismay, nihilism, or apathy is not at all 'tragic'. Tragedy is the confrontation between being and the ultimate nature of our 'thrownness', our being-unto-death, and if this is to be achieved in art, what is required is a powerful sense of the importance of meaning. If we examine the greatest tragedies, such as *King Lear*, what we find is a profound sense of the value and importance of life, of the significance of being. It therefore follows that I do not consider many modern works, some of which are acclaimed as 'tragic', as tragic at all. I find, for example, that the paralysed sense of non-being, non-becoming, futility and apathy in the works of Samuel Beckett is unfit to be called tragic. They are said to be comic, but they are ultimately, to me, boring and sentimental, since there is nothing they can say about human existence in a positive sense at all—and this can offer nothing of the tragic kind to express the nature of our confrontation with the problem of meaning in existence. (One only has to compare Mahler to indicate the difference; Beckett lacks utterly that kind of courage, to come to terms with being human and to find the capacity for gratitude for having existed.)

Where expression such as that of the schizoid author can have value may be seen by looking at a report by Victor Frankl. He tells us he was telephoned by a lady who told him she was determined to commit suicide but 'was curious to know what I would say about it'. He talked to her for half an hour, and she finally agreed not to commit suicide but to come to him at the hospital.

> The only reason she had decided not to commit suicide was the fact that, rather than growing angry because of having been disturbed in my sleep in the middle of the night, I had patiently listened to her and talked with her for half an hour, and a world, she found, in which this can happen, must be a world worth living in. (*The Will to Meaning*, p. 8)

That is, the nihilistic work, even in its moral inversion, may have the beneficial effect of enabling us to feel that we all, too, at times, have such feelings—and we see expressed in it certain inclinations of our own—for, as Fairbairn points out, we all have schizoid characteristics, and all move up and down an imaginary scale of schizoid proclivities. The danger is that, since the schizoid individual is so impelled towards false solutions based on hate rather than love, he may seduce others into his very cunning inversions, and his energetic, sometimes dreadfully *logical*, falsifications. (See my *Sylvia Plath: Poetry and Existence*.) Again, the worst effect of the development of the schizoid view of human existence as futile into a dogma has come to mean that such false solutions cannot be exposed to the necessary scrutiny and dialogue—to the discourse of love or human interactivity, which would expose them as false, and prompt the discovery, beyond them, of truth.

The atmosphere which a predominantly schizoid culture generates, therefore, is one in which there develops a new form of the 'taboo on tenderness' which Ian D. Suttie found prevalent in our society. There has developed now what might be called a 'taboo on being'. The expression of a sense of meaninglessness, of the futility of trying to overcome apathy (as enacted in Beckett's plays), and the idolization instead of the false solutions of hate (as in Genet), has led to a tendency to reinforce false solutions, and to resist insights. As Rollo May reports, individuals in America have even taught themselves to have sexual intercourse without having their feelings involved, and he reports in his work many instances of the dissociation of feeling from reality. While in the consulting-room patients report their horror of feeling and acting as if they were

162

automata, in order to cope with a dehumanized society, outside they deliberately adopt the function of an automaton, a false self. The mechanistic 'model' which comes over to us from 'science' seems to justify this schizoid split between the whole life of being and consciousness, and the physical body. Having adopted this dissociation as a way of living, it becomes too painful to recognize the real problem, which is that we exist as whole beings. So a strong defence arises in our thinking, to defend ourselves against the very problem of life itself, and our deeper needs. This kind of dissociation has become a theme of the modern novel, and its modes and language endorse this falsification of experience. In Erica Jong's *Fear of Flying*, for example, she implies that the highest form of sexual experience is that in which the man and the woman do not know each other as persons. Doris Lessing, one of our most esteemed authors, shows her protagonist Martha Quest, in the last of her series of novels about this protagonist, to be fascinated and compelled by a sexual relationship with a promiscuous stud-like man ('Jack') with whom she has experienced a 'marvellous' dissociation of body and being (in *The Four-gated City*). Although, on the principle of such dissociation, this man has come to develop a project in which he seeks to humiliate women in a kind of perverted brothel, and although he is known to her as a man who seeks to destroy women by such predatory activity, she still continues to go back to him, in appreciation of his marvellous body 'intelligence', while her experience of his seductions are the major feature of her (otherwise dismal) novel. (Her only other positive is another form of dissociation, a kind of telepathy.) That there is no critical rejection of such celebrations of dissociation is a significant feature of the scene in which the 'modern novel' exists and thrives. I shall say more later about aspects of this scene which trouble the teacher of English. For what are we to do, when a form of art which is, as from the past, a major instrument of thought about the nature of being and existence, becomes an instrument for pressing false solutions on to the reader? When I talk with a sensitive student about Frances Hodgson Burnett's *The Secret Garden*, she tells me in the next breath that she wants to go on to do an M.A. Course at the University of East Anglia, because it was from there that Clive Sinclair and Ian McEwan came. Can someone who appreciates *The Secret Garden* really turn cheerfully to *The Concrete Garden?* A student who appreciates *Middlemarch* writes a dissertation on Doris Lessing, and is mystified that I find so much that fills me with doubt, in her later work. And, of course, novelists who are the focus of such doubts are invited to student societies, and are the subject of acclaim in the pages of the newspapers and journals. There is, indeed, a whole system of approval, or works which, to my principles, insult humanness and promote falsity, stretching from the review pages to professionals in my own English faculty. The universal dissociation has become a gift for those who simply use the situation to exploit it with their own debasements.

In a moment, I will give some examples of what I mean, about the way in which the development of the 'modern novel' has led to a certain kind of ethos, in which, by the corruption of language, expectation, attitude to existence, and to the vehicle itself, it has become virtually impossible to object to what amounts to moral stupidity and decadence. But first it is important to be quite clear about the moral and philosophical grounds upon which one makes discriminations. These can be made in relation to the novel itself, as it was at its best. It is also important to see how things have gone wrong.

We may take the problem of existence to be as the existentialist therapist sees it; Rollo May quotes Ernest Keen:

> Emerging out of my self-consciousness is my experience of myself as a 'valuing self' and a 'becoming self'. . . . This 'emerging' involves an integration or synthesis of my bodily awareness and my self-consciousness, or, one might say, of my wish and my will. . . . decision is neither a wish nor an act of will . . . making a decision is a commitment. It always involves the risk of failure, and it is an act that all my Being is involved in.

May's chapter is about 'intentionality' and describes the way the therapists help patients to make choices which involve their whole being and their responsibility to the world. The assumption, as behind most therapy, is that a primary need in the human being is love, and that therapy can help the patient to discover the I-Thou for himself or herself. May quotes Søren Kierkegaard, 'In love every may starts from the beginning.' The beginning is the relationship between people which we call

164

care. Though it goes beyond feeling, it begins there. It is a feeling denoting a relationship of concern when the other's existence matters to you. In ultimate terms, it involves one not only in being willing to get delight in, but also to suffer for, the other. As May says, today philosophers and psychologists are becoming increasingly interested in *feeling* as the basis of human existence; we cannot *know* except as we *feel*. We may relate this emphasis to Leavis's assertion that *the novel* represents a certain whole way of knowing—as about this feeling which is the basis of thought. May wants '*sentio ergo sum*' to replace '*cogito ergo sum*' as a motto for human experience of the world.

To May's observation, I believe we may add some insight from Victor Frankl, in his *The Will to Meaning*. He says that psychotherapy owes a good deal to Ludwig Binswanger who reinstalled and reinstated the human being in his humanness, through his concept of 'being-in-the-world'. And through the influence of Martin Buber, 'the I-Thou relationship can be regarded as the heart of the matter.' It is, of course, the heart of the matter in the true novel.

> Yet even beyond this is another dimension still to be entered. The encounter between I and Thou cannot be the whole truth, the whole story. The essentially self-transcendent quality of human existence renders man a *being reaching out beyond himself*. Therefore, if Martin Buber, . . . interprets human existence basically in terms of a dialogue between I and Thou, we must recognise that this dialogue defeats itself unless I and Thou transcend themselves to refer to a meaning outside themselves.

Daseins-analysis has freed the partners in a relationship from their ontological blindness, by revealing to them that in their encounter they may find the meaning of being. And it has freed them from their ontological deafness by indicating that from this I-Thou meeting, they need to turn out to seek a sense of meaning in life-tasks that can triumph over being-unto-death. We find a profound sense of meaning in the meeting of one unique being with another in love; then we have to turn out to find this sense of meaning fulfilling itself in our destiny. (Lawrence, seeking the first ontological escape, never found the second—his lovers remain in a sexual *huis clos*.)

This view of our primary needs from *Daseins*-analysis marks a

165

radical departure from the implications of Freudian psycho-analysis, and the difference between these two views of human life and need is crucial to my discriminations in the field of literary criticism. We may bring together problems of language, attitude, morality and the philosophy of being. We may relate the question to wider problems of philosophy. 'The exalted melancholy of our fate', declared Martin Buber, 'lies in the fact that every *Thou* inevitably becomes an *It*.' As Leslie Farber puts it, 'if we inspect the moment, it becomes an article of knowledge' (*The Ways of the Will*, p. 136). I should like to follow Farber's argument here, from his chapter on 'Martin Buber and Psychoanalysis'. We may relate what he says about knowledge here, to the problem of the novel. Self-consciousness belongs to the world of *It*. Even as we reflect on experience, we bring our knowledge into that realm. In the moment, we are alive, and our consciousness is full of intentionality. We are involved in creative living, in the moment as it unfolds, in our unique being. As soon as we reflect on that experience, we move into the *It*. We have continually to remember the sphere of the *I-Thou*, and what Buber calls 'the eternal *Thou*', our relationship with all that is beyond us and to what Leavis called the *Ahnung*.

Farber takes modern psychology to be an example of the world of the *It*, as, indeed, is every form of trying to impose comprehension and order on experience. The realm of the *I-It*, says Farber, is the typical subject-other relationship of traditional epistemology, as well as of modern psychology. Our way of experiencing even comes to belong to the *I-It*. But there is another dimension, in which there is a recognition of un-knowable states, and spheres of being which cannot be brought to explicitness. As Farber argues, in modern psychology, even in psychiatry, there is a division between 'fact' and 'feeling', as if feelings were unreal, while the physical self were an 'animated clod'. The problems which arise from this come from the way in which natural science approaches, like behaviourism, make physicalistic investigations of phenomena which belong to human subjectivity and experience, to being and consciousness. The effect of such investigations is to objectify the subject. The most striking fact about human experience is that so much of it is invisible. Yet today's psychologists make physical experi-ments on animals, and suppose that these 'objective' studies can be applied to phenomena which belong to the inner life of persons. From this arises a mode of thought that obscures 'being'. Farber sees that Freud's model led him to make interpretations of human experience which were essentially reductive. He and his Freudian followers have ever tended to define such manifestations as love: as though it were 'nothing but anxiety'. Examining a definition by Sullivan, Farber says that not only does it imply this, but also 'an anxiety that needs to be relieved is not very different from an *instinctual or libidinal drive that needs to be discharged.*'

> . . . through these reductive views of man, current philosophy has arrived at both a biological and a steam-engine psychology of motive. Love is nothing but a physiological drive that needs outlet—nothing but an emotional tension that needs relief. (p. 141)

When Martin Buber described the experience of the *I-Thou* in infant and mother, he was imagining the experience of the mother towards her child and of the child towards his mother. He was imagining this to be a mutual experience of reciprocity— of shared relation. This is a truly phenomenological approach, attending to consciousness and the inward life, by imagination. He also discusses the way the child finds reality, in the same vein. Buber thus pointed in *I and Thou* to a way of understanding human experience not in the language of the physical sciences, which tends always to find objects, and so to reduce living beings to mechanisms, but in the way of the imaginative investigation of beings, by such means as projection—throwing oneself into the experience of others.

This kind of philosophical anthropology (Farber makes the point that Buber's enterprise *does* represent a philosophical anthropology, a term also used for his work by Maurice Friedman) requires a different language—and Farber here discusses the very important question of the language of psychoanalysis itself. Its terms (such as *cathexis* and *libido*) seem to imply a scientific mode, as if it were dealing with physical entities and objects. But of course there is the other dimension of therapy—the rôle of the therapist in offering a kind of love, and the generation and discussion of dreams and their meanings, which is a phenomenological, poetic discipline.

We may extend these considerations to the world of the novel. The implication of the work of Buber, like that of Frankl, Farber, Rollo May and others, is that the primary human need is relationship in Buber's sense of the *I-Thou*: 'from man to man the heavenly bread of self-being is passed.' The 'model' here is one which finds consciousness and experience, and the search for meaning, as primary. By this model, *one would not expect to find that the satisfaction of instinctual needs satisfies the patient's needs*. The fundamental need is for that *I-Thou* experience, from which it is possible to relate to a meaningful world.

At the time he transposed his honeymoon experience into art in *Mr. Noon*, D. H. Lawrence was being lured by Frieda into new European perspectives on sexuality, under the influence of Otto Gross. Gross, of course, in turn, was in engagement with the Freudian attitudes of his time. But what Lawrence picked up from the German sexual revolution was an attitude to human needs which was essentially based upon instinct theory. The truth, in the world of psychotherapy, has painfully come to be seen, that strictly Freudian psychoanalysis may produce an individual who is capable of sexual activity without guilt, while it leaves the existential problems unsolved. This is so because all that the instinctual model can offer is sensual satisfaction, and since the end of sexual hunger is detumescence and the loss of appetite, the existential yearning may, by this, be even more exacerbated. Since Ian D. Suttie's critique in *The Origins of Love and Hate* it has become clear that the instinctual model, which supposes that 'release' is the goal, is itself based upon Freud's need to satisfy the demands of the medical profession of his time for an 'organic' model. It thus fails to find the real existential problem. And in any case, in Freud's metapsychology lurked the death instinct in the background, as though the organism sought first the detensioning of sexual urges, and then a kind of ultimate detensioning, related to entropy, in death; the urge towards dead equilibrium became a principle of human existence as well as of the universe. But this left the individual in the same meaningless flux of matter as the implicit bleak philosophy of existence inherent in scientific positivism.

Although D. H. Lawrence recognized, as an artist, other needs, for love, and for a sense of the uniqueness of the other, as we have seen, as in his poems, he was also attracted, obviously,

to the instinctual model, at least the appetitive model. His letter
to Ernest Collings of 17 January 1913 is a significant one. The
question arises: Lawrence wanted to attend to the needs of
'being', but he tended to equate this with 'the body'; by this, did
he mean the deeper life of the individual as a whole being, or
did he mean the (instinctual) impulses of 'the blood'? This
letter suggests that he did identify 'the body' with the 'hunger'
of the instinctual life and appetite:

> My great religion is a belief in the blood, the flesh, as being wiser
> than the intellect. We can go wrong in our minds. But what our
> blood feels and believes and says, is always true. . . . I conceive of
> a man's body as a kind of flame, like a candle flame, forever
> upright and forever flowing, coming God knows from out of
> practically nowhere, and being *itself.* . . .

He speaks of how, instead of chasing the mystery in the fugitive
things outside us, we ought to look at ourselves, and say, 'My
God, I am myself!' He wants to live in Italy, where the people are
so unconscious. This all sounds as though it might fit in with the
existentialist view, and the emphasis on being. But Lawrence
goes on:

> The real way of living is to answer to one's wants. Not 'I want to
> light up with my intelligence as many things as possible' but 'For
> the living of my full flame—I want that liberty, I want that
> woman, I want that pound of peaches, I want to go to sleep, I want
> to go to the pub and have a good time, I want to kiss that girl, I
> want to insult that man.'

Despite his disclaimers about the importance of what he is
saying, it is clear from this that Lawrence thought of 'listening
to the blood' very much in Freudian terms of listening to the
'instincts' and appetitive needs.

   Farber, in his essay on Buber, goes on to discuss some specific
problems of psychoanalysis. He believes it is important to get
both forms of thought together, both the capacity to explore
experience by the I-Thou, but also the I-It. Since much of his
work has to do with the schizophrenic, he is concerned that this
often involves an 'extreme withering of the *Thou* capacity'
leading to a 'crippling of the intellect'.

> I mean intellect not in the narrow sense of a measurable reason of
> intelligence, but in a larger sense—experience informed with

imagination, and imagination ordered by knowledge and judgement. (p. 148)

The problem with schizophrenics is that their imaginative powers and intellectual powers may be severely limited, so that their capacity for recovery is impaired. But he also speaks of the 'pseudo-Thou', and a state of 'pseudo-grace', which sometimes occurs especially in therapy with hysterics. I believe that what he says may also be applied to the situation in which a *culture* has come to be caught up in a condition of placing emphasis on the *pseudo-Thou* and *pseudo-grace*, or, in my terms, when the goal of Thou experience is conceived in terms of satisfying 'the wants'. That is, if the solving of problems is conceived within the framework of the Freudian kind of emphasis on instinct or 'the blood', and on sexual fulfilment, we have a culture of false solutions. The central theme is false; the underlying need for meaning in the *I-Thou* is avoided; the mode becomes an impoverished one because of the separation of the two modes of understanding, and the imaginative power becomes impoverished. It is that to which the influence of Freud and Lawrence, himself under the influence of Otto Gross, has brought us; we move towards what Frankl calls 'a thoroughly decadent sensualism' in the novel and attitudes to life.

Leslie Farber's phrases here have always struck me as most telling, when applied to the cultural situation in which we have a powerful schizoid (if not schizophrenic) element, and a parallel manifestation to that ('usually hysterical') syndrome which he is discussing, both of which come from a dissociation of the *I-Thou* from the *I-It*[2]:

> it is sex and sex metaphor that so willfully force the pseudo-Thou. Thus what was formerly one of the expressions of relation or love becomes an idolatry, fragmented endlessly in the world of *It*—each article of the sexual act carrying the willful burden. In a sexological age where man is defined by his sexual competence, love has been relegated to a device for achieving orgasm.

And Farber quotes Buber himself:

> Many years I have wandered through the land of men, and have not yet reached an end of studying the varieties of the 'erotic man'. . . . There a lover stamps around and is in love only with his passion. There is one wearing his differentiated feelings like

170

medal ribbons. There is one enjoying the adventures of his own fascinating effect. There is one collecting excitement. There is one displaying his 'power'. There is one preening himself with borrowed vitality. There one is delighting to exist simultaneously as himself and as an idol very much like himself. There is one warming himself at the blaze of what has fallen to his lot. There is one experimenting. And so on and on—all the manifold monologists with their mirrors, in the apartment of the most intimate dialogue. (*Between Man and Man*, p. 29)

This could be a description of the 'modern novel', not, I hasten to add, of the way in which modern man is 'placed' or 'diagnosed' in the modern novel in the light of a deeper understanding—but rather as such postures are approved in the novel *in themselves*, and as we are involved in them by it. Buber's point is that none of these postures leads to the true discovery of the I-Thou, of love or meaning, through the most intimate dialogue. Indeed, they are all 'monologues', and the essence of the atmosphere of the 'modern novel' is that it endorses the *monologue*, and endorses the egotism by which the posturer in his monologue moves further and further away from the engagement with his true needs. The implicit model behind the modern novel reinforces this, and the language goes with it. It is that 'frank' language which Lawrence sought to purify, and which seems to be vindicated by Freudian 'realism'; what we fail to see is the degree of hostility, hate and contempt inherent in that language, and the way in which these dynamics in it tend to contribute to an atmosphere in which the discussion of true needs in the realm of the I-Thou becomes impossible. That is, the language contributes to the taboo on tenderness and on being and true need, while, by its implicit invocation of the 'instinct' model, it spoils the complex in which discourse can take place.

> Everyone at Kane's has fucked her. Everyone at Tarka's has fucked her. Everyone everywhere has fucked her. Everywhere we go people have fucked her. Just walking down the street— everyone has fucked her! I've never met anyone who hasn't fucked her. The partner's probably fucked her. The liftman's definitely fucked her. (*Success*, Martin Amis, p. 9)

This situation cannot be 'discussed' unless we examine the way this prose promotes indifference, creating an essential *contempt* for human being, not least by its confident tone. And, of course, such a tone, which invites a certain kind of indulgence in outrageousness, draws the reader with it into a tendency to indulge in the mental hostility, and the taboo on being.

I once tried out a paragraph from this novelist at a conference of distinguished people working in such disciplines as psychotherapy, education and the arts. I quoted a paragraph which will be discussed in full below, though here I need only to draw attention to one line: 'The bed was now beginning to look like a butcher's apron.' There was no need to labour the question; one (socialist) psychotherapist pronounced that the passage showed the writer to be 'not only decadent but *degenerate*'. Yet at the time the author was the respected literary editor of our only socialist weekly, and belongs to a whole movement in our contemporary literature which receives serious commendatory attention. (At the time of writing this author is advertised as our 'leading novelist'.)

Anthony Thwaite tells us that *The Rachel Papers*, this author's first novel, was written 'with disdainful wit, ingenious obscenity, astute literariness, loathing, lust, anxiety . . .', as though these were commendable, and the book is described as 'very funny, fairly nasty'. Auberon Waugh describes *Dead Babies* as 'nothing less than brilliant'.

The language, the tone and 'voice' of the whole paragraph may be compared with the writing of the novelists quoted earlier in this book:

> Then: I flattened her on her back and, straddling her waist with my thighs, placed her arms behind her head. Both stimulated and amused, by her look of B-movie prostration, I began to slide peelingly up her midriff, and went on to make delightful play with the tumescent trio beneath me, digging, gliding and bending long after her nipples had started to throb for mercy. Inching up further, seated comfortably on the bench of her breasts and supporting my diagonal torso against the head-rest with my hands, I dipped at my own slow leisure into that ravenous O.
>
> A quarter of an hour of that and, with another display of skilful athleticism, I had executed a 180-degree pivot, offering my face up to her hooked-over thighs (I had already reckied the area, naturally, paddling a finger and covertly sniffing it—it was warm, wet and sweet), while she continued to shower my dock

with her saliva and her tears. Now mind you I wasn't down there just for the hell of it: after a few messy moments—adequately beguiled by her tonguey doings—I did another expert turnabout, swivelling my legs under my chest like a gymnast and concurrently upending the girl's body, so that in a flash she was on her tummy—haunches aloft—and I was tensed mightily behind her. She tensed too. She tensed too late.

After a perfectly civil, and in fact somewhat tedious, phased entry, I buggered her quite pitilessly for—oh—a good twenty-five minutes, wrenching at her hair whenever she made some coquettish attempt to wriggle free. Roots, roots. Why, the bottom sheet was looking like a butcher's apron by the time I flipped her on to her back, surged forward into the hot crush, and gouged myself empty to her screams. (*Success*, p. 136)

The particular tone of this piece conveys an outrageous implication that we are undisturbed by the most atrocious language describing the most outrageous acts. Lawrence's enthusiasm for sodomy has, in this, come to its nemesis, for what can be indulged here is an evident contempt for woman.[3] It is supposed to be ironic about sexual fantasy, but it manages to get it both ways by, as it were, revelling in the exuberant language of sadistic fantasy itself. Yet if one compares it with the prose of a de Sade, it is revealed as phoney, even in its own non-seriousness. Though in de Sade (as Masud Khan has pointed out in *Alienation in Perversion*) the fantasy loses all touch with reality, since the physical atrocities could not be carried out without causing serious damage to the bodies of the participants, there is a gruesome sense in his work that the fantasies *have* to be indulged, for a life or death unconscious reason; they represent a grotesque kind of authenticity, albeit an authenticity of false solutions. Here the inauthenticity is betrayed by the absence of all such impelling need; it is rather a trivial and loutish joke, attempting to involve the reader in a ironic indulgence in mental lust and rage. What the language and the fantasy establish, therefore, is a confused moral inversion, inhibiting the very processes of response by which authenticity can be sought. By such prose the access to 'being', which may be fostered by the novel as art, is crippled, as the expectations of the reader, and the nature of the novel, are brutalized.

As a further representative example we may take this, from the much praised novel *The White Hotel*:

> Even the chef, the portly beaming chef, took a hand in the refurbishment—embarrassingly, for one day the lovers were disturbed by a scraping at their window and when they looked across they saw the jolly chef beaming in, paint brush in hand. The young woman was being mounted from behind; pink with shame, she tried to pretend she was kneeling in prayer. But they were too far gone, and he gave them such a jolly wink, that there seemed no harm in calling him in and asking him to join them. And he must have been good for more things than steaks, because, with her eyes closed and her face buried in the pillow, she could not tell which of them was making love to her, it was all equally rare, tender, and full of good juice. She felt happy that part of her body was occupied by someone else. The spirit of the white hotel was against selfishness.

The passage is supposed to come from a self-revealing fantasy, shown by a young woman to her doctor Sigmund Freud. But on examination, the prose displays a particular kind of oily pimpish tone which is derived from pornography, and which displays a certain gloating eagerness, in the cruel triumph over the victim—the invasion of privacy, the destruction of normal values, the outrage to authenticity ('she could not tell which of them . . .'). Anyone who has studied the case-histories of sexual perversion will know that here we have a concoction manufactured from such histories, and given an added spice, as by the references to steak ('equally rare, tender and full of good juice'). The dissociation from reality which the prose displays goes with an abandonment to moral inversion.

I should like to put my discussion of *The White Hotel* in a context. I was in McMaster University, Hamilton, Toronto, for a fortnight in the spring of 1984. A class of graduates which I attended was puzzled by a number of things in the novel: why, for instance, was Freud's analysis of the character 'Lisa' shown to be so erroneous? What was the purpose? The analysis is dismissed, in favour of one which shows her dreams to have been a foreboding of the future; thus (the novel suggests) our dreams and other meanings should be examined in terms of what is going to happen to us. Can this be anything but an irrational form of occult mumbo-jumbo, like the present vogue for horoscopes? And then, when one intelligent student suggested that the book be looked at in terms of what we learn in the last chapter, which takes place in a kind of purgatory, we pondered the revelation in an interview that Thomas added this chapter as an afterthought, because he felt his novel had so far neglected the 'spiritual' element in Lisa? As the class discussed the novel and the interview, a number of underlying things emerged, which may be indicated by quotations from the interview[4]:

> Just because someone finds an erotic fantasy in something very dark doesn't mean that he or she is going out to do it. It is better, in that case, to confront it, as Freud was doing, to try to bring up these dark forces, to bring them to the light. . . . I think there must be an awful lot of hysteria or nervous tension now as a result of our fears about a nuclear holocaust. . . . I decided there ought to be some kind of spiritual fantasy at the end, as there is a sexual fantasy, and as there is Freud's fantasy of who she is. . . . It is the association, the closeness of sex and death, of Eros and Thanatos—the great Freudian and great human forces— which, I think, either made people very strongly for it, or in some cases made them revolted by it. . . . (D. M. Thomas)

What we discussed was what lay behind these words: certain assumptions evidently dear to today's literary following. There is, for example, an acceptance of the Freudian model, of the sexual instincts so 'powerful' that they are almost impossible to control, with the death instinct in the background. There is the 'release' theory that it is better to drag these dark forces out into the light and 'confront' them. And there is the attitude that we must, as it were, be free and able to indulge the wildest fantasies, as part of the art of the twentieth century, because of our 'nuclear' predicament. At McMaster I was able to argue, as it is difficult to argue at large, that possibly this popularization of Freud instinct-theory is seriously wrong, and that, in the light of much that has happened in psychoanalytical thinking since, not only is the 'model' a false one, but the licence it gives to untrammelled exploitation of brutal fantasies is itself vicious. It could be that, because of these falsities, we are enclosing our-selves further and further in the darkness itself. As Guntrip argues, the Freudian model of our savage dark inner forces disguises the true picture, which is revealed by the schizoid diagnosis. Our real problem is that we are weak and are afraid of our human weakness of identity. To this the existentialists have added the insight that this sense of the weakness of identity is mingled with our anxiety about whether our lives have any meaning, whether we have sufficient, by way of symbolic achievement in our lives, to feel the sense of *Dasein*, the sense of *being there*, in a meaningful way, before we are swept away into death.

So we find in the interview just quoted a sense that, in Thomas's attitudes to his own notorious book, there is something disturbingly false. The violence in the book is hideously devastating, and it is given a particular sexual quality, sadistic and coloured by a contrasting insistence on the vulnerability of the victims which draws out as much as possible the reader's sense of outrage. That is, it is impossible to read the book without violent feelings, without the extreme of mental rage. And that, of course, is the danger of following the supposedly 'Freudian' procedure of seeking to 'release' the 'dark side' of the inner life. In Freudian practice there are two factors which are not taken into account, in this fashionable misinterpretation of psychoanalytical theory. While the therapist trusts that destructive fantasies and impulses may emerge in therapy, he does not provoke them. Moreover he trusts also that he will establish a firm personal relationship within which they can be borne and endured—and engaged with—modified. There are thus elements of love in therapy which are missing from the exploitations of 'realism' in culture for which justification is sought on 'Freudian' lines. As Ian D. Suttie pointed out, while Freudian theory seemed to be based unduly on hate, the practice was based on love, and on the creative intersubjectivity of transference. Moreover, the violence released in patients' dreams is generated in the context of that phenomenological discipline, the interpretation of dreams, which itself draws out in the patient that positive search for harmony and order which psychoanalysis collaborates with, as a 'talking cure'.

But the most significant revelation in the interview with D. M. Thomas comes at the beginning of the transcript:

> I suppose, for many readers, it created a breakthrough into what must have seemed to them *rather forbidden sexual territory*. Through that, they began to feel that they knew the heroine intimately:

176

they identified with her fantasies and her preconceptions and her outlook on life. Therefore, when she met the Holocaust, it had a more personal effect on them. . . . (My italics.)

So, perhaps we can look at the book as a particular kind of calculated fantasy. We are engaged in the most intimate analysis of the meanings of the heroine's consciousness; then, all the interpretations are ripped away, and she is massacred, by having a bayonet ripped into her genitals. The 'excuse' for this indulgence is the Holocaust. This, for the reader, represents a 'breakthrough'. And there can be a full 'Freudian' false justi-fication for it all:

> Freud said that the sexual instinct is where the highest and the lowest are closest together. He quoted Goethe from 'Heaven Across the World to Hell'. I think the sexual instinct does embrace totality; I think it does embrace everything. You have extremes: St. Theresa feeling the arrows of God; a Jack the Ripper or necrophilia—again an unimaginable horror. . . . in our own sexuality, at times we touch both extremes in a way, if only through fantasy. We touch apprehensions of the divine and at times we are aware of dark forces in us, a desire to be cruel, or sado-masochistic, if only as a kind of brief shadow. Whether this embraces the Holocaust, I don't know, but it certainly embraces death and violence; and as that is an extreme form of violence, there is a possibility that it might touch our imagination in that way, which I think is a horrific thought if it is true. I think it is thrown up by *The White Hotel* in some way, and that maybe is why some people become very agitated by it. But it is human, perhaps it is better to confront that.

Here, there seems to me to be just a little expression of doubt, or even guilt, since the implication is that to make use of the Holocaust as a stimulus to the 'imagination' can itself be 'horrific'; and yet that is what he has done in *The White Hotel*. But, again, the 'Freudian' excuse is taken to justify what is really a deplorable ploy—a seduction of the reader into identi-fying with a heroine who is then raped—to gain maximum 'effect'.

But suppose we take the lesson of later forms of psycho-analytical thought, and insist that the real problem is that of *finding the courage to be human*, which means confronting not the 'dark' bestial forces within us, but engaging with the sense of emptiness and meaninglessness which the black machismo—a defence—covers up and diverts us from. What happens if we suggest that the preoccupation with sexual perversion, sadism and violence in art is in fact a new form of *sentimentality*, that is, of false feeling, 'taking out on yourself feelings you haven't got', to disguise the real problems from ourselves by a kind of indulgence in manic mental rage? That all this horror ('ripped the corset from her body . . . screaming, bleeding . . . some became old in minutes . . . soundless howl . . . faces covered in blood . . . white soft flesh being flailed . . . sea of bodies covered in blood . . . unpleasant smell told her he had lost control of his bowels . . .') is essentially decadent, and a moral stupidity?[6]

Yet a dogmatic preservation of the (roughly-speaking) 'Freudian' ideology seems entrenched, even in the world of publishing itself[7]: and it was my recent experience of McMaster which brought this home to me again. There, because of an open and continuing debate on psychoanalysis, on Freud and Freudianism, together with 'subjective' philosophy, there is sufficient of an 'open' intellectual centre to enable those in literary studies to approach to predominant works and themes of contemporary literature with the deepest suspicion: a suspicion which turns out, from time to time, to be profoundly justified.

It was a relief to work in such a way at McMaster, because in Britain the atmosphere is strongly cohesive, among those who endorse the ethos in which the kind of 'modern novel' I am discussing may flourish. One of the influential figures there was Professor Andrew Brink, the author of *Creativity as Repair* and *Loss and Symbolic Repair*. In the former he writes:

> There are thus forces in our society which want to normalize what is probably a psychopathology. . . . we may well be in an era when reparative art may be at a discount. . . . (p. 45)

By contrast, in Cambridge, the sometime Edward VII Professor of English Literature endorses the novel writing of Ian McEwan. McEwan's work was discussed in an issue of *The Gadfly*. Sex, the contributor declared, is often presented in this author's work as 'a degrading cross between the butcher's counter and the gynaecologist's couch' (G. L. Gibbs, Vol. 6, No. 1, p. 72, February 1983):

Mary muttered her intention of hiring a surgeon to amputate Colin's arms and legs. She would keep him in a room of her house, and use him exclusively for sex, sometimes, lending him out to friends.

The human body is reduced to a sensation-organism, and the psychopathological depersonalization is emphasized by the phrase 'lending him out to friends'. We have a paradigm of the (schizoid) dissociation, of which Rollo May writes, between the emotional life and being and the physical organism, a focus of mere sensation. The way in which the matter is put, in a tone of jestful cynicism, compounds the dehumanization, and attempts to involve the reader in a coarse grotesquery which borders on the insane.

This 'jokey' tone may be studied in itself for the way in which it is clearly meant to inhibit objection. Indeed, the atmosphere has become one in which, to use the phrase from Polanyi again, moral inversion is so 'immanent' that discourse and discrimination are impossible. The tone of newspaper reviewers here is very revealing. Here, for instance, is an extract from a review on the literature pages of *The Times*. The face of the woman reviewer appears on the cover of the Arts Council list of writers who are willing to go into schools to talk about their work. She is reviewing a novel by John Barth, *Sabbatical*:

> For all its cleverness, the only time I found myself laughing out loud was unquestionably inappropriate. Susan's sister Mimsi is gang-raped and variously maltreated by a group of youths who strip her naked and tie her hands behind her back. When she at last succeeds in finding her way out of that wilderness, and stands at the roadside naked, in the hope of finding rescue, her plight stops a pick-up truck whose driver rushes to her side, but not to help. He rapes her again. . . .

At what, exactly, was the reviewer laughing? I take the point of her 'unquestionably inappropriate'. But her tone is wrong, and is surely confusing. It implies that 'We sophisticated readers are so used to violent sexual scenes in novels that we are only amused by yet another clever bit of outrageous brutality.' It is noticeable that she can assume that her middlebrow audience in *The Times* will share her view, and know that it is the deliberate reversal of hopes, that human good will prevail, that comes in for cynical comic deflation—in the name of the exposure of sentimentality, and of 'unmasking'. But why is a cruel rape so funny in a novel, when, in the news pages, it would be seen as a monstrous offence against a human being? Why is the calculation of such fantasies, for entertainment, so up-roarious, and to be commended?

I am particularly interested in this example because it illuminates the perplexities of our situation over questions of criticism and art today. So successful has the influence of moral inversion been that it has now established what may be called a dogma. With Freudian instinct theory in the background, it is almost a matter of required belief, that it is valuable for human nature to be 'unmasked' by the new 'realism' of the brutal book. What is heretical is to doubt the dogma, and to be shocked. I found the reviewer's report on her laughter shocking, and have used the instance in one or two places. When I quoted her in this vein in another manuscript, it came back with a note from the publisher's reader; breaking all the customary rules of confidentiality, he protested through the university press that the reviewer was a respectable wife and mother, and who was I to question her critical lapse?

There is a remarkable cohesion thus maintained, among those who share the ethos of commercial publishing in this respect, and endorse the kind of trend in the novel which I am examining. A representative example of such a proponent is Professor Malcolm Bradbury. I will quote a review, in the *Times Literary Supplement* of 14 December 1979, of Clive Sinclair's *Hearts of Gold*. Bradbury applauded Sinclair's first novel *Bibliosexuality*, though he admits it was 'a little bit too much an extended verbal pun, and had something of the over-brilliance of a twenty-year-old author who has penetrated, almost in weariness, the reflective issues of modern art'.

> The condition to which the title refers is a disorder of the senses in which an unnatural relation with a book is desired or obtained. It is much concerned with 'the erotic tensions of text', and much is made of the decadent equation that links the grammar of narrative to the grammar of desire. It is only through indirection laid over direction, only through the prolonging of anticipation and the deferral of satiety, only through angled moves through

space to the final oblique outcome, that either sex or text acquire anything like complexity or pleasure. . . .

What can such nonsense mean? Nothing here accords with my experience either of sexual love, or of literature; but with its clever air it manifests an idolization of lust and perversion, in some sinister way. 'Indeed, it is really only on the page that sex comes anywhere near its full potential; art, though useless, is not as useless as life. . . .' Surely, there must have been a time when a man would be too ashamed to write thus? 'The author glowered at us off the dust-jacket, photographed with a naked girl in the background, and a low gleam in his eye; he works, of course, on a book.' In this kind of publicity, we surely have something akin to the profitable cult of the lout in 'pop' culture. The postures are recognizable as postures, and it seems we can no longer bring up against them anything meant or real. We do not expect sincerity, but what we no longer recognize is the essentially perverted nature of the offering:

> Clearly the novel came from that dark and seamy Soho of the soul wherein so much of literature arises, from that half-world of decadence where mind and body are locked in a farcical intercourse—as are, also, text and reader.

Indeed, one might suggest that here Bradbury displays a fascination for that which transforms the creative exchange between literary work and reader, which is a matter of love, and its related symbolism of being, into an act of perversion. So, he goes on, Sinclair has developed his obsessions, just like McEwan; both were products of Bradbury's own East Anglia:

> Indeed, it is not an inappropriate link to make, since both McEwan and Sinclair participated in a creative writing group at the University of East Anglia; in this respect I must declare an interest, but equally a firm judgement that both are outstanding. Like McEwan's, Sinclair's narrators in these tales are usually perverse figures . . . sexual fantasists, schlemiels, vampires, and even a Jewish giraffe. . . . They are all seedy exploiters of their own intelligence, experts in the art of playing victim. . . . They live in a world where we carry heads, but vote with our loins; mind contends with body in endless dialogue—so the professor of philosophy in 'Tittilatio', struggling, in the act itself, between Spinoza and spermatozoa, Kant and cunt.

Behind this, perceptibly, lies the Freudian instinct model, vindicating the cynicism, and seeming to justify the mechanistic dissociation, to endorse the division of sexuality from meaning and emotion. Bradbury's coarse jests simply deepen the indulgence in verbal and mental sex, but the tone also suggests a confused indulgence in the tolerance of brutal egoism. Yet Bradbury can declare that it is all very moral: 'Meanwhile a pathos of outflanked desire haunts everything, and functions almost like a morality; though some will not like them, these are in fact moral stories.' They are, it would seem, only moral because of the degree of weariness and disgust they manifest; the striking aspect of them which Bradbury commends is their mental rage, what he calls 'the arts of titillation'—'it is a meal of fine sensations served from the decadent table':

> . . . it narrates the hero's desire to plant his seed in contemporary Israel by bedding a Jewish girl. . . . he is always comically interrupted by the universe: . . . some are highly erotic. The narrator of 'Among School Children' has nymphet-ish tastes, while that of 'Le Docteur Enchainé', a psychiatrist, finds that he is the pimp and pandar of sex, offering Socratic rather than Biblical orgasms. His heroes . . . end up back in fiction: as one narrator says, the pen is mightier than the penis. . . . the stories are not only very finely poised but genuinely contemporary, stylistically serious. . . .

We note in the tone a new aestheticism, a new and jokier ironic detachment, from meaning and human values; any indulgence is permissible, so long as it is stylish—the ghost of Prince Daniyal[8] haunts the decline into sinister triviality. How can the above writer be the same Malcolm Bradbury who writes, in his splendid essay on Jane Austen's *Emma* in Volume Five of the *Pelican Guide to English Literature*, thus:

> . . . we have learned of the duty of the individual to immerse himself in the events about him and to accept his obligations to his acquaintance finely and squarely; we have learned of the value of the 'serious spirit', involved and totally responsible. We have been persuaded in fact of the importance of true regard for others, persuaded to see the full human being as full, fine, morally serious, totally responsible, entirely involved, and to consider every human action as a crucial, committing act of self-definition. If literary artists construct not only their work but their reader,

Jane Austen, a great artist working in a small compass, has constructed one who, however remote from her social and moral world, is capable of recognising and recovering an experience of life as serious and intense as even Henry James could have wished for. (pp. 185–86)

Why should there be such a split between the values implicit here and those adopted in the previous quotations?

The confusion of language, discourse and sensibility matters, because the novel at best is a particular kind of thought about human experience. I have tried to show that the novel is concerned in the gravest way, as art, with authenticity of being, in a manner parallel to the work of the therapist. As E. K. Ledermann says, morality lies at the heart of medical practice, and is related to questions of human worth, value and meaning. He believes that the therapist should lead the patient to become confronted with his conscience, and to the question, 'What can I do to acquire a more authentic existence?' Surely this is the kind of process we go through, when we become absorbed in a good novel, as when we identify with a 'Pip' or a Maisie, or a Nanda Brookenham? In *Mental Health and Human Conscience*, Ledermann goes on to say that 'the existentialist postulates an unconscious ethical force'—thus pointing to that daemonic urge we seem to have within us, to find and realize our true self. We may debate to what degree this urge is 'unconscious'; if it were unconscious, we would surely be too little aware of its promptings. If we have volition, then there must be a sense in which we are continually engaged in trying to *listen* to this conscience, to submit, in Leavis's sense, to 'the *Ahnung*'.

The problem, arises, of course: how do we know the true *Ahnung* when we hear it? How do we distinguish between those voices of the true self-being of which Peter Lomas writes, and those false solutions which offer other promptings? Those confusions he confronts as psychotherapist? Those effective false solutions which we may have constructed to deal with the world, on a false basis—constructs which we know, fundamentally, to be wrong for us, but which have enabled us to survive, and so can be relinquished only in some discomfort and even dread?

This is the moral problem, and it makes it clear that there is always a possibility that individuals may be encouraged to take to false solutions. There is an obligation on us all to consider whether we are helping others to fulfil their true selves, or whether we are reinforcing their attachment to false solutions. Moreover, this is made more difficult by the problem that often we are inclined to idealize our own deeper myths, even though they belong to the false patterns in our lives. Even Lawrence fell into confusion over what he meant by 'blood'.

But surely there is something terribly wrong, when in a Humanities department of a university, students are introduced to works which confuse them morally, and which tend actually to endorse the false solutions of hate and barbarity? This is one of the chief embarrassments today, for anyone concerned with literature and the Arts. Perhaps the process came to a head with the emergence of the 'campus' novel, not least with *Lucky Jim*[9]; its author, after all, was appointed as Director of English Studies at a Cambridge college (though prevented from being invited to lecture by the heroic intervention of Leavis himself). I feel this problem particularly when, in an educational institution, my students enthuse about writers whom I reject. The 'campus' novel is itself a focus of this dismay; from *Lucky Jim*, through the work of Malcolm Bradbury, to that of Howard Jacobson, to Tom Sharpe and David Lodge, there has been a theme in this genre, which seeks to portray the English academic at the university as a lustful fool, whose values are impotent and hypocritical, and who is 'really' driven by lust, ambition and egoism. The effect, as Boris Ford has pointed out to me, is that the public's view of the Humanities in the universities has been seriously damaged, and, more important, the view held by politicians of the status of the Humanities on the campus. There is no doubt that many now see us as incompetents who do not subscribe to the values we are supposed to uphold, not the least despicable because we seem to regard the intellectual life with an air of superior disdain and ironic self-interest. A somewhat diffident but indicative article appeared on this theme in *The Use of English*, Vol. 37, No. 2 (Spring 1986), by Anthony Kearney: 'Campus Novels and the English Teacher'. He sees that Tom Sharpe's disgusting novels express the sense that 'teaching English is a pointless business' while he and Jacobson are 'paying off old scores' and ridiculing the academic life 'with savage glee'. Sharpe is 'cynical' in setting out to 'destroy the pieties of academic life' and 'airy idealism'. Jacobson's hero sets out to 'revenge himself on his dimwit students'. In Bradbury's novel, English is not represented by any teachers of personality or conviction, but by a man who passes nervously through the campus aware that 'there is no more moral scruple and concern.' The wishy-washy woman who teaches the subject is 'defenceless' and is soon seduced by the ruthless and ambitious 'history man'. This novel chronicles 'the demise of English as a convincing discipline' and the demise of the educational institution as a focus of moral concern. This depressing novel, says Kearney, is fascinated by confidence and power; to some it might seem a profound act of treachery to human meaning. *Small World* is 'less playful'. Lodge finds a 'compulsive attraction' in a frenzy of movement of new ideas, but has undercurrents of defeat and failure, showing academics as impotent, or doomed to disappointment; a lecture on striptease suggests that the search for ultimate meanings is 'enticing but pointless'. Criticism has deconstructed itself, and 'the old authority has gone'. The hero, Gordon Swallow, puts up a defence of the old Arnoldian traditions, but it is hard to know what status he has—a slightly ludicrous figure, a subject of irony, and not making much impact. The result is a 'complete impasse'—yet Kearney, though he sees these campus novels as 'sometimes murderous' in their impulse to dismiss and revenge themselves upon the academic life, as 'important and entertaining'—even useful. He cannot see (the English critical atmosphere being so cohesive in its acclaim of such works) that the genre is a focus of intellectual disaster—of the failure of confidence in the Humanities as sources of meaning and hope, in our society.

Because of all this perplexity, it was heartening to read Q. D. Leavis's essay 'The Englishness of the English Novel'[10] a few days before her death. She points out that 'the English novel', which we take so much for granted, was the product of a number of special circumstances: the influence of Shakespeare, for example, and the effect of a special kind of sociological tradition—also, a *moral* tradition. She claims the novel as a unique national product, of which other nations must be envious. But in our time, Mrs. Leavis believed, this tradition has been sadly diminished:

> What strikes me with apprehension for the future of the English novel is how diminished the tradition has become in the hands of

the well-known practitioners of this age, who have uncritically been accepted as classics.

As Mrs. Leavis says, some novelists today admire the brutally selfish and anti-social man, or glorify the untrammelled female egoist, or like Kingsley Amis (and his son, Mrs. Leavis might have added) inculcate a 'militant philistinism'. These represent a complete rejection of the English tradition. Mrs. Leavis quotes Dr. Johnson's 'want of tenderness is want of parts, and no less a proof of stupidity than depravity'. No one who cares for the English novel can expose himself to these rejections and stupidities without pain. And even more painful is the fact, which Mrs. Leavis also records, that these writers command an educated public and approval among them.

When a tradition has declined as the tradition of the novel has declined, what hope can there be of sustaining serious interest in the genre at the same level as a serious interest in music or painting?

The 'novel' is, of course, studied in schools and at the university. But even here, it is difficult to maintain critical discourse. For students who appreciate Thomas Hardy take up with equal enthusiasm the kind of spurious concoction John Fowles made on lines borrowed from Hardy, *The French Lieutenant's Woman*. The strange complacent ('Freudian') 'realism' about sexuality in that book and its confusion of the problems of integrity, its essential grossness about the sexual act, do not strike them as questionable.

The mechanistic, 'Freudian' model clearly lies behind this novel, together with all the assumptions that go with it, about our superior state of 'liberation' in the personal life.

Indeed, Fowles uses this model as a basis to offer a claim for our moral superiority over the 'Victorians'. The novel has become very well known as a piece of 'literature' and has even been set for 'A'-level school examinations. It seemed to me an unpleasant book, not least because of its knowingness, which intrudes—a knowingness which, above all, *knows* that the current ('60s) attitude to sexuality is so much more healthy and 'uninhibited' than that of the late nineteenth century. There is a continual movement backwards and forwards, between the present day and 'then', to underline this point—a movement which destroys the integrity of the imaginative realization of the 'then' because one is continually reminded of the present and its arrogant assumption of a superiority of sensibility. The result is again to destroy the capacity for tragic experience, to avoid the very reference to authenticity that makes for the art of the novel.

There was a valuable analysis of this novel by Richard Gill in *The Use of English*, Vol. 33/3, p. 13, Summer 1982. It is, says Gill, an unquestioning, and therefore uninteresting, reflection of ideas that were fashionable in self-consciously intellectual circles in the 1960s. The attraction between the hero and the heroine, understood throughout in the language of the 1960s, passes beyond a cramping present into an open future where people can 'be themselves'. ('Doing your own thing is never far below the surface.') But in this there is that confident assumption that the attitude to sexual morality and to self-fulfilment of our time is triumphantly superior, which, in the light of the work of therapists like Rollo May, is simply not true. The therapist knows the disasters behind it all, and reveals the confidence as a misplaced disguise of deeper problems than ever before.

The French Lieutenant's Woman announces itself as an 'existentialist' work. But that, alas, is simply what it is not. As Gill says, this assertion is only on the level of rhetoric. The references to existentialism ('the thin walls stood between him and nothingness, an ultimate vacuity, a total purposelessness') are simply meant to meet a latent receptiveness in an audience, and are merely a gesture to a prevailing fashion. The real existentialist predicament of the characters is not felt, in all its living immediacy, because of the intrusions of the author's sense of our time being so much further advanced and so much more able to understand what makes human beings act as they do. For instance, Fowles invokes Darwinian theory and the new materialism of science; but the theme is pursued without critical intelligence, in language which is faded and tired—for the reason that the author has made up his mind on the point and writes from a thesis in which the issue has been decided, including that of 'freedom'. The characters do not live out their quest for freedom; the outcome has already been decided, as by the contrast between the intended bride for the hero, and the woman he is tempted by. The outcome is heavily pre-empted by the author. The woman, as Gill points out, is a rebel, and is conceived therefore in terms of the girl of the swinging '60s; she is indifferent to standard fashion and is even blessed with a modern look: 'we can sometimes recognize the looks of a century ago in a modern face: but never those of a century to come.' Her intelligence is of that delicate, intuitive kind, says Gill, with 'instinctive profundity of insight' which was so valued in the '60s as being more interesting than that which was 'analytic or problem-solving'. In all this, says Gill, Fowles is sharply critical, even hostile, to the Victorians, but naïvely uncritical about the 1960s. His dealings with freedom, determinism, sexuality and repression are closely related to his self-conscious intellectualism. The self-conscious double ending with its air of 'experiment' actually represents a form of trivialization. Contrary to his protestations, that he is not a novelist of the traditional kind, claiming omniscience, Fowles is actually more than that; he does move through the novel like God, and Gill quotes instances in which a kind of petulant hostility and even hatred is displayed in his presentation of 'bad' characters. Is not there in this, Gill suggests, a kind of self-loathing? This, I believe, is a useful insight into the falsities of the confidence of the 'enlightened' 1960s; it hides something, and what it hides are untruths. Love, freedom, sexuality are not like that, and we know it. The confidence about being so 'liberated' has to do with an impulse to be liberated from being human, from human needs, and from one's own essential problems—from being human. The air of superior 'enlightenment' and a new freedom emerges from a fear of life and being. Gill finds Fowles's novel a 'dangerous' one, because of these self-deceiving falsities, and I agree.[11]

By contrast, we could point to the novels of Elizabeth Gaskell, which were written more or less in the period (if not of the period) to which Fowles refers with such a sense of superiority. There is nothing explicit about the sexual life, of course, in her books. The attention is to authenticity, how each character comes to discover 'that which in himself or herself he or she wishes to truly fulfil'. In *Wives and Daughters* there is a marvellously profound contrast between Cynthia Kirkpatrick and Molly Gibson, the one emotionally superficial if essentially good-hearted, and the latter true to herself and her integrity, whatever pain this may bring; yet the two girls

188

have sympathy and affection for one another, and for Cynthia her love for Molly is a major and positive experience in her life. The married life of Molly's father and Mrs. (Clare) Kirkpatrick is superbly and ironically done; he cuts his losses, as married people do when they are dependent upon a difficult partner and need them more than mere independence and peace of mind. Yet there are some principles he will not abandon—concerning his rôle as a doctor and concerning his deep love for his daughter. It is a subtle portrayal of a marriage with which we can identify, to our advantage; we learn something, about our own motives and conflicts, even if our own relationships are quite different. The same is true of the Hales's marriages in *North and South*; and in both books Mrs. Gaskell is unflinchingly realistic, about disease and death, and in the latter, about social conditions. Above all, her heroines are superb—superb in their determination to operate from inner integrity, as free independent beings—at a time when, of course, everything in society was loaded against woman making her free moral choices and social determination. In this her work obviously draws largely on Jane Austen; Elizabeth Bennett, Fanny Price and Emma Woodhouse are clearly behind Molly Gibson. But Mrs. Gaskell's heroines have a wider range of passion and free intelligence, and the world of woman's consciousness and charm is rendered in her novels with exceptional power. Take, for instance, her insightful comments on Cynthia Kirkpatrick:

> in the short time they had met, Cynthia's unconscious power of fascination had been exercised upon her. Some people have this power. Of course, its effects are only manifested in the susceptible. A schoolgirl may be found in every school who attracts and influences all the others, not by her virtues, nor her beauty, nor her sweetness, nor her cleverness, but by something that can neither be described nor reasoned upon. . . .
>
> A woman will have this charm, not only over men but over her own sex; it cannot be defined, or rather it is so delicate a mixture of many gifts and qualities that it is impossible to decide on the proportions of each. Perhaps it is incompatible with very high principle; as its essence seems to consist in the most exquisite power of adaptation to varying people and still more various moods: 'being all things to all men'. (pp. 254–55, Penguin edition)

This is an incidental (and sadly inadequate) tribute to only one great woman writer. One learns so much from such a writer, not only about social conditions and *moeurs*, or about the personal predicament of the time—but about universal problems of consciousness and emotion, about existential choice and the inevitable anguish (as of bereavement, secret marriage, sickness, the care of children, social opprobrium, conflict in the organization of affairs), but always in the context of a generous feeling about humanity and its joys and sufferings (in *Wives and Daughters* there is a real delight in Roger Hamley's intellectual achievements, a real sympathy with Osbourne Hamley's secret marriage and occupational perplexities).[12]

There are many 'modern novels' which I cannot read, not least because I shudder over the first few pages. I found *The History Man* a revolting book, because of its implicit attitude to human beings. I read Beryl Bainbridge's *The Bottle Factory Outing* and was appalled by the low and cruel attitude to human beings, in its cold-blooded black comedy about death. I can read and enjoy Saul Bellow and recognize in him a striving decency, aware of the dangers of a developing fear of being in us, and dissatisfaction with all the possible states of existence we know. I can identify in respect with his heroes, like Herzog, and can follow them into their anguished bewilderment in the modern world. But at the centre of his work I find little more than bewilderment, and, despite the groping, a moral emptiness and confusion. This enables me to think further about what has happened to the modern American consciousness, and I believe that there has been serious collapse at the centre of the existentialist question—of by what values may we survive, not least by the predominance of the bleak scientific world-view. I can respect Bellow, as I can respect Robert Lowell and Theodore Roethke in recording this bewilderment—but there are many modern American writers whom I could not read at all, and others who fill me with foreboding, like Norman Mailer, because, it seems to me, they have taken the path of false solutions and promote these in their civilization.

The social dangers of moral inversion sometimes surface. Recently, as an American journal, *Chronicles of Culture*, pointed out, Mr. Norman Mailer and Mr. Robert Silvers, the Editor of the *New York Review of Books*, arranged parole for a convicted killer in whom they detected all the supreme moral sensitivity and subtlety of feelings to which a modern American can pretend. Soon thereafter their *trouvaille* monstrously slew an innocent man. The *New York Times*, in its book section, on this, under the heading, 'Editor's Choice' (16 August 1981) announced, 'In the Belly of the Beast' by Jack Henry Abbott: 'The author's 20 years in American prisons: introduction by Norman Mailer.' In his introduction Mr. Mailer said:

> Out of Abbott's letters, however, came an intellectual, a radical, a potential leader, a man obsessed with a vision of more elevated human relations in a better world that revolution could forge. His mind, at its happiest, wanted to speak from his philosophical height across to yours. . . . It is that not only the worst of the young are sent to prison, but the best—that is, the proudest, the bravest, the most daring, the most enterprising, the most un-defeated of the poor. . . . If you can conceive of a society (it is very difficult these days) that is more concerned with the creative potential of violent young men than with the threat they pose to the suburbs, then a few solutions for future prisons may be there. Somewhere between the French Foreign Legion and some prodigious extensions of Outward Bound may lie the answer, at least for all those juvenile delinquents who are drawn to crime as a positive experience—because it is more exciting, more mysterious, more transcendental, more religious than any other experiences they have known.

As *Chronicles of Culture*, the journal relating this episode, concludes, some may feel that such idolization represents something like being an accessory to manslaughter. What we certainly have, in this mode of literary fashion, is a profound and penetrating inversion of values and an idolization of false solutions, which does not stop at literature, but exerts its influence on life at large.

The consequence has been that situation which M. B. Kinch referred to thus, writing about Q. D. Leavis:

> A combination of technical facility and fashionable cynicism or brutality or sexual explicitness (often all three) [which] seems to constitute a reliable formula for the achievement by a late twentieth century novelist of critical as well as commercial success. (*Q. D. Leavis, an Appreciation*, Brynmill, 1982)

191

As Mrs. Leavis said, discussing the 'campus' novel, these objectionable works 'deal with artificial worlds inhabited by cardboard characters whose behaviour is arbitrary, so one forgets each novel immediately after reading it'. Moreover, 'our novelists seem to have abdicated from moral responsibility, to have become sub-human.' This has become possible, because there is no philosophy behind criticism which would enable it to reject either brutality or moral irresponsibility, while the predominant philosophy of brutal determinism (or Naked Apery) seems to vindicate the exploitation of cynicism and hate by commercial publishing.

Fortunately, there are a few exceptions, and I should like to pay tribute to one of these—John Harvey, who is a Cambridge author. His writing may be taken as an example that the novel as art is not dead, and will go on being created by those who wish to use the form as a serious mode of exploration of experience.

John Harvey has taken a path in his writing which is completely apart and individual among the swamps and wastelands of the present-day novel. He did this to some extent in his first novel, *The Plate Shop*, which was about work, its satisfactions and human perplexities. It had a certain purity of scope and intention, a humane realism. *Coup d'Etat*[13] is on a much bigger scale, but it displays the same rectitude and, at the same time, a passionate concern for how human beings can survive and live in an age like ours. There is nothing of that destructive sardonic energy, and nothing of that offensive falsity and grossness about emotional life, sexuality and meaning. Yet there is nothing sentimental about his view of existence; the book is a terrible one, often painful, often racking, not only because of the torture and massacre, but also because of the situations in which the protagonists cannot solve their problems of emotional need, but act out of bewilderment in their desire to live, to *have* their lives, when circumstances seem to deny that simple possibility.

Coup d'Etat is about the events in Greece between 1967 and Autumn 1974, traced, as it were, from the ground, from the streets and flats of those living under the régime of the colonels, from the islands, the villages, and Athens. The protagonists are an intelligent, graceful and charming Greek girl, Chryssa, and two men, Vangelis, a law student, and Michael, a linguist who is English. They meet first as students in London. Later, Vangelis becomes Chryssa's husband, and Michael finds himself a journalist in Athens. Vangelis, now a lawyer, becomes involved in defending victims of the Junta, and in resistance. He is taken up and tortured to find out the secrets of the underground. Michael has come to find out about the régime, and to do what he can to expose it abroad.

Chryssa is devoted to Greece; she is profoundly Greek, and the woman's background is superbly done—her father, for example, is a hugely comic and sad character. Although she is devoted to her incarcerated husband, Chryssa becomes tenderly drawn to Michael, and they enter into an affair. This relationship is done with great poignancy and tenderness; for both, it is as if this is what they would have wished for, if everything had been different, if, as it were, there could have been another life. So, at times, they try to keep this life of love and joy apart, but this is an impossible dream and, occasionally, their guilt and anguish break out. It is as if the madness of the time, the impossible and awful viciousness of the power-struggle and the dictatorship cannot allow human beings to live in simple sanity and fulfilment. At the end, when Vangelis is released, there is nothing else for it but for Chryssa to go back to him and to relinquish Michael, who flies back to England for ever. The whole complex problem is done throughout with great delicacy and realism, and it has the quality of total authenticity, written out of a deep respect for the quest between emotional needs and moral scruples, to live responsibly and truly, so it is deeply moving.

By contrast, Harvey gives us the daily life of those who belong to the world of the 'authorities'. They are not caricatured, but given us as human beings, subtly placed but poignant in their turn. John Harvey's antecedents are evident and, in the torture scenes, perhaps too much so—I found at times an insistence, where Conrad, for example, would have created a sense of horror more by understatement. Also, I felt that the descriptions of deaths were often descriptions of deaths seen on television or on film, rather than an immediate witness; but then, again, it is a tribute to his imagination that they are mostly so convincing. Another weakness I must mention is the stiffness of some of the dialogue. John Harvey gives us interior monologue superbly, and we are very much with his characters. Somehow, at times, the imaginative power fails, and one is not 'hearing' the rhythm of the characters' words to one another—as, say, one hears the rhythms of Grandcourt and Mrs. Glasher, or Rosamond and Dorothea talking to one another in George Eliot.

But these are minor reservations, when one's main feeling in response to this gripping novel is gratitude. John Harvey has shown us what the novel can and should be in our time. He undertook an enormous task, and has constructed a novel of accomplished craftsmanship to carry it out. It is moving and harrowing, and it is *sound*.

Novels which have a genuine attention to authenticity, then, do come to be created in our time, and do get published. But they are against the general trend, and all the atmosphere, taste and commercial considerations are against such true novels getting into print. A certain kind of substantial, genuine discourse has come to be abused.

This is not only a 'cultural' matter, of taste. There are serious political questions which arise here. They were extremely well dealt with in an article by Dr. R. D. Grant in an issue of the *Salisbury Review* on 'the Politics of Sex' (Dr. Grant is a University lecturer in English at the University of Glasgow and he has written on L. H. Myers and Shakespeare). Dr. Grant draws a distinction (which has been seriously lost sight of) between lust and love; love, he declares, has nothing to do with 'possessive individualism'. Lust, of which pornography is a manifestation, reduces people and sexual acts to mere *things*. The way in which lust, in extremity, is not concerned with any person whatever may be linked with the lust for power; rape is an indulgence in the exercise of power (and pornography is visual rape, and teaches such impulses). Lust leaves the subject, however, in a solipsistic void, and so leaves the indulging individual further than ever from the goal which drives him. It is this solipsistic void which is deepened, not only by the sexual fantasies indulged in the present-day novel, but also in their enthusiastic and amused endorsement.

Love, by contrast, seeks the other as the focus of trust, and Dr. Grant's political point develops from here. If we follow him, we will find lust to be the 'antithesis of society and of culture'; and so, by implication, the liberal establishment who find no harm in the unleashing of lust, or in the use of powerful media to educate the population in lust, are in fact, ironically, endorsing the destruction of both society and culture. Pornography, Dr. Grant believes, is the greatest threat to our society, in the sphere of sexual politics, because it frees lust from moral scruple, and this has an impact on attitudes which stretches far beyond the question of immediate 'impact'. (Novels by Tom Sharpe, Martin Amis and Clive Sinclair are clearly pornographic, while Robert Nye has declared in *The Times*, of which he is Poetry Editor, his intention to write pornography in *Falstaff*.)

Grant uses the concept of innocence, which he develops from examining the important aspect of human life, which is that secret and creative intimacy that develops between man and woman in love. It is, as in the love poems of John Donne, a submission to 'a new, third, emergent thing'. This has a profound meaning, and this surrender to a mutual meaning has links which stretch out into society, not least through marriage. (That shame is a natural protection for the committed, and secret creativity of lovers is a point made by Erwin Straus in *Phenomenological Psychology*.)

We see all human beings with whom we come into contact as potential intimates, says Grant; so our attitude to the most intimate of contacts, in which man and woman actually become one, colours our attitudes to all our fellows, and thus to society. In love there develops a fundamental innocence, which is the innocence of absolute trust. This trust is the very basis of social bonds, and damage in this sphere could be socially disastrous. 'Dissolve that and society becomes reduced to an aggregate of angry, self-seeking, defensive individuals.' Grant says that it was Keynes who declared that the quickest way to bring a country to its knees was to debase its currency. 'He might have added that a more insidious method is to permit its debauchery.' Moreover, under the rule of lust, says Grant, our greatest art, indeed our whole past, would become incomprehensible; and he suggests that some very significant works of literature, important for the contributions they have made to our consciousness and civilization, are already inaccessible to us, because 'liberal enlightenment', over sexuality, has corrupted our essential innocence. One of these is *The Tempest*; another is Schumann's *Dichterliebe*, No. 4, 'Wenn Ich in Deine Augen Seh'.

I have often felt this strongly myself. Who, after reading the 'modern' novel, with its endless preoccupation with sexual gymnastics and its 'irony' (of the kind that makes the reviewer laugh), who, steeped in this, can really understand the subtle moral criticism in the sphere of personal relationships, of *Mansfield Park* or *The Awkward Age?* So, in a sense we are disinherited, while the implicit politics of lustful egotism corrupts us.

It becomes a question of the quality and richness of our civilization. Shall we simply allow our consciousness to be left to commercial exploitation, vindicated by 'liberal' obtuseness? 'Too much is at stake to allow the ethos of the free market to dominate completely', says Dr. Grant:

> Constantly to expand 'alternative' networks, subject to no control except that which the market provides, is to create a monstrous octopus of communications, whose tentacles reach into every living room, and whose interest in the moral life of the entire nation may be wholly malign.

The power of other media here is now formidable, but the taking over of the novel by the promoters of forms of egoism and inauthenticity is a serious perversion of a significant art form. A serious corruption of consciousness threatens not least because we regard the novel still as an influential genre. But the fact is now that *the novel*, once a great art form contributing to our understanding of human nature, our insights, our sense of proper moral choice, our sympathy, our sense of authenticity and freedom in a powerfully *moral* way, is often drawn into the falsification of human truth and become with many an instrument of corruption.

NOTES

1. 'D. H. Lawrence and the Tradition of Authenticity: *Mr. Moon*', to be published in *Encounter*, 1987.
2. What I am suggesting here is that so much explicit sex in culture has pathological characteristics both of a schizoid and hysteric kind, and is so a sickness rather than a 'liberation'.
3. '[H]er raw-liver kisses and her sweet-sherry tongue, about the ghostly

smells that issue from her pouches and vents, about the underworld effluvia she leaves glistening on your sheets' (ibid., p. 17).

4. *Art Out of Agony: The Holocaust Theme in Literature, Sculpture and Film*, Stephen Lewis, C.B.C. Enterprises (Montreal, 1984).

5. See *The Origins of Love and Hate*, Ian D. Suttie, 1935; and Marion Milner's reports at the end of *In The Hands of The Living God*, 1969.

6. Incidentally, as Boris Ford points out to me, there is much more to condemn in this novel than is relevant to my purposes here: its calculated pornography repeated twice over, its shameful concoction of a 'case-history' as a preamble to the horrific experiences of a real person borrowed, for instance. Since I go on to relate *The White Hotel* to Plath's *Journals*, it is perhaps also worth pointing out that she was at least grappling with her own tragic problems, not concocting them for fictional work.

7. Returning to a study of D. H. Lawrence, I believe he cannot be absolved from some influence here. His 'dark sensual ithyphallic gods' often seem very like Freud's powerful instincts, as the basic reality, while the implication that 'naked desire' is more important than meaning in personal relationships (as in *The Virgin and the Gipsy*) is a gift to the ethos of the acquisitive society, since its basis can only be appetitive; 'I want that woman, I want that pound of peaches', as he put it in the letter quoted above declaring this to be our fundamental mode.

8. Prince Daniyal is the sinister aesthete in L. H. Myers's distinguished novel *The Near And The Far*.

9. Mrs. Leavis, it may be noted, describes *Lucky Jim* as 'only a puerile scenario for a cinema-type farce', though it 'astonishingly made him an immediate reputation' even though it is one of those 'university' novels which are 'irresponsible and advance no argument'.

10. *New Universities Quarterly*, Vol. 35, No. 2 (Spring 1981): now published as the title essay in the first volume of her criticism, by Cambridge University Press (1983).

11. Fowles's most recent novel, *Mantissa*, opens with cheap sexual sensationalism: a ridiculous episode of a female doctor and a female nurse giving sexual therapy for amnesia—again surely a schizoid manifestation. Later in the novel there is an exchange (author speaking first): 'The curse of fiction'/—'Which is?' 'All those boring stretches between the sexy bits.' This perhaps indicates the harm the present fashion has done the novel; readers have become mere barbarians, impatient with any human *content*, addicted only to the mental rage and excitements of lust. The quotations here are very revealing.

12. *Ruth*, a story about a woman who is seduced and has a baby which she brings up herself, is an extremely brave novel. It caused such a stir that Mrs. Gaskell's husband's congregation actually burnt it—not because it dealt with illegitimacy, but because the heroine stays in society and raises her child, prompted by her deepest conscience.

13. John Harvey, *Coup d'État* (Collins, 1985).

Bibliography

Novels mainly examined:

AUSTEN, JANE, *Emma* (1815)
———, *Mansfield Park* (1814)
FORSTER, E. M., *A Passage to India* (1924)
HARVEY, JOHN, *Coup d'Etat* (1985)
JAMES, HENRY, *What Maisie Knew* (1897)
———, *The Awkward Age* (1899)
LAWRENCE, D. H. *Mr. Noon* (1985)
SILLITOE, ALAN, *Saturday Night and Sunday Morning* (1958)

Other books:

BERLAND, ALWYN, *Culture and Conduct in the Novels of Henry James* (Cambridge, 1981)
BREWER, D. S., *Symbolic Stories* (Brewer and Boydell, 1980)
BRINK, ANDREW, *Creativity as Repair* (Cromlech, 1982)
CROSS, J. W., *George Eliot's Life*, ed. G. S. Haight (Oxford, 1968)
FAIRBAIRN, W. R. D., *Psychoanalytical Studies of the Personality* (Tavistock, 1952)
GRENE, MARJORIE, *Approaches to a Philosophical Biology* (Basic Books, 1968)
GUNTRIP, HARRY, *Personality Structure and Human Interaction* (Hogarth, 1961)
GUNTRIP, HARRY, *Schizoid Phenomena, Object Relations and the Self* (Hogarth, 1968)
HEIDEGGER, MARTIN, *Being and Time* (S.C.M., 1962) (For a discussion of Heidegger and Daseinsanalysis see Herbert Spiegelberg, *Phenomenology in Psychology and Psychiatry* (Northwestern, 1972), especially on Ludwig Binswanger, pp. 193–232. See also David Holbrook, *Further Studies in Philosophical Anthropology* (Gower, 1987). See also *Being-in-the-World*, papers of Ludwig Binswanger, ed. Needleman (Souvenir, 1963))
HOLBROOK, DAVID, *Evolution and the Humanities* (Gower, 1987)
———, *Gustav Mahler and the Courage to Be* (Vision, 1973)

————, *Human Hope and the Death Instinct* (Pergamon, 1971)

————, *The Masks of Hate* (Pergamon, 1971)

HUSSERL, EDMUND, *The Crisis of European Sciences and Transcendental Phenomenology* (Northwestern, 1970)

KHAN, MASUD, *Alienation in Perversion* (Hogarth, 1979)

KINCH, M. B., *Q. D. Leavis, an Appreciation* (Brynmill, 1982)

KNIGHTS, L. C., *Explorations* (Chatto, 1946)

KROOK, DOROTHEA, *The Ordeal of Consciousness in Henry James* (C.U.P., 1967)

LAING, R. D., *The Divided Self* (Tavistock, 1960)

LANGER, SUSANNE, *Mind: An Essay in Human Feeling* (Hopkins, 1967)

LEAVIS, F. R., *The Great Tradition* (Chatto, 1948)

————, *Mill on Bentham and Coleridge* (Chatto, 1950)

————, *Nor Shall My Sword* (Chatto, 1972)

LEAVIS, Q. D., *Collected Essays I: The Englishness of the English Novel* (C.U.P., 1983)

LEDERMANN, E. K., *Mental Health and Human Conscience, the True and False Self* (Avebury, 1984)

LOMAS, PETER, *True and False Experience* (Allen Lane, 1973)

MAY, ROLLO, *Love and Will* (Souvenir, 1969)

————, Ernest Angel and Henri Ellenberger (eds.), *Existence: A New Dimension in Psychiatry and Psychology* (Basic Books, 1958)

MERLEAU-PONTY, MAURICE, *The Phenomenology of Perception* (Routledge, 1962)

MILNER, MARION, *The Hands of the Living God* (Hogarth, 1969)

NAEVESTAD, MARIE, *The Colours of Rage and Love* (Universitetsforlaget, Oslo, 1979)

POLANYI, MICHAEL, *Personal Knowledge* (Routledge, 1958)

SECHEHAYE, M., *Symbolic Realisation* (International University Press, 1971)

STERN, KARL, *The Flight from Woman* (Unwin, 1970)

STOLLER, ROBERT, *Perversion: The Erotic Form of Hatred* (Harvester, 1976)

STRAUS, ERWIN, *The Primary World of Senses* (Free Press of Glencoe, 1963)

SUTTIE, IAN D., *The Origins of Love and Hate* (Kegan Paul, 1935)

WINNICOTT, D. W., *Playing and Reality* (Tavistock, 1971)

Articles:

BEWLEY MARIUS, and LEAVIS, F. R., on *What Maisie Knew*, and Mrs. Wix, *Scrutiny*, Vol. XVII, *passim*

Bibliography

BRINK, ANDREW, 'Bertrand Russell: the Angry Pacifist', *Journal of Psychohistory*, Vol. 12, No. 4 (1985) p. 497

GORDON, ROSEMARY, 'D. H. Lawrence, Women and Individuation', *Journal of Analytical Psychology*, Vol. 23, No. 3 (July, 1978)

HARDING, D. W., 'Regulated Hatred: An Aspect of the Work of Jane Austen', *Scrutiny*, VIII, 346–62

HOLBROOK, DAVID, 'D. H. Lawrence and the Tradition of Authenticity: *Mr. Noon*', *Encounter*, 1987: a chapter from a forthcoming book, *Where D. H. Lawrence was Wrong About Woman*

LEWIS, STEPHEN, 'Art Out of Agony: The Holocaust Theme in Literature, Sculpture and Film', C.B.C. Enterprises (Montreal, 1984)

TRILLING, LIONEL, *Mansfield Park*, *Pelican Guide to English Literature*, Vol. V, ed. Boris Ford

Index

203

Index